The Insecurity of Freedom

Essays on Human Existence

The
INSECURITY
of FREEDOM

by Abraham Joshua Heschel

SCHOCKEN BOOKS · NEW YORK

To
Wolfe

Acknowledgments

"Religion in a Free Society," a paper presented at a seminar on Religion in a Free Society, May 9, 1958, sponsored by the Fund for the Republic. First printed as "The Religious Message" in *Religion in America,* edited by John Cogley. Published by Meridian Books, 1958, for the Center for the Study of Democratic Institutions.

"The Patient as a Person," a paper presented to the American Medical Association, 113th annual convention, in San Francisco, California, on June 21, 1964; printed in *Ramparts,* October, 1964, under the title "The Sisyphus Complex," and in *Conservative Judaism,* Vol. XIX, No. 1.

"Children and Youth," a paper presented to the White House Conference on Children and Youth, March 28, 1960; printed in *Law and Order,* Vol. 8, No. 5, May, 1960.

"Idols in the Temples," a paper presented to the 62nd annual convention of the Rabbinical Assembly of America, and to the national convention of the Religious Education Association, in Chicago, Illinois, November 18–20, 1962; printed in the *Proceedings* of the Rabbinical Assembly 1962, Vol. XXVI, and in *Religious Education,* March–April, 1963.

"To Grow in Wisdom," a paper presented to the 1961 White House Conference on Aging, Washington, D.C., January 9, 1961. Published separately by The Synagogue Council of America; most of it also included in *Geriatric Institutional Management,* edited by Morton Leeds and Herbert Shore, G. P. Putnam's Sons, 1964.

"Religion and Race," the opening address at the National Conference on Religion and Race, Chicago, January 14, 1963. Printed in *Race: Challenge to Religion,* edited by Mathew Ahmann, Henry Regnery Company, 1963. Partly incorporated in "Centenary of Emancipation Proclamation" in *The Proceedings of the Golden Jubilee Convention,* the United Synagogue Convention, November 17–21, 1963.

"The White Man Is on Trial," a paper presented to the Metropolitan Conference on Religion and Race, February 25, 1964. Printed in the *Proceedings* of the conference; reprinted in *The Jewish World,* March, 1964.

"Depth Theology," first of a series of lectures delivered at the University of Minnesota, Minneapolis, where the author was a visiting professor in the spring of 1960. Printed in *Cross Currents,* Fall, 1960.

"Confusion of Good and Evil," published in *Reinhold Niebuhr,* edited by Charles W. Kegley and Robert W. Bretall, The Macmillan Company, 1956, under the title "A Hebrew Evaluation of Reinhold Niebuhr."

"Sacred Image of Man," based on a paper presented to the national convention of the Religious Education Association, November 24–26, 1957, Chicago, Illinois. Printed in *The Christian Century,* Vol. LXXIV, No. 50, December 11, 1957, and in *Religious Education,* Vol. LIII, No. 2, March–April, 1958. Also in *What Is the Nature of Man?,* the Christian Education Press, Philadelphia, 1959, under the title "Man as an Object of Divine Concern." The paper appears here in expanded form and includes material from the author's essay "The Concept of Man in Jewish Thought" in *The Concept of Man,* edited by S. Radhakrishnan and P. T. Raju, Allen and Unwin, Ltd., London, 1960.

"Protestant Renewal: A Jewish View," written at the invitation of the editor of *The Christian Century,* and published in *The Christian Century,* Vol. LXXX, No. 49, December 4, 1963.

"The Ecumenical Movement," delivered at the dinner for Augustin Cardinal Bea, New York, N.Y., April 1, 1963. Printed in the

Catholic News, Vol. LXXVIII, No. 14, New York, April 4, 1963.

"The Individual Jew and His Obligations," a paper presented in Hebrew to the Jerusalem Ideological Conference, convened at the Hebrew University in Jerusalem in August, 1957. Printed in *Forum IV,* Jerusalem, 1959; in *Conservative Judaism,* Vol. XV, Spring, 1961; in Hebrew, *Hazuth, IV,* Jerusalem, 1958.

"Israel and the Diaspora," a paper presented to the 58th convention of the Rabbinical Assembly of America. Printed in *Proceedings of the Rabbinical Assembly of America,* Vol. 22, (1958).

"Jewish Education," a paper presented to the Pedagogic Conference of the Jewish Education Committee of New York City, February 15, 1953; printed in *Jewish Education,* Vol. XXIV, No. 2, Fall, 1953.

"The Vocation of the Cantor," a paper presented to the 10th annual convention of the Cantors Assembly of America. Printed in the *Proceedings of the 10th Annual Conference-Convention,* 1957, and in *Conservative Judaism,* Winter, 1958, Vol. 12, No. 2.

"Prayer as Discipline," the transcription of a talk given at Union Theological Seminary in the spring of 1958. Printed in *Union Seminary Quarterly Review,* Vol. XIV, No. 4, May, 1959.

"The Jews in the Soviet Union," a paper presented to the Conference on the Moral Implications of the Rabbinate, at the Jewish Theological Seminary of America on September 4, 1963. Printed in *The Day—Jewish Journal,* September 12–13, and October 12; also as a broadside by the Synagogue Council of America.

"A Declaration of Conscience," a paper read to the New York Conference on Soviet Jewry, October 28, 1964, at Hunter College, New York.

An abbreviated version of "The Last Days of Maimonides" was published by Erich Reiss, Berlin, 1935.

The books of the Pentateuch are quoted from the translation of the Torah published by the Jewish Publication Society of America in 1962. Other biblical quotations are from the Revised Standard Version of the Bible, except in a few instances where the author's own translation is used.

Contents

I

II

III

I

1 / Religion in a Free Society

Little does contemporary religion ask of man. It is ready to offer comfort; it has no courage to challenge. It is ready to offer edification; it has no courage to break the idols, to shatter callousness. The trouble is that religion has become "religion"—institution, dogma, ritual. It is no longer an event. Its acceptance involves neither risk nor strain. Religion has achieved respectability by the grace of society, and its representatives publish as a frontispiece the *nihil obstat* signed by social scientists.

There is no substitute for faith, no alternative for revelation, no surrogate for commitment. This we must remember in order to save our thought from confusion. And confusion is not a rare disease. We are guilty of committing the fallacy of misplacement. We define self-reliance and call it faith, shrewdness and call it wisdom, anthropology and call it ethics, literature and call it Bible, inner security and call it religion, conscience and call it God. However, nothing counterfeit can endure forever. Theories may intensify oblivion, yet there is a spirit in history to remind us.

It is customary to blame secular science and antireligious philosophy for the eclipse of religion in modern society. It would be more honest to blame religion for its own defeats. Religion declined not because it was refuted, but because it became irrelevant, dull, oppressive, insipid. When faith is completely replaced by creed, worship by discipline, love by habit; when the crisis of today is ignored because of the splendor of the past; when faith becomes an heirloom rather than a living fountain; when religion speaks only in the name of authority rather than with the voice of compassion, its message becomes meaningless.

Religion is an answer to ultimate questions. The moment we become oblivious to ultimate questions, religion becomes irrelevant, and its crisis sets in. The primary task of religious thinking is to rediscover the questions to which religion is an answer, to develop a degree of sensitivity to the ultimate questions which its ideas and acts are trying to answer.

Religious thinking is an intellectual endeavor out of the depths of reason. It is a source of cognitive insight into the ultimate issues of human existence. Religion is more than a mood or a feeling. Judaism, for example, is a way of thinking and a way of living. Unless we understand its categories, its mode of apprehension and evaluation, its teachings remain unintelligible.

It is not enough to call for good will. We are in desperate need of good thinking.

Our theme is religion and its relation to the free society. Such a relation can be established only if we succeed in rediscovering the intellectual relevance of the Bible.

The most serious obstacle which modern men encounter in entering a discussion about the ideas of the Bible, is the absence from man's consciousness of the problems to which the Bible refers. This, indeed, is the status of the Bible in modern society: it is a sublime answer, but we no longer know the question to which it responds. Unless we recover the question, there is no hope of understanding the Bible.

The Bible is an answer to the question, What does God require of man? But to modern man, this question is suppressed by another one, namely, What does man demand of God? Modern man continues to ponder: What will I get out of life? What escapes his attention is the fundamental, yet forgotten question, What will life get out of me?

Absorbed in the struggle for the emancipation of the individual we have concentrated our attention upon the idea of human rights and overlooked the importance of human obligations. More and more the sense of commitment, which is so essential a component of human existence, was lost in the melting pot of conceit and sophistication. Oblivious to the fact of his receiving infinitely more than he is able to return, man began to consider his self as the only end. Caring only for his needs rather than for his being needed, he is hardly able to realize that rights are anything more than legalized interests.

Needs are looked upon today as if they were holy, as if they contained the totality of existence. Needs are our gods, and we toil and spare no effort to gratify them. Suppression of a desire is considered a sacrilege that must inevitably avenge itself in the form of some mental disorder. We worship not one but a whole pantheon of needs and have come to look upon moral and spiritual norms as nothing but personal desires in disguise.[1]

Specifically, need denotes the absence or shortage of something indispensable to the well-being of a person, evoking the urgent desire for satisfaction. The term "need" is generally used in two ways: one denoting the actual lack, an objective condition, and the other denoting the awareness of such a lack. It is in the second sense, in which need is synonymous with interest, namely "an unsatisfied capacity corresponding to an unrealized condition" that the term is used here.

Every human being is a cluster of needs, yet these needs are not the same in all men or unalterable in any one man. There is a fixed minimum of needs for all men, but no fixed maximum for any man. Unlike animals, man is the playground for the unpredictable emergence and multiplication of needs and interests, some of which are indigenous to his nature, while others are induced by advertisement, fashion, envy, or come about as miscarriages of authentic needs. We usually fail to discern between authentic and artificial needs and, misjudging a whim for an aspiration, we are thrown into ugly tension. Most obsessions are the perpetuation of such misjudgments. In fact, more people die in the epidemics of needs than in the epidemics of disease. To stem the expansion of man's needs, which in turn is brought about by technological and social advancement, would mean to halt the stream on which civilization is riding. Yet the stream unchecked may sweep away civilization itself, since the pressure of needs turned into aggressive interests is the constant cause of wars, and increases in direct proportion to technological progress.

We cannot make our judgments, decisions, and directions for action dependent upon our needs. The fact is that man who has found out so much about so many things knows neither his own heart nor his own voice. Many of the interests and needs we cherish are imposed on us by the conventions of society; they are not indigenous to our essence. While some of them are necessities, others, as I pointed out before, are fictitious, and adopted as a result of convention, advertisement, or sheer envy.

The contemporary man believes he has found the philosopher's stone in the concept of needs. But who knows his true needs? How are we going to discern authentic from fictitious needs, necessities from make-believes?

Having absorbed an enormous amount of needs and having been taught to cherish the high values, such as justice, liberty, faith, as private or national interests, we are beginning to wonder whether needs and interests should be relied upon. While it is true that there are interests which all men have in common, most of our private and national interests, as asserted in daily living, divide and antagonize rather than unite us.

Interest is a subjective, dividing principle. It is the excitement of feeling, accompanying special attention paid to some object. But do we pay sufficient attention to the demands of universal justice? In fact, the interest in universal welfare is usually blocked by the interest in personal welfare, particularly when it is to be achieved at the price of renouncing one's vested interests. It is just because the power of interests is tyrannizing our lives, determining our views and actions, that we lose sight of the values that count most.

Short is the way from need to greed. Evil conditions make us seethe with evil needs, with mad dreams. Can we afford to pursue all our innate needs, even our will for power?

In the tragic confusion of interests, in which every one of us is caught, no distinction seems to be as indispensable as the distinction between right and wrong interests. Yet the concepts of right and wrong, to be standards in our dealing with interests, cannot themselves be interests. Determined as they are by temperament, bias, background, and environment of every individual and group, needs are our problems rather than our norms. They are in need of, rather than the origins of, standards.

He who sets out to employ the realities of life as means for satisfying his own desires will soon forfeit his freedom and be degraded to a mere tool. Acquiring things, he becomes enslaved to them; in subduing others, he loses his own soul. It is as if unchecked covetousness were double-faced; a sneer and subtle vengeance behind a captivating smile. We can ill afford to set up needs, an unknown, variable, vacillating, and eventually degrading factor, as a universal standard, as a supreme, abiding rule or pattern for living.

We feel jailed in the confinement of personal needs. The more we indulge in satisfactions, the deeper is our feeling of oppressiveness. To be an iconoclast of idolized needs, to defy our own immoral interests, though they seem to be vital and have long been cherished, we must be able to say No to ourselves in the name of a higher Yes. Yet our minds are late, slow, and erratic. What can give us the power to curb the deference to wrong needs, to detect spiritual fallacies, to ward off false ideals, and to wrestle with inattentiveness to the unseemly and holy?

This, indeed, is the purpose of our religious traditions: to keep alive the higher Yes as well as the power of man to say, "Here I am"; to teach our minds to understand the true demand and to teach our conscience to be present. Too often we misunderstand the demand; too often the call goes forth, and history records our conscience as absent.

Religion has adjusted itself to the modern temper by proclaiming that it too is the satisfaction of a need. This conception, which is surely diametrically opposed to the prophetic attitude, has richly contributed to the misunderstanding and sterilization of religious thinking. To define religion primarily as a quest for personal satisfaction, as the satisfaction of a human need, is to make of it a refined sort of magic. Did the thunderous voice at Sinai proclaim the ten Words in order to satisfy a need? The people felt a need for a graven image, but that need was condemned. The people were homesick for the fleshpots of Egypt. They said: "Give us flesh." And the Lord gave them spirit, not only flesh.

The Bible does not begin with man, or the history of religion, or man's need for God. "In the beginning God created the heaven and the earth." To begin with human needs is a sign of man's pitiful perspective.

Religion is spiritual effrontery. Its root is in our bitter sense of inadequacy, in a thirst which can only be stilled by greater thirst, in the embarrassment that we really do not care for God, in the discovery that our religious need is utterly feeble, that we do not feel any need for God.

We must beware of converting needs into ends, interests into norms. The task is precisely the opposite: it is to convert ends into needs, to convert the divine commandment into a human concern.

Religion is not a way of satisfying needs. It is an answer to the question: Who needs man? It is an awareness of being needed, of man being a need of God. It is a way of sanctifying the satisfaction of authentic needs.

It is an inherent weakness of religion not to take offense at the segregation of God, to forget that the true sanctuary has no walls. Religion has often suffered from the tendency to become an end in itself, to seclude the holy, to become parochial, self-indulgent, self-seeking; as if the task were not to ennoble human nature but to enhance the power and beauty of its institutions or to enlarge the body of doctrines. It has often done more to canonize prejudices than to wrestle for truth; to petrify the sacred than to sanctify the secular. Yet the task of religion is to be a challenge to the stabilization of values.

Religion is not for religion's sake but for God's sake Who is "gracious and merciful . . . good to all, and His compassion is over all that He has made" (Psalm 145:8 f.).

II

The mind of the prophets was not religion-centered. They dwelt more on the affairs of the royal palace, on the ways and views of the courts of justice, than on the problems of the priestly rituals at the temple of Jerusalem.[2]

We today are shocked when informed about *an increase* in juvenile delinquency, or *an increase* in the number of crimes committed in our city. The normal amount of juvenile delinquency, the normal number of crimes does not cause us to be dismayed. At this very moment somewhere throughout the nation crimes are being committed.

The sort of crimes and even the amount of delinquency that fill the prophets of Israel with dismay do not go beyond that which we regard as normal, as a typical ingredient of social dynamics. A single act of injustice—to us it is slight, to the prophet it is a disaster.

Turning from the discourses of the great metaphysicians to the orations of the prophets, one may feel as if he were going down from the realm of the sublime to an area of trivialities. Instead of dealing with the timeless issues of being and becoming, of matter and form, of definitions and demonstrations, one is thrown into orations about widows and orphans, about the corruption of judges and affairs of the market place. The prophets make so much ado about paltry things, employing the most excessive language in speaking about flimsy subjects. So what if somewhere in ancient Palestine poor people have not been treated properly by the rich? So what if some old women found pleasure and edification in worshiping "the Queen of Heaven"? Why such immoderate excitement? Why such intense indignation?

Their breathless impatience with injustice may strike us as hysteria. We ourselves witness continually acts of injustice, manifestations of hypocrisy, falsehood, outrage, misery, but we rarely get indignant or overly excited. To the prophets a minor, commonplace sort of injustice assumes almost cosmic proportions.

> Be appalled, O heavens, at this,
>   be shocked, be utterly desolate, says the Lord.
> For My people have committed two evils:
>   they have forsaken Me,
> the fountain of living waters
>   and hewed out cisterns for themselves,
> Broken cisterns
>   that can hold no water.
>   Jeremiah 2:12–13

They speak and act as if the sky were about to collapse because Israel had become unfaithful to God.

Is not the size of their indignation, is not the size of God's anger in disproportion to its cause? How should one explain such moral and religious excitability, such extreme impetuosity?

The prophet's words are outbursts of violent emotions. His rebuke is harsh and relentless. But if such deep sensitivity to evil is to be called hysterical, what name should be given to the deep callousness to evil which the prophet bewails? "They drink wine in bowls, and anoint themselves with the finest oils; but are not grieved over the ruin of Joseph" (Amos 6:6).

The niggardliness of our moral comprehension, the incapacity to sense the depth of misery caused by our own failures, is a fact which no subterfuge can elude. Our eyes are witness to the callousness and cruelty of man, but our heart tries to obliterate the memories, to calm the nerves, and to silence our conscience.

The prophet is a man who feels fiercely. God has thrust a burden upon his soul, and he is bowed and stunned at man's fierce greed. Frightful is the agony of man; no human voice can convey its full terror. Prophecy is the voice that God has lent to the silent agony, a voice to the plundered poor, to the profaned riches of the world. It is a form of living, a crossing point of God and man. God is raging in the prophets' words.

The prophets had disdain for those to whom God was comfort and security; to them God was a challenge, an incessant demand. He is compassion, but not a compromise; justice, but not inclemency. Tranquillity is unknown to the soul of a prophet. The miseries of the world give him no rest. While others are callous, and even callous to their callousness and unaware of their insensitivity, the prophets remain examples of supreme impatience with evil, distracted by neither might nor applause, by neither success nor beauty. Their intense sensitivity to right and wrong is due to their intense sensitivity to God's concern for right and wrong. They feel fiercely because they hear deeply.

The weakness of many systems of moral philosophy is in their isolationism. The isolation of morality is an assumption that the good is unrelated to the morally neutral values. However, there is an interrelatedness between the moral and all other acts of man, whether in the realm of theory or in the realm of aesthetic or technical application, and the moral person must not be thought of as if he were a professional magician, moral in some situations and immoral in others.

Consequently the moral problem cannot be solved as a moral problem. It must be dealt with as part of the total issue of man. The supreme problem is all of life, not good and evil. We cannot deal with morality unless we deal with all of man, the nature of existence, of doing, of meaning.

The prophets tried to overcome the isolationism of religion. It is the prophets who teach us that the problem of living does not arise with the question of how to take care of the rascals, of how to prevent delinquency or hideous crimes. The problem of living begins with the realization of how we all blunder in dealing with our fellow men. The silent atrocities, the secret scandals, which no law can prevent, are the true seat of moral infection. The problem of living begins, in fact, in relation to our own selves, in the handling of our emotional functions, in the way we deal with envy, greed, and pride. What is first at stake in the life of man is not the fact of sin, of the wrong and corrupt, but the neutral acts, the needs. Our possessions pose no less a problem than our passions. The primary task, therefore, is not how to deal with the evil, but how to deal with the neutral, how to deal with needs.

The central commandment is in relation to the person. But religion today has lost sight of the person.

Religion has become an impersonal affair, an institutional loyalty. It survives on the level of activities rather than in the stillness of commitment. It has fallen victim to the belief that the real is only that which is capable of being registered by fact-finding surveys.

By religion is meant what is done publicly rather than that which comes about in privacy. The chief virtue is social affiliation rather than conviction.

Inwardness is ignored. The spirit has become a myth. Man treats himself as if he were created in the likeness of a machine rather than in the likeness of God. The body is his god, and its needs are his prophets. Having lost his awareness of his sacred image, he became deaf to the meaning: to live in a way which is compatible with his image.

Religion without a soul is as viable as a man without a heart. Social dynamics is no substitute for meaning. Yet, the failure to realize the fallacy of such substitution seems to be common in our days.

Perhaps this is the most urgent task: to save the inner man from oblivion, to remind ourselves that we are a duality of mysterious grandeur and pompous dust. Our future depends upon our appreciation of the reality of the inner life, of the splendor of thought, of the dignity of wonder and reverence. This is the most important thought: God has a stake in the life of man, of every man. But this idea cannot be imposed from without; it must be discovered by every man; it cannot be preached, it must be experienced.

When the Voice of God spoke at Sinai, it did not begin by saying, "I am the Lord your God Who created heaven and earth." It began by saying, "I am the Lord your God Who brought you out of the land of Egypt, out of the house of bondage." Judaism is not only deliverance from external slavery, but also freedom from false fears and false glories, from fashion, from intellectual will-o'-the-wisps. In our souls we are subject to causes; in our spirits we are free, beholding the uncompromising.

The most commanding idea that Judaism dares to think is that freedom, not necessity, is the source of all being. The universe was not caused, but created. Behind mind and matter, order and relations, the freedom of God obtains. The inevitable is not eternal. All compulsion is a result of choice. A tinge of that exemption from necessity is hiding in the folds of the human spirit.

We are not taught to feel accused, to bear a sense of boundless guilt. We are asked to feel elated, bred to meet the tasks that never end.

Every child is a prince; every man is obliged to feel that the world was created for his sake. Man is not the measure of all things, but the means by which to accomplish all tasks.

As a free being the Jew must accept an enormous responsibility. The first thing a Jew is told is: You can't let yourself go; get into harness, carry the yoke of the Kingdom of Heaven. He is told to bear loads of responsibility. He is told to abhor self-complacency, to enjoy freedom of choice. He has been given life and death, good and evil, and is urged to choose, to discriminate. Yet freedom is not only the ability to choose and to act, but also the ability to will, to love. The predominant feature of Jewish teaching throughout the ages is a sense of constant obligation.

We are taught to prefer truth to security, to maintain loyalty even at the price of being in the minority. It is inner freedom that gives man the strength to forgo security, the courage to remain lonely in the multitude.

Judaism is forever engaged in a bitter battle against man's deeply rooted belief in fatalism and its ensuing inertia in social, moral, and spiritual conditions. Abraham started in rebellion against his father and the gods of his time. His great distinction was not in being loyal and conforming, but in defying and initiating. He was loved by the Lord not for ancestral worship but because he taught his descendants to "keep the way of the Lord by doing what is just and right" (Genesis 18:19).

III

We all share a supreme devotion to the hard-won freedoms of the American people. Yet to be worthy of retaining our freedoms we must not lose our understanding of the essential nature of freedom. Freedom means more than mere emancipation. It is primarily freedom of conscience, bound up with inner allegiance. The danger begins when freedom is thought to consist in the fact that "I can act as I desire." This definition not only overlooks the compulsions which often lie behind our desires; it reveals the tragic truth that freedom may develop within itself the seed of its own destruction. The will is not an ultimate and isolated entity, but determined by motives beyond its own control. *To be* what one wants to be is also not freedom, since the wishes of the ego are largely determined by external factors.

Freedom is not a principle of uncertainty, the ability to act without a motive. Such action would be chaotic and subrational, rather than free.

Although political and social freedom must include all this, even the freedom to err—its true essence is in man's ability to surpass himself, even to act against his inclinations and in defiance of his own needs and desires, to sacrifice prejudice even if it *hurts*, to give up superstition even when it claims to be a doctrine.

Freedom is the liberation from the tyranny of the self-centered ego. It comes about in moments of transcending the self as an act of spiritual ecstasy, of stepping out of the confining framework of routine reflexive concern. Freedom presupposes *the capacity for sacrifice.*

Although all men are potentially free, it is our sacred duty to safeguard all those political, social, and intellectual conditions which will enable every man to bring about the concrete actualization of freedom which is the essential prerequisite of creative achievement.

The shock of radical amazement, the humility born in awe and reverence, the austere discipline of unremitting inquiry and self-criticism are acts of liberating man from the routine way of looking only at those features of experience which are similar and regular, and opening his soul to the unique and transcendent. This sensivity to the novel and the unprecedented is the foundation of God-awareness and of the awareness of the preciousness of all beings. It leads from reflexive concern and the moral and spiritual isolation which is the result of egocentricity to a mode of responding to each new and unique experience in terms of broader considerations, wider interests, deeper appreciation and new, as yet unrealized values.

As the object of divine transitive concern *man is;* knowing himself to be the object of divine concern and responding through acts of his own transitive concern *he is free.*

The meaning of freedom is not exhausted by deliberation, decision, and responsibility, although it must include all this. The meaning of freedom presupposes an openness to transcendence, and man has to be *responsive* before he can become *responsible.*

For freedom is not an empty concept. Man is free to be free; he is not free in choosing to be a slave; he is free in doing good; he is not free in doing evil. To choose evil is to fail to be free. In choosing evil he is not free but determined by forces which are extraneous to the spirit. Free is he who has decided to act in agreement with the spirit that goes beyond all necessities.

Freedom is a challenge and a burden against which man often rebels. He is ready to abandon it, since it is full of contradiction and continually under attack. Freedom can only endure as a vision, and loyalty to it is an act of faith.

There is no freedom without awe. We must cultivate many moments of silence to bring about one moment of expression. We must bear many burdens to have the strength to carry out one act of freedom.

Man's true fulfillment cannot be reached by the isolated individual, and his true good depends on communion with, and participation in, that which transcends him. Each challenge from beyond the person is unique, and each response must be new and creative. Freedom is an act of engagement of the self to the spirit, a spiritual event.

Loyalty to freedom means loyalty to the substance of freedom. But such loyalty must be actualized again and again. Here our way of living must change: it must open the sight of sublime horizons under which we live.

Refusal to delegate the power to make ultimate decisions to any human institution, derives its strength either from the awareness of one's mysterious dignity or from the awareness of one's ultimate responsibility. But that strength breaks down in the discovery that one is unable to make a significant choice. Progressive vulgarization of society may deprive man of his ability to appreciate the sublime burden of freedom. Like Esau he may be ready to sell his birthright for a pot of lentils.

A major root of freedom lies in the belief that man, every man, is too good to be the slave of another man. However, the dynamics of our society, the cheapening and trivialization of existence, continues to corrode that belief. The uniqueness and sacred preciousness of man is being refuted with an almost cruel consistency. I do not mean the anthropological problem whether or not we are descendants of the monkeys. What I have in mind is the fact that we are being treated as if there were little difference between man and monkey. Much that is being done, e.g., in the name of entertainment, is an insult to the soul. What is involved is not demoralization; much of it may be morally neutral. What is involved is dehumani-

zation; so much of it is a continual process of intellectual deprivation. Sensitivity to words is one of the many casualties in that
process.

Words have become pretexts in the technique of evading the
necessity of honest and genuine expression. Sometimes it seems as if
we were all engaged in the process of liquidating the English
language. But words are the vessels of the spirit. And when the
vessels are broken, our relationship to the spirit becomes precarious
(see "Prayer as Discipline," p. 259).

To be free one must attain a degree of independence. Yet the
complexities of society have enmeshed contemporary man in a web
of relationships which make his independence most precarious.

Inherent in man is the desire to be in agreement with others. Yet
today with a mass of miscellaneous associations and unprecedented
excitements, it is a grim task, indeed, to agree with all and to retain
the balance of integrity.

Loaded with more vulnerable interests than he is able to protect,
bursting with fears of being squeezed by a multiplicity of tasks and
responsibilities, modern man feels too insecure to remain upright.

Good and evil have always had a tendency to live in promiscuity,
but in more integrated societies man, it seems, found it easier to
discriminate between the two, while in our turbulent times circumstances often stupefy our power of discernment; it is as if many of
us have become value-blind in the epidemics of needs.

The glory of a free society lies not only in the consciousness of *my*
right to be free, and *my* capacity to be free, but also in the realization of *my fellow man's* right to be free, and *his* capacity to be free.
The issue we face is how to save man's belief in his capacity to be
free. Our age may be characterized as the *age of suspicion*. It has
become an axiom that the shortest way to the understanding of man
is to suspect his motives. This seems to be the contemporary version
of the Golden Rule: *Suspect thy neighbor as thyself*. Suspicion
breeds suspicion. It creates a chain-reaction. Honesty is not necessarily an anachronism.

The righteous man shall live by his faith. Can he live by his suspicion and be righteous? It is dangerous to take human freedom for granted, to regard it as a prerogative rather than as an obligation, as an ultimate fact rather than as an ultimate goal. It is the beginning of wisdom to be amazed at the fact of our being free.

Freedom is a gift which may be taken away from us. It is not an absolute but a relative possession, an opportunity. We are free only when living in attachment to the spirit.[3] The blessings and opportunities of living in a free society must not make us blind to those aspects of our society which threaten our freedom: the tyranny of needs, the vulgarization of the spirit are a particular challenge.

The insecurity of freedom is a bitter fact of historical experience. In times of unemployment, vociferous demagogues are capable of leading the people into a state of mind in which they are ready to barter their freedom for any bargain. In times of prosperity hidden persuaders are capable of leading the same people into selling their conscience for success. Unless a person learns how to rise daily to a higher plane of living, to care for that which surpasses his immediate needs, will he in a moment of crisis insist upon loyalty to freedom?

The threat to freedom lies in the process of reducing human relations to a matter of fact. Human life is no longer a drama; it is a routine. Uniqueness is suppressed, repetitiveness prevails. We teach our students how to recognize the labels, not how to develop a taste. Standardization corrodes the sense of ultimate significance. Man to his own self becomes increasingly vapid, cheap, insignificant. Yet without the sense of ultimate significance and ultimate preciousness of one's own existence, freedom becomes a hollow phrase.

We are losing our capacity for freedom. New forces have emerged which regulate our actions. Modern man is not motivated anymore, he is being propelled; he does not strive anymore, he is being driven.

The principle of majority decision, the binding force of a majority, depends upon the assumption that the individuals who make up the majority are capable of discerning between right and wrong. But we are gradually led to believe that man is incapable of making a significant moral judgment.

We have made great contributions to the spiritual defamation of man. Far from eliminating the fear of man, our novels and theories depict man as untrustworthy, passion-ridden, self-seeking, and disingenuous.

Reverence for man has been strenuously refuted as sentimental eyewash. We all ride on the highways of debunking. There seems to be no question in our mind that there is no depth to virtue, no reality to integrity; that all we can do is to graft goodness upon selfishness, to use truth as a pragmatic pretext, and to relish self-indulgence in all values.

Contemporary man is told that his religious beliefs are nothing but attempts to satisfy subconscious wishes, that his conception of God is merely a projection of self-seeking emotions, an objectification of subjective needs; God is the Ego in disguise. We have not only forfeited faith; we have also lost faith in the meaning of faith. This tendency to question the genuineness of man's concern for God is a challenge more serious than the tendency to question God's existence.

One of the chief problems of contemporary man is the problem: What to do with time? Most of our life we spend time in order to gain space, namely things of space. Yet when the situation arrives in which no things of space may be gained, the average man is at a loss as to what to do with time.

With the development of automation the number of hours to be spent professionally will be considerably reduced. The four-day week may become a reality within this generation. The problem will arise: What to do with so much leisure time? The problem will be *too much* time rather than too little time. But too much time is a breeding ground for crime (see "To Grow in Wisdom," pp. 79 ff.).

The modern man has not only forgotten how to be alone; he finds it even difficult to be with his fellow man. He not only runs away from himself; he runs away from his family. To children, "Honor your father and your mother," is an irrational suggestion. The normal relationship is dull; deviation is where pleasure is found.

The modern man does not know how to stand still, how to appreciate a moment, an event for its own sake. When witnessing an important event or confronted with a beautiful sight, all he does is take a picture. Perhaps this is what our religious traditions must teach the contemporary man: to stand still and to behold, to stand still and to hear.

Judaism claims that the way to nobility of the soul is the art of sanctifying time. Moral dedications, acts of worship, intellectual pursuits are means in the art of sanctification of time. Personal concern for justice in the market place, for integrity in public affairs and in public relations is a prerequisite for our right to pray.

Acts of worship counteract the trivialization of existence. Both involve the person, and give him a sense of living in ultimate relationships. Both of them are ways of teaching man how to stand alone and not be alone, of teaching man that God is a refuge, not a security.

But worship comes out of wisdom, out of insight, it is not an act of oversight. Learning, too, is a religious commandment. I do not mean the possession of learning, erudition; I mean the very act of study, of being involved in wisdom, and of being overwhelmed by the marvel and mystery of God's creation (see "Idols in the Temples," p. 57).

Religion's major effort must be to counteract the deflation of man, the trivialization of human existence. Our religious traditions claim that man is capable of sacrifice, discipline, of moral and spiritual exaltation, that every man is capable of an ultimate commitment.

Ultimate commitment includes the consciousness of being accountable for the acts we perform under freedom; the awareness that what we own we owe; the capacity for repentance; that a life without the service of God is a secret scandal.

Faith in God cannot be forced upon man. The issue is not only lack of faith but the vulgarization of faith, the misunderstanding and abuse of freedom. Our effort must involve a total reorientation about the nature of man and the world. And our hope lies in the certainty that all men are capable of sensing the wonder and mystery of existence, that all men have a capacity for reverence. Awe, reverence precedes faith; it is at the root of faith. We must grow in awe in order to reach faith. We must be guided by awe to be worthy of faith. Awe is "the beginning and gateway of faith, the first precept of all, and upon it the whole world is established."

The grandeur and mystery of the world that surrounds us is not something which is perceptible only to the elect. All men are endowed with a sense of wonder, with a sense of mystery. But our system of education fails to develop it and the anti-intellectual climate of our civilization does much to suppress it. Mankind will not perish for lack of information; it may collapse for want of appreciation.

Education for reverence, the development of a sense of awe and mystery, is a prerequisite for the preservation of freedom.

We must learn how to bridle the outrageous presumption of modern man, to cultivate a sense of wonder and reverence, to develop an awareness that something is asked of man. Freedom is a burden that God has thrust upon man. Freedom is something we are responsible for. If we succeed, we will help in the redemption of the world; if we fail, we may be crushed by its abuse. Freedom as man's unlimited lordship is the climax of absurdity, and the central issue we face is man's false sense of sovereignty.

Tragic is the role of religion in contemporary society. The world is waiting to hear the Voice, and those who are called upon to utter the word are confused and weak in faith. "The voice of the Lord is powerful; the voice of the Lord is full of majesty" (Psalm 29:4). Where is its power? Where is its majesty?

A story is told about a community where a man was accused of having transgressed the Seventh Commandment. The leaders of the community went to the Rabbi and, voicing their strong moral indignation, demanded stern punishment of the sinner. Thereupon the Rabbi turned his face to the wall and said: "O, Lord, Thy glory is in heaven, Thy presence on earth is invisible, imperceptible. In contrast to Thy invisibility, the object of that man's passion stood before his eyes, full of beauty and enravishing his body and soul. How could I punish him?"

Rabbi Simon said: "When the Holy One, blessed be He, came to create Adam, the ministering angels formed themselves into groups and parties, some of them saying, 'Let him be created,' whilst others urged, 'Let him not be created.' Thus it is written, Love and Truth fought together, Righteousness and Peace combatted each other (Psalm 85:11): Love said, 'Let him be created, because he will dispense acts of love'; Truth said, 'Let him not be created, because he is compounded of falsehood'; Righteousness said, 'Let him be created, because he will perform righteous deeds'; Peace said, 'Let him not be created because he is full of strife.' What did the Lord do? He took Truth and cast it to the ground. Said the ministering angels before the Holy One, blessed be He, 'Sovereign of the Universe! Why dost Thou despise Thy seal? Let Truth arise from the earth!' Hence it is written, Let truth spring up from the earth (Psalm 85:12)."[4]

God had to bury truth in order to create man.

How does one ever encounter the truth? The truth is underground, hidden from the eye. Its nature and man's condition are such that he can neither produce nor invent it. However, there is a way. If you bury the lies, truth will spring up. Upon the grave of the specious we encounter the valid. Much grave digging had to be done. The most fatal trap into which religious thinking may fall is *the equation of faith with expediency*. The genuine task of our traditions is to educate a sense for the expedient, a sensitivity to God's demand.

Perhaps we must begin by disclosing *the fallacy of absolute expediency*. God's voice may sound feeble to our conscience. Yet there is a divine cunning in history which seems to prove that the wages of absolute expediency is disaster. We must not tire of reminding the world that something is asked of man, of every man; that the value of charity is not to be measured in terms of public relations. Foreign aid, when offered to underdeveloped countries for the purpose of winning friends and influencing people, turns out to be a boomerang. Should we not learn how to detach expediency from charity? The great failure of American policy is not in public relations. The great failure is in private relations.

The spirit is a still small voice, and the masters of vulgarity use loudspeakers. The voice has been stifled, and many of us have lost faith in the possibility of a new perceptiveness.

Discredited is man's faith in his own integrity. We question man's power to sense any ultimate significance. We question the belief in the compatibility of existence with spirit.

Yet man is bound to break the chains of despair, to stand up against those who deny him the right and the strength to believe wholeheartedly. Ultimate truth may be hidden from man, yet the power to discern between the valid and the specious has not been taken from us.

Surely God will always receive a surprise of a handful of fools— who do not fail. There will always remain a spiritual underground where a few brave minds continue to fight. Yet our concern is not how to worship in the catacombs but rather how to remain human in the skyscrapers.

NOTES

1. Portions of this section are based on Heschel, *Man Is Not Alone* (New York: Farrar, Straus, 1951).

2. Portions of this section are based on Heschel, *The Prophets* (New York: Harper & Row, 1962), Chap. 1.

3. "The Torah says: 'The tables were the work of God and the writing was the writing of God, engraved upon the tablets' (Exodus 32:16). Read not *harut* (meaning 'engraved') but *herut* meaning freedom, for none can be considered free except those who occupy themselves with the study of the Torah" (*Aboth*, VI, 2).

4. "The seal of God is truth" (*Shabbut*, 55b).

2 / The Patient as a Person

I wish I could extend the theme of this session—"The Patient as a Person"—and speak about the person as a patient. We are all patients, regardless of whether we have studied medicine or not. We all have suffering in common. Scratch the skin of any human being and you come upon some degree of helplessness, misery, or even agony. Being a person involves the ability to suffer himself, to suffer for others; to know *passio*, passion, as well as compassion. But I must adhere to the topic and speak as suggested to me: *The Patient as a Person*.

What is human about a human being?

Biologically man is properly classified as a type of mammal, and defined as an animal with a distinguishing attribute. And yet, such definitions prove to be meaningless when you stand with man face to face.

It is reported that after Plato had defined man to be a two-legged animal without feathers, Diogenes plucked a cock and brought it into the Academy. . . .

The zoomorphic conception of man enables us to assign his place in the physical universe, yet it fails to account for the infinite dissimilarity between man and the highest animal below him. The gulf between the human and the nonhuman can be grasped only in human terms. The very question we ask: What is human about a human being? is not an animal problem but a human problem.

What we seek to ascertain is not the animality but the humanity of
man. The common definitions, for all the truths they contain, are
both an oversimplification and an evasion.

Human being is being *sui generis*. The only adequate way to
grasp its meaning is to think of man in human terms. Human is
more than a concept of fact; it is a category of value, of the highest
of all values available to us.

What is the worth of an individual man? According to a rabbinic
dictum, "he who saves one man is regarded as if he saved all men;
he who destroys one man is regarded as if he destroyed all men."

It is beyond my power to assess the worth of all of humanity.
What would a Life Insurance Company charge for the insurance of
the entire human race? Now it is just as staggering to ponder the
worth of one human being.

In terms of statistics the individual man is an exceedingly insignificant specimen compared with the totality of the human species.
So why should the life and dignity of an individual man be regarded
as infinitely precious?

Because human being is not just being-around, being-here-too, a
being to be assessed and classified in terms of quantity. Human
being is a disclosure of the divine. The grandeur of human being is
revealed in the power of being human.

What is the meaning of human being? In dealing with a particular man I do not come upon a generality but upon an individuality,
upon uniqueness, upon a person. I see a face, not only a body; a
special situation, not a typical case. The disease is common, the
patient is unique.

Most conspicuous is the variety and inner richness of the human
species. Not only do individuals differ widely; the individual himself
is not always the same. Look at a dog. Once a dog always a dog. Yet
man may be a sinner today and a saint tomorrow. Perhaps the most
amazing aspect about man is what is latent in him.

One thing that sets man apart from animals is a boundless,
unpredictable capacity for the development of an inner universe.
There is more potentiality in his soul than in any other being

known to us. Look at the infant and try to imagine the multitude of events it is going to engender. One child named Johann Sebastian Bach was charged with power enough to hold generations of men in his spell. But is there any potentiality to acclaim or any surprise to expect in a calf or a colt? Indeed, the essence of human being is not in what he is, but in what he is able to be.

What constitutes being human, personhood? The ability to be concerned for other human beings. Animals are concerned for their own instinctive needs; the degree of our being human stands in direct proportion to the degree in which we care for others. The word "cure" comes from the word "care."

The truth of being human is gratitude, the secret of existence is appreciation, its significance is revealed in reciprocity. Mankind will not die for lack of information; it may perish for lack of appreciation.

Being human presupposes the paradox of freedom, the capacity to create events, to transcend the self. Being human is a surprise, a flash of light; a moment in time rather than a thing in space. It has no meaning, no genuine reality, or validity within the context of the categories of space. It cannot be validated or kept alive within scientific empiricism.

The ultimate significance of human being as well as the ultimate meaning of being human may be wishful thinking, a ridiculous conceit in the midst of a world apparently devoid of ultimate meaning, a supreme absurdity.

It is part of the cure to trust in Him who cures.

Supreme meaning is therefore inconceivable without meaning derived from supreme being. Humanity without divinity is a torso. This is even reflected in the process of healing.

Without a sense of significant being, a sense of wonder and mystery, a sense of reverence for the sanctity of being alive, the doctor's efforts and prescriptions may prove futile.

I am born a human being; what I have to acquire is being human.

The tragedy is that our way of thinking and living leads to a gradual liquidation of the riches of the inner man. We are losing any understanding of the meaning of being human.

The contemporary man is bored, bitter, blasphemously disgruntled. His scientific goal is to quantify the soul. The human as a category is becoming meaningless, a linguistic aberration.

To be human we must know what humanity means, how to acquire, how to preserve it. Being human is both a fact and a demand, a condition and an expectation. Our being human is always on trial, full of risk, precarious; man is always in danger of forfeiting his humanity.

One of the most frightening prospects we must face is that this earth may be populated by a race of beings which, though belonging to the race of *homo sapiens* according to biology, will be devoid of the qualities by which man is spiritually distinguished from the rest of organic creatures.

Just as death is the liquidation of human being, dehumanization is the liquidation of being human.

America's problem number one is not the use of insecticide but the promotion of spiritual homicide, the systematic liquidation of man as a person.

Decay sets in inconspicuously, not dramatically. Is it not possible that we are entering a stage in history out of which we may emerge as morons, as an affluent society of spiritual idiots? Doctors will disappear, veterinarians may take over the practice of medicine.

A baby was born in the hospital, and the father's first chance to see his first-born child was after it was brought home and placed in the crib. His friends saw how he leaned over the crib and an expression of extreme bewilderment was in his face. Why do you look so bewildered? Impossible, he answered, how can they make such a fine crib for $29.50?

We cannot speak about the patient as a person unless we also probe the meaning of the doctor as a person. You can only sense a person if you are a person. Being a person depends upon being alive to the wonder and mystery that surround us, upon the realization that there is no ordinary man. Every man is an extraordinary man.

Technocracy is growing apace. Soon the doctor may be obsolete. The data about the patient would be collected by camera and dictaphone, arranged by typists, processed into a computer. Diagnosis and treatment would be established by a machine, and who then would need doctors?

The mother of medicine is not human curiosity but human compassion, and it is not good for medicine to be an orphan. Physics may be studied as a pure science, medicine must never be practiced for its own sake.

In contrast to times gone by, the doctor's role has broadened from healing the sick to serving all men, ill and well. However, I will limit myself to the role of the physician as a healer, a supreme test of his role in the life of society.

What manner of man is the doctor? Life abounds in works of achievement, in areas of excellence and beauty, but the physician is a person who has chosen to go to the areas of distress, to pay attention to sickness and affliction, to injury and anguish.

Medicine is more than a profession. Medicine has a soul, and its calling involves not only the application of knowledge and the exercise of skill but also facing a human situation. It is not an occupation for those to whom career is more precious than humanity or for those who value comfort and serenity above service to others. The doctor's mission is prophetic.

Humanity is an unfinished process, and so is religion. The law, the teaching, and the wisdom are here, yet without the outburst of prophetic men coming upon us again and again, religion may become fossilized. Nature has marvelous recuperative power, yet without the aid of the art of medicine the human species might degenerate.

There is a prophetic ingredient in the calling of the doctor. His vocation is to prevent illness, to cure disease, to lessen pain, to avert death. The doctor is a prophet, a watchman, a messenger, an assayer, a tester.

The weight of a doctor's burden is heavy and often grave. In other professions mistakes, inadvertency, blunders may be pardonable, even remediable; the doctor, however, is often like an acrobat, a ropewalker; precision, meticulousness are imperative; one mistake and the patient may be dead.

While medical science is advancing, the doctor-patient relationship seems to be deteriorating. In fairness to physicians, the relationship has changed because medicine has changed. The doctor of old may have had little more to offer the patient than understanding, sympathy, personal affection.

The great advances in medicine have made it necessary for men to specialize if they wish to remain abreast of any particular field of medicine, and this specialization has forced a change in the image of the practitioner. Involved as he must be in the technical minutiae of his practice, he is one to dim down the sick to uniformity, to become oblivious to the personal aspect of human being.

The blunder in much of primitive medicine was in the tendency to personalize disease; the error in much of contemporary medicine is the tendency to depersonalize the patient, to treat the disease and to ignore the person. Is it really so that specialization and compassion, the use of instruments and personal sensitivity are mutually exclusive?

The failure is due to the loss of awareness of what it means to be a person, of what it means to be human and to the distortion of the concept and image of being a doctor.

What many of us fear is a collapse of the old and traditional esteem for the character of the doctor, an increasing alienation between the healer and the sick. By many people the doctor is alleged to act like an executive, and the patient is only a consumer.

Generalizations are unfair. Such an image may apply to a minority of men in this great profession. Yet attitudes of some may reveal a condition of concern to many.

The crisis in the doctor-patient relationship is part of the ominous, unhealthy, livid condition of human relations in our entire society, a spiritual malaria, a disease of which high powered commercialism and intellectual vulgarity are only premonitory symptoms. Let me offer an example of intellectual vulgarity.

What is the meaning of being a person? According to the philosophy of a dog, to quote Bradley, what smells is; what does not smell is not real and does not exist. According to the philosophy of logical positivism, what is verifiable is meaningful; what is not verifiable is meaningless. Thus, the term "person" should be regarded as a misnomer, unverifiable, indefinable, vague, mystical, and therefore both meaningless and worthless. Since we must think in terms which are both clear and exact, man must be regarded as a collection of tubes and cells, of pipes and wires. This is a scientific fact, accessible to our instruments.

Strictly speaking, what is a patient? A human machine in need of repair; all else is accidental. Or, as has been suggested, man could best be defined as an ingenious assembly of portable plumbing.

As a patient, what do I see when I see a doctor? Since I am essentially a machine, I see the doctor as a plumber, whose task is to repair a tube in my system. What does the doctor encounter when he examines a patient? He sees a case, a urinary case, an intestinal case, but not a person. This, then, would be our philosophy: The world is a factory, man a gadget, and the doctor a plumber; all else is irrelevant.

While such a philosophy of medicine may seem plausible, it is being refuted by the grandeur and agony of man. And no one sees so much agony as you, gentlemen.

To accept such a philosophy would be to perpetrate euthanasia on the spirit of medicine itself. The mechanics of medicine must not be mistaken for the very essence of medicine, which is an art and not alone a science.

The human organism can accept an artificial leg or a transplanted kidney. But will a patient retain his identity if his brain is removed and a mechanized brain is put in instead? Will medicine retain its identity if reduced to engineering?

The doctor-patient relationship comes to pass in the dimension of personhood as it does in the dimensions of time and space. There is no escape.

It is not true that diagnosis or treatment of a patient comes about in a way completely unaffected by religious and philosophical commitments. The doctor's commitments are as much a part of it as scientific knowledge and skill. His attitudes are either sensitive or cruel, human or inhuman; there is no middle course. Indifference is callousness.

The doctor is not simply a dispenser of drugs, a computer that speaks. In treating a patient he is morally involved. What transpires between doctor and patient is more than a commercial transaction, more than a professional relationship between a specimen of the human species and a member of the American Medical Association. Medicine is not simply merchandise, and the relationship between doctor and patient is blasphemously distorted when conceived primarily in terms of economics: the doctor a merchant, the patient a customer. What comes to pass in the doctor's office is a profoundly human association, involving concern, trust, responsibility. The doctor is commander-in-chief in the battle for survival.

Disease has been defined by Spencer as a state which prevents an organism from relating itself to the conditions of its environment. A doctor who lacks the ability to relate himself to a patient must be regarded as suffering from a serious deficiency.

The doctor enters a covenant with the patient; he penetrates his life, affecting his mode of living, often deciding his fate. The doctor's role is one of royal authority, while the patient's mood is one of anxiety and helplessness. The patient is literally a sufferer, while the doctor is the incarnation of his hope.

The patient must not be defined as a client who contracts a physician for service; he is a human being entrusted to the care of a physician.

The physician is the trustee holding the patient's health in trust. In return, the patient's earnest is reliance, commitment. In other relationships trust may be replaceable by shrewdness or caution, in the doctor-patient relationship trust is the essence; distrust may spell disaster.

The work of a teacher is being judged by a host of students. The books of a scholar are critically examined by reviews published in magazines. Yet the work of the practicing physician is seldom subject to public evaluation. The patient's reliance upon his doctor is often due to blind faith.

In our democratic society where every individual insists upon being independent, and authoritarianism is abhorrent, the doctor is the only person whose authority is accepted and even cherished and on whose judgment we depend. Sickness, like sin, indicates frailty, deficiency, scantity in the make-up of man. The survival of the patient does not depend on the pharmacist alone.

The doctor's position is formidable. He gives orders and demands strict obedience. The doctor is not alone in his effort to conquer disease. The patient is a partner, not a bystander.

Disease is an assault, and healing is war. The doctor as an autocrat would be like a general without an army. The patient is both battlefield and soldier. Chemistry supplies the weapons, but who will decide whether the enemy is defeated by strategy or valor?

The patient is a person. A person is not a combination of body and soul but rather body and soul as one. The human body is personal.

Health is profoundly related to one's way of thinking, to one's sense of values. And physical well-being, the chemistry of the body are not independent of the condition of the inner man.

The doctor must find out the pressure of the blood and the composition of the urine, but the process of recovery also depends on the pressure of the soul and the composition of the mind.

Diet and physical exercise are important, but so are the capacity to praise, the power to revere, self-discipline and the taste of self-transcendence—these are qualities of being human.[1]

Sickness, while primarily a problem of pathology, is a crisis of the total person, not only a physical disorder. There is a spiritual dimension to sickness. At a moment in which one's very living is called into question, the secretions of character, commitments of the heart, the modes of answering the ultimate question, of what it means to be alive, are of supreme importance.

How to be sick gracefully? The process of healing is war, and the first casualty when war comes is moral pretentiousness. Peevishness, resentfulness, suspicion are not restrained by constipation. How to grow spiritually in distress?

Sickness ought to make us humble. In a world where recklessness and presumption are the style of living, and callousness dominates relationships between man and man, sickness is a reminder of our own neediness and extremity, an opportunity for the cynic to come upon the greatness of compassion.

Life is mystery, the reflection of God's presence in His self-imposed absence. Jacob on his sickbed bowed his head (Genesis 47:31) in acknowledging the invisible presentness of the Lord. God's presence is at the patient's bed. His chief commandment is, "Choose life" (Deuteronomy 30:19). The doctor is God's partner in the struggle between life and death. Religion is medicine in the form of a prayer; medicine is prayer in the form of a deed. From the perspective of the love of God, the work of healing and the work of religion are one. The body is a sanctuary, the doctor is a priest.

Medicine is a sacred art. Its work is holy. Yet the holy disappears when reverence is disused. Reverence for the doctor is a prerequisite for the sanity of all men. Yet we only revere a human being who knows how to revere other human beings.

It is a grievous mistake to keep a wall of separation between medicine and religion. There is a division of labor but a unity of spirit. The act of healing is the highest form of *imitatio Dei*. To minister to the sick is to minister to God. Religion is not the assistant of medicine but the secret of one's passion for medicine.

No honor is adequate and no reward is too high for those who have chosen to live in the areas of distress, at the sickbeds, in the clinics. However, not all rewards are benign. Some are like narcotics, poisonous, habit-forming.

In our acquisitive society the ambition to get rich is generally regarded as a most respectable trait. I am not going to make a judgment on that. However, there are some callings where such an ambition is a dangerous impediment, among these I would include ministers, teachers, lawyers, and physicians.

Acquisitiveness is an insidious disease; among its effects are hardening of the arteries of love and understanding, perversion of one's sense of values. It poisons every vocation in our society, including those in which sensitivity to suffering humanity or dedication to the exercise of law and justice should be paramount.

The mortal danger faced by all of us is to succumb to the common virus of commercialism—the temptation to make a lot of money.

The motivation to dedicate one's life to the great calling of medicine has its source in the depth of the person. Yet a great calling, whether teaching, healing, or writing, is a jealous mistress; she requires complete devotion, supreme appreciation. Medicine, teaching, and the ministry are not sinecures; nor are patients, students, and parishioners shares to be traded at the stock exchange.

May I suggest a therapy for the virus of commercialism: a personal decision to establish a maximum level of income.

Luxuries are expensive, but making money is even more expensive. We pay for it dearly. Making money may cost us values that no money can buy.

The flesh is weak, temptations are strong. But the sign of intelligence is the capacity to delay the satisfaction of desire and above all to exercise preference, to make an option, when the integrity of one's vocation is in danger of being corrupted.

The doctor must realize the supreme nobility of his vocation, to cultivate a taste for the pleasures of the soul. There is no more thrilling adventure than to alleviate pain, no greater pleasure than to restore health. Perhaps no more beautiful life has ever been conceived than a life devoted to healing the sick.

Striving for personal success is a legitimate and wholesome ingredient of the person. The danger begins when personal success becomes a way of thinking, the supreme standard of all values. Success as the object of supreme and exclusive concern is both pernicious and demonic. Such passion knows no limit. According to my own medical theory, more people die of success than of cancer.

The goal is to protect or to restore the patient's health. But do we not create a *Sisyphus complex* if we cure him physically and destroy him economically? Is it a triumph when the appendix is removed and bitterness is imbued?

It is no secret that the image of the doctor in the mind of the public and in the profession itself is deteriorating. The admiration for medical science is increasing, the respect for its practitioners is decreasing. The depreciation of the image of the doctor is bound to disseminate disenchantment and to affect the state of medicine itself. What should motivate a serious and dedicated student to commit himself to the study and practice of medicine?

Should the medical profession forfeit its nobility of purpose and the doctor become a status-seeker, it will lose its attraction, and only inspire gifted students to prepare themselves for better paid positions in business and industry. Is not the deplorable scarcity of nurses, and the poor quality of service in many hospitals, a foretaste of what may be expected?

Is dehumanization and commercialization the price we must pay for technical progress? If medicine is not to lose its calling, it must be concerned with its own health. I invite you to understand your predicament a little better.

Let us think of the helpless and the poor languishing in the wards, in the clinics and dispensaries, of the private hospitals who refuse to admit a human being in agony, unless cash is offered in advance.

The nightmare of medical bills, the high arrogance and callousness of the technicians, splitting fees, vested interests in promoting pharmaceutical products, suspicion that the physician is suggesting more surgery than absolutely necessary—all converge to malign the medical profession. Man is often sick, and medicine is indispensable for survival. But medicine today is believed to be itself in need of therapy.

Socialized medicine may be a dangerous thing. But what shall we think of socialized sickness, of socialized despair of the aged?

It is both sterile and dangerous to be involved in defensive and obsolete thinking. We must be open to the situation and seek to make available to all men the blessings that the genius of medicine has discovered.

It is not enough to battle socialism. What is needed is fresh creative thinking, openness to the situation.

We must not be enslaved to conceptual clichés, not remain in the rut of outworn ideas, not do what other people do, simply justifying our present economic practice.

The marvelous achievements of medicine must not make us blind to the problems that continue to arise as a result of the socioeconomic revolution. It is terribly embarrassing to know that some individual doctors seem to think that it is highly improper for a patient to get sick during weekends. (Night calls are as fashionable as horse and buggy.) The patient is haunted with fear, but some doctors are in a hurry, and above all impatient. They have something in common with God; they cannot be easily reached, not even at the golf course.

A subject that requires most careful, dispassionate study is medical care for the aged. The expense of modern methods of therapy is high and often beyond the financial means of many citizens. The economics of medicine is a field about which I have no competence to speak. Yet it is certainly the obligation of the medical profession to see to it that every patient receives the care he needs. The task of the physician is to treat the whole man, the total individual. But is not the economic situation a part of the condition of the whole man? Can it be ignored in facing the patient as a person?

Doctors occupy a privileged position in society and it is their duty to rise above the standards of society and to herald a new ethical vision! The word "doctor" means teacher. We are in the midst of many revolutions. Above all, man's sense of the meaning of his being must change. This problem must become the doctor's concern. He has a stake in the battle against the decay of conscience.

Many of us, doctors and patients alike, are expecting the A.M.A. to serve as a major moral force in the life of our society. Whatever affects the health of man—the care for the aged, the prevention of illness, the use of nuclear weapons—is within the scope of the A.M.A.

Physical vigor alone does not constitute total health. Nor is longevity the only purpose of living. Quality of living is as important as quantity of living. The achievement of personhood, being human, is as important for health as all medical inventions put together.

For the doctor to carry out his part, he must be concerned with his own personhood. In addition to his efforts in enhancing his scientific knowledge and skill, his daily concern must be with enhancing his own qualities of living.

You might say that this is a task to be left to religion. Let the minister do it! No, I would not let him do it alone. Maintaining and conserving total health involves quality, and it is the doctor's duty to do it.

I feel humble in your presence. The least of you has to his credit the merit of soothing pain, of preventing grief and tears. All I can do is to labor in the mineworks where God and man are intermingled and to use the power of ideas to raise the mind, to unfreeze the heart. What I say in words, you proclaim in deeds.

To save human life is to do the work of God. To heal is to do the holy. There is nothing greater. The glory of God is reflected in the majesty of medicine. It is for this reason that we must strive for this majesty to remain immaculate, without fault, without blemish.

Moral sensitivity is neither inherent as grist in our bones, nor does it float in the air as an idea; it is radiant energy, waves of a divine light. Our moral substance depends upon the process of emission and absorption, upon the witnessing or receiving, upon the outpouring of the goodness done by human beings.

Eclipse of sensitivity is the mark of our age. Callousness expands at the rate of nuclear energy, while moral sensitivity subsides.

The calling and conduct of the doctor is care for others, and the meeting of doctor and patient is a supreme occasion for being human. The doctor is a major source of moral energy affecting the spiritual texture and substance of the entire society.

Character is shaped by experiences of quality, particularly by what we come upon in times of anxiety. A patient is a person in crisis and anxiety, and few experiences have such a decisive impact upon our ability to understand the meaning of being human as the way in which the doctor relates himself to us at such times.

The doctor is not only a healer of disease, he is also a source of emanation of the spirit of concern and compassion. The doctor may be a saint without knowing it and without pretending to be one.

NOTE

1. For discussion of these ideas see Heschel, *Who Is Man?* (Stanford: Stanford University Press, 1965).

3 / Children and Youth

The problem of our youth is not youth. The problem is the spirit of our age: denial of transcendence, the vapidity of values, emptiness in the heart, the decreased sensitivity to the imponderable quality of the spirit, the collapse of communication between the realm of tradition and the inner world of the individual. The central problem is that we do not know how to think, how to pray, how to cry, how to resist the deceptions of too many persuaders. There is no community of those who worry about integrity.

The problem will not be solved by implanting in the youth a sense of belonging. Belonging to a society that fails in offering opportunities to satisfy authentic human needs will not soothe the sense of frustration and rebellion. What youth needs is a sense of significant being, a sense of reverence for the society to which we all belong.

The mainspring of tenderness and compassion lies in reverence. It is our supreme educational duty to enable the child to revere. The heart of the Ten Commandments is to be found in the words: *Revere thy father and thy mother.* Without profound reverence for father and mother, our ability to observe the other commandments is dangerously impaired. The problem we face, the problem I as a father face, is why my child should revere me. Unless my child will sense in my personal existence acts and attitudes that evoke reverence—the ability to delay satisfactions, to overcome prejudices, to sense the holy, to strive for the noble—why should she revere me?

Reverence for parents is the fundamental form of reverence, for in the parent is incarnated the mystery of man's coming into being. Rejection of the parent is a repudiation of the mystery. Only a person who lives in a way which is compatible with the mystery of human existence is capable of evoking reverence in the child. The basic problem is the parent, not the child.

We are all conscious of a supreme crisis in history. We are all exposed to a progressive corrosion of our moral and spiritual sensibilities, in the process of which we may lose our freedom, and even our lives.

Hard-won insights of the Western tradition are falling into oblivion. Timeless values are going out of fashion. The joys of inner living are denied to most of us. *Sensitivity is a luxury,* but *entertainment is becoming a compulsion.*

Home, inwardness, friendship, conversation are becoming obsolete. Instead of insisting: my home is my castle, we confess: my car is my home. We have no friends; we have business associates. Conversation is disappearing; watching television substitutes for the expression of ideas.

Our nation's spiritual plight embarrasses its best sons, its finest friends. What goes on in the homes of America has a profound effect upon the state of the world.

What is the spirit of the age? It is, I believe, the instrumentalization of the world, the instrumentalization of man, the instrumentalization of all values.

Others may suffer from degradation by poverty; we are threatened by degradation through power. Small is the world most of us pay attention to, and limited is our concern. What do we see when we see the world? There are three aspects of nature that command our attention: its *power,* its *beauty,* and its *grandeur.* Accordingly, there are three ways in which we may relate ourselves to the world—we may exploit it, we may enjoy it, we may accept it in awe. In the history of civilization different aspects of nature have drawn forth the talents of man; sometimes its power, sometimes its beauty and occasionally its grandeur have attracted his mind. Our age is one in which usefulness is thought to be the chief merit of nature; in which the attainment of power, the utilization of its resources is taken to be the chief and only purpose of man in the universe. Man has indeed become primarily a tool-making animal, and the world is now a gigantic tool-box for the satisfaction of his needs.

The Greeks learned in order to comprehend. The Hebrews learned in order to revere. The modern man learns in order to use, accepting the maxim which declares: "*Knowledge is power.*" This is how people are urged to study: knowledge means success. We no longer know how to justify any value except in terms of expediency. Man is willing to define himself as "a seeker after the maximum degree of comfort for the minimum expenditure of energy." He equates value with that which avails. He feels, acts, and thinks as if the sole purpose of the universe were to satisfy his needs.

The obsession with power has completely transformed the life of man and dangerously stunted his concern for beauty and grandeur. We have achieved plenty, but lost quality; we have easy access to pleasure, we forget the meaning of joy. But what is more serious is the fact that man's worship of power has resurrected the demon of power.

Not only do we distort our sight of the world by paying attention only to its aspect of power; we are reducing the status of man from that of *a person* to that of *a thing*. We have locked ourselves out of the world by regarding it only as material for the gratification of our desires. There is a strange cunning in the fact that when man looks only at that which is useful, he eventually becomes useless to himself. In reducing the world to an instrument, man himself becomes an instrument. Man is the tool, and the machine is the consumer. The instrumentalization of the world leads to the *disintegration of man.*

The world is too sublime to be a tool, and man is too great to live by expediency alone. The mode of living which is becoming universal is rapidly depriving man of his sense of significance.

According to an ancient Hebrew saying, the world rests upon three pillars: upon *learning,* upon *worship,* and upon *charity.* Learning meant having a share in divine wisdom; the object of worship was the Creator; charity meant both openness to and active sympathy with our fellowman's suffering.

In our civilization these pillars become instruments. Learning is pursued in order to attain power; charity is done not because it is holy, but because it is useful for public relations. And the supreme object of our worship and adoration is our own ego.

An extreme crisis calls for radical efforts, for a radical reorientation. Power is an instrument, not the end of living. Learning, worship, charity are ends, not means. It is wrong to define education as *preparation* for life. Learning *is* life, a supreme experience of living, a climax of existence.

The teacher is more than a technician. He is the representative as well as the interpreter of mankind's most sacred possessions. Learning is holy, an indispensable form of purification as well as ennoblement. By learning I do not mean memorization, erudition; I mean the very act of study, of being involved in wisdom.

Genuine reverence for the sanctity of study is bound to invoke in the pupils the awareness that study is not an ordeal but an act of edification; that the school is *a sanctuary,* not a factory; that study is *a form of worship.* True learning is a way of relating oneself to something which is both *eternal* and *universal.* The experience of learning counteracts *tribalism* and *self-centeredness.* The work of our hands is *private* property; the fruits of the intellect belong *to all men.* The ultimate meaning of knowledge is not power, but the realization of a unity that surpasses all interests and all ages. Wisdom is like the sky, belonging to no man, and true learning is the astronomy of the spirit.

Learning, education, must not be equated with a curriculum we complete upon graduation. No one ever thinks that entertainment is a stage in one's life which is completed once a person has passed the test of being entertained. The meaning of existence is found in the experience of education. Termination of education is the beginning of despair. Every person bears a responsibility for the legacy of the past as well as the burden of the future.

We have come to accept compulsory military service in peacetime for the sake of national security. Am I too bold in suggesting the idea of compulsory adult education in leisure time for the sake of spiritual security?

To find a parallel to the situation of man in the atomic age we must go back to a prehistoric age when man living in the jungle had to be on the alert against continual threat to his very existence. The source of danger today is not the brutality of the beast but the power of man.

Constant danger requires constant vigilance. What is needed is *defense in depth,* in the depth of every person. For the holocausts are caused not only by atomic explosions. Holocausts are caused wherever a person is put to shame. *Daily living is brinkmanship.*

The burning issue is not things to come, but the things that happen here and now. The only way to prevent public scandals is to avoid involvement in private scandals. International disasters begin in individual crimes.

We have denied our young people the knowledge of the dark side of life. They see a picture of ease, play, and fun. That life includes hardships, illness, grief, even agony; that many hearts are sick with bitterness, resentfulness, envy—are facts of which young people have hardly an awareness. They do not feel morally challenged, they do not feel called upon.

The young person of today is pampered. In moments of crisis he transfers his guilt to others. Society, the age, or his mother is blamed for his failure. Weakened by self-indulgence, he breaks down easily under hardship.

The glorification of fun as the chief purpose of existence—education must be fun—failure to understand the meaning of tribulation, unwillingness to cope with privation, suffering, disappointment, or humiliation—these are major factors responsible for the huge divorce rate, the vast number of nervous breakdowns, and for escape into self-pity as a typical response to the challenge of trial.

What is there about our life that accounts for the plethora of morbidity and gloom in the works of the contemporary artists? There are jobs, opportunities for success, comfort, security, but there is no exaltation, no sense for that which is worthy of sacrifice, no lasting insight, no experience of adoration, no relatedness to the ultimately precious.

Demands which were made of the individual in earlier periods are now considered excessive. Self-discipline is obsolescent, self-denial unhygienic, metaphysical problems irrelevant. The terms of reference are emotional release and suppression, with little regard for remorse and responsibility.

Basic to man's existence is a sense of indebtedness, of indebtedness to society, of indebtedness to God. What is emerging in our age is a strange inversion. Modern man believes that the world is indebted to him, that society is charged with duties toward him. His standard and preoccupation: *What will I get out of life?* Suppressed is the question: *What will life, what will society get out of me?* (See "Religion in a Free Society," pp. 4 f.)

The basic issue is how young people can be brought up with a proper sense of responsibility in an affluent society. Yet, how can we expect the young to be noble if we ourselves continue to tolerate the ignoble? This is the advice given by a director of a large plant to his managers: Do not associate with unsuccessful people.

There is no sense of responsibility without reverence for *the sublime in human existence,* without a sense of dignity, without loyalty to a heritage, without an awareness of the transcendence of living. Self-respect is the fruit of discipline, the sense of dignity grows with the ability to say No to oneself.

We underestimate the nature of man. Even the form in which we ask the question about man is biased by our own conception of man as a thing. We ask: *What is man?* Yet the true question should be: *Who is man?*[1]

As a thing man is explicable, as a person he is both a mystery and a surprise. As a thing he is finite, as a person he is inexhaustible.

In order to explain man in terms of our categories, we were forced *to reduce the spiritual size of man* and, as a result, adjusted our spiritual norms and standards to our reduced size. Now we build machinery on a grand scale, and treat our soul as if it were a miniature toy.

The cardinal sin of our educational philosophy is that we have asked too little. Its modest standards are unfair to the potentialities of man. Is it true that man is capable of profundity, of sacrifice, of love, of self-denial?

Fundamental problems are ignored. To whom does man owe ultimate allegiance? Who is the object of worship? How to relate our deeds to a source of eternal meaning? What is lasting in our existence?

Perhaps this is the central issue: the instrumentalization of values. "Appraising Ideals and Values in Their Changing World" is the theme of this session of the White House Conference on Children and Youth. Are we truly committed to the notion that ideals and values vary and alter in accordance with changing conditions? Should we not question such a relativistic dogma? Is it not the degree of our sensitivity to the validity of the ultimate ideals and values that fluctuates rather than the ultimate ideals and values?

The agony of the contemporary man is *the agony of a spiritually stunted man*. The image of man is larger than the frame into which he has been compressed. In order to be human, man has to be more than a man. There is a divine stake in human existence.

We prepare the pupil for employment, for holding a job. We do not teach him how to be a person, how to resist conformity, how to grow inwardly, how to say No to his own self. We teach him how to adjust to the public; we do not teach him how to cultivate privacy.

How to save the inner man from oblivion—this is the major challenge we face. To achieve our goal, we must learn how to activate the soul, how to answer the ultimate, how to relate ourselves to the spirit.

We train the outward man; we must not neglect the inner man. We impart information; we must also foster a sense of appreciation. We teach skills, we must also stimulate insight. We are involved in numerous activities; we must not forget the meaning of stillness. We set a premium on togetherness; we should also acknowledge the value of solitude. Eloquence is important, but so is stillness. Skills are vital, but so is self-restraint.

We are not true to our own selves. We are afraid to formulate as norms the insights we cherish most. We are afraid of insisting upon norms lest they interfere with the conclusions of descriptive psychology, since only observations and descriptions of behavior are regarded as objective and impartial ways of knowing. However, we overlook the fact that what is seen and disclosed in our observations is strongly slanted by our own intellectual perspective and spiritual level.

Our foremost task is to drive out the darkness of ignorance from the minds of man, to impart knowledge about nature and history, individual and society. Yet we blunder into pretending that scientific information alone is capable of giving us a complete picture of man and of answering the ultimate problems of meaning and value, of solving the mystery of life and death.

Teachers complain about the listlessness and the lack of intellectual excitement of their students. Is it the fault of the students? If I understand correctly what goes on in our schools the sequence seems to call for information to be digested by the student, questions presented by the teacher, and answers to be supplied by the student. We evaluate the student by his ability to answer questions rather than to understand problems. Cribs and ponies become a major source of edification.

The truth, however, is that the valid test of a student is his ability to ask the right questions. I would suggest that we evolve a new type of examination paper, one in which the answers are given—the questions to be supplied by the student.

Our system of training tends to smother *man's sense of wonder and mystery,* to stifle rather than to cultivate his sense of the unutterable. I shudder to think of a generation devoid of a sense of wonder and mystery, devoid of a sense of inadequacy and embarrassment. I am terrified at the thought of being governed by people who believe that the world is all calculated and explained, who have no sense either of quality or of mystery.

We are fostering a type of man who lives by *borrowed words* rather than by his own innate *sense of the unutterable,* by the stirring in his own heart which no language can declare.

The human mind is in quest of *explanation.* Yet man is also in need of *exaltation.* Our tendency to make everything explicit, to explain the world as though everything were level and smooth, flat and bare, deprives the world of its aspect of grandeur which is indispensable to the ennoblement of man.

This is the legacy of the wisdom of the ages: this is a world we apprehend and cannot comprehend. There is a dimension of reality that lies within our reach but beyond our grasp. Just as no flora has ever fully displayed the hidden vitality of the earth, so has no work of art and no system of philosophy ever brought to expression the depth of the unutterable, in the sight of which creative power of man is evoked.

The knowledge of explanations makes a person strong. Does it make him *noble?* Is it not our duty as teachers to share the awareness of the ineffable, to cultivate a stillness in the soul? Stand still and behold! Behold not only in order to explain, to fit what we see into our notions; behold in order to stand face to face with the beauty and grandeur of the universe.

Talent, knowledge, success are important to human existence. Yet talent without dedication, knowledge without reverence, success without humility may end in futility. Important is the premise that a life unexamined is not worth living, yet it is just as vital to realize that life without a commitment to what is greater than life is not worth living.

Man has to choose between awe and anxiety, between the divine and the demonic, between radical amazement and radical despair. A time without awe becomes an age of anxiety; blindness to the presence of the divine leads to being possessed by the demonic.

Our society is fostering the *segregation of youth,* the separation of young and old. The adult has no fellowship with the young. He has little to say to the young, and there is little opportunity for the young to share the wisdom of experience, or the experience of maturity.

We, the adults, have delegated our moral responsibility to the schools, the social agencies, or community funds. We have time for hobbies, for watching baseball; we have no time to help the needy, to sustain the sick, to offer companionship to the lonely, no time to offer guidance to our children. Many of us have a fear of growing up and seem to cherish the idea of perpetual adolescence. Significantly, the biblical injunction does not say that we are to appoint a teacher to train our children. The biblical injunction is that the parent be the teacher.

School education is a supplement. The problem is not only the scarcity of teachers; the problem is the absence of parents. Education is not only a business for professionals. It is the vocation of all men at all times.

What we need are not only more school buildings and more playgrounds, but also the restoration of the home, the resurrection of the parent as a person worthy of being revered, as an example of devotion and responsibility.

One of the supreme principles which we all regard as essential to American democracy is the *sanctity of human life.* However, the regard for the sanctity of human life is contingent upon the *sanctity of human living.* If the ways of living become perverted, the idea of the sanctity of life is in danger of becoming meaningless.

An essential attribute of sanctity is transcendence. Sanctity points to something greater than itself. What it stands for is more than I am able to imagine or to appreciate. A sacred object is perceptible, but not completely available. It is in our custody, but not at our disposal. We may enjoy it; we must neither abuse nor consume it. Such is life, both my own and the life of my fellow man. I can only have regard for the sanctity of others if I insist upon cultivating sanctity in my own living.

Sanctity of life means that man is a partner, not a sovereign, that life is a trust, not a property. To exist as a human is to assist the divine.

What is the meaning of the statement that to exist as a human is to assist the divine? It means to be a witness to the holy, to give testimony to the grandeur of honesty, to the glory of righteousness, to the holiness of truth, to the marvel and mystery of being alive. We have all caught a glimpse of the mystery of the world. We have all experienced the wonder of love, the glory of compassion. To be human is to celebrate a greatness which surpasses the self.

The creation of the world is an unfinished process. The goals are not attained.

There is a cry for justice which only man must answer. There is a need for acts of compassion that only man must satisfy.

There is no hope for the survival of humanity unless we realize the absurdity of man's false sense of sovereignty as well as the fallacy of absolute expediency. Some of us may find it difficult to believe that God created the world, yet most of us find it even more difficult to act as if man had not created the world.

Time has come to revise the notion of adjustment to society as the preoccupation of the educational process. Many of the values and mores of our present-day society are imposed upon it by narrow-minded vested interests, and must not be regarded as sancta. The ideal of adjustment has resulted in unconditional conformity.

Together with adjustment to society we must cultivate a sense for injustice, impatience with vulgarity, a capacity for moral indignation, a will *to readjust society itself* when it becomes complacent and corrupt.

In this age the term "society" is too narrow. This is one world. A commitment to all mankind rather than the adjustment to one affluent society, a commitment to help the poor in the slums, the underprivileged in Asia and Africa must become imperative in American education. No one with a sensitive conscience can feel well adjusted to a self-indulgent society which is indifferent to the misery of millions of people.

What is the concrete and practical consequence of the change of attitude I am pleading for? But first I must propose a revision of the term "practical." The term "practical" is usually associated with activities capable of being described in terms of charts and statistics. I should like to stress that acts that occur within the inner life of man, a thought, a moment of sensitivity, a moment of stillness and self-examination, the acquisition of a spiritual insight, this is supremely practical.

What I plead for is that education is an end rather than a means; a life-long process rather than a passing stage. We have been guilty of underestimating the mind and soul of man. We must restore him to his true stature, we must become aware of the dangerous grandeur and the infinite capacity of man.

The task of counteracting the deflation of man and the trivialization of human existence is incumbent upon every man. But it is the duty of every teacher to teach and to live the claim that every man is capable of genuine love and compassion, of discipline and universality of judgment, of moral and spiritual exaltation.

We will have to adjust our educational standards to an enhanced conception of man; to rise to an understanding of values compatible with the grandeur of man and compatible with the challenge and danger of our age; to endeavor to develop an aptitude and personal responsibility in every student for the preservation of the humanistic tradition of the West, a reverence for what man has thought concerning universality, justice, and compassion; that right living consists not only in the satisfaction of personal needs, but also in responding to moral and spiritual demands.

Our greatest threat is not the atomic bomb. Our greatest threat is the callousness to the suffering of man. The most urgent task faced by American education is to destroy the myth that accumulation of wealth and the achievement of comfort are the chief vocations of man. How can adjustment to society be an inspiration to our youth if that society persists in squandering the material resources of the world on luxuries in a world where more than a billion people go to bed hungry every night? How can we speak of reverence for man and of the belief that all men are created equal without repenting the way we behave toward our brothers, the colored people of America?

We betray our youth if we fail to teach and to live by the principle that the destiny of man is to aid, to serve. We have to master in order to serve; we have to acquire in order to give away.

For *the high standard of living* the young people enjoy we must demand in return a *high standard of doing,* a *high standard of thinking.* Charity, being personally involved in relieving the sufferings of man, is as important to education as the acquisition of technical skills. We must implant in the pupil a sensitivity to the challenging questions: What shall I do with power? What shall I do with prosperity, with success, or even with competence?

A radical revision of attitudes is the call of the hour. It is a question of life and death. This is the supreme challenge to education. Will man rise to the emergency?

There are more marvels hidden in the soul of man than we are able to imagine. He will act, if he is inspired; he will respond, if called upon.

NOTE

1. For discussion of this problem see Heschel, *Who Is Man?* (Stanford: Stanford University Press, 1965).

4 / *Idols in the Temples*

What is religious about religious education?

Only scoundrels are modest. There is one thing we, as Jews, must never surrender: our high standards of education. None of us here can rest content with his intellectual, moral, or spiritual state of living.

Contemporary religious education stands in sharp contrast to general education. Contemporary general education, all strictures notwithstanding, must be credited with remarkable accomplishments in the teaching of science as well as in other subjects. In comparison, religious education must be regarded as having fallen short of its goals. It would be irresponsible to conceal what most of us acknowledge.

The Bible may be found in the hotels, but it is not to be found in the homes or in the minds. Few of our contemporaries have ever absorbed the challenge of the prophets or the grandeur of the Book of Genesis, though they have attended Sunday school and were thrilled with the confirmation ceremonies. What prevails in the field of religion is intellectual as well as spiritual illiteracy, ignorance as well as idolatry of false values. We are a generation devoid of learning as well as sensitivity.

Why has attendance at religious school in most cases not shaped the character and attitudes of our children? What are the factors to be blamed for such ineffectiveness? Without minimizing the corroding influence of the general social climate, I insist that the *vapidity and trivialization of religious instruction* is the major cause of this failure.

There are numerous forces that neutralize the effect of religious instruction. We may in our teaching extol the value of learning, compassion, and faith, yet the child lives most of the time in an atmosphere obsessed with commercialism, boastfulness, and cynicism. The environment has never been particularly favorable to any attempt to serve the will of God. We must learn to survive in spite and because of adverse spiritual conditions. It would be suicidal to live by the maxim that unless the climate favors our principles, they will have to be discarded.

General studies are taught on a high level of learning, while religious education is satisfied with clichés buttered with sentimentality. As a result, religious instruction acquired in childhood fades away when exposed to the challenge and splendor of other intellectual powers in an age of scientific triumphs.

For many people the Sunday school has proved to be more of a hindrance than a help in their effort to attain a deeper understanding for God.

What young people need is not religious tranquilizers, *religion as a diversion, religion as entertainment,* but *spiritual audacity, intellectual guts, power of defiance!*

Another malady is the intellectual irrelevance of tradition to the person, the collapse of communication between personal problems of the individual and the message of our heritage.

An education which continues to evade intellectual problems or which ignores emotional obtuseness is doomed to failure.

We tell the pupil many things, but what has our instruction to do with his inner problems, with the way he is going to behave or think outside the classroom?

In our classroom we shy away from fundamental issues. How should one deal with evil? What is our relation to the enemy?

What shall one do about envy? What is the meaning of honesty? How should one face the problem of loneliness? What has religion to say about war and violence? About indifference to evil?

Surely religious education is vital, and the advice to study is not hard to give. Yet the tragedy is that our generation does not know how to study, how to relate itself to the classical sources of our tradition. Thus the chief problem of religious education is not only what to do with the children who do not attend religious schools but what to do with those who do attend. The secret of religious education is learning, passion, and conviction. To teach means to impart *information* as well as to let the pupil share one's *appreciation*. The problem is not only more hours, more knowledge, but also more relevance, more understanding.

The story of how Abraham smashed his father's idols is something that impresses itself deeply upon the minds of our children. Many of them, however, never get to Chapter 32 of the Book of Exodus where the story of the Golden Calf is reported.

"Love thy neighbor as thyself" is, according to Rabbi Akiba, the essence or epitome of the Torah. However, according to Rabbi Ishmael, the epitome and the design of the Torah is the design to keep our people away from idolatry.

Rabbi Akiba's view is known to all of us; Rabbi Ishmael's view is forgotten.

Manasseh, we are told, placed an idol in the Temple. Is it not possible that there are idols in our homes, in our minds, in our temples?

Religion finds itself in a continuous battle with idolatry. It is bound to reject as vulgar and destructive certain values that our own people cherish and worship!

Another ailment that plagues us is the monopoly of education. Actually, education is a matter which rests primarily with the parent, with the father. The teacher is but a representative of the father, according to Jewish tradition. Thou shalt teach them diligently, not vicariously. Now parents act as they please, commercialism and vulgarity blare from the loudspeakers—and little children are expected to listen to the voice of the spirit. Religious instruction, like charity, begins at home.

The depersonalization of teaching is another outstanding weakness. I refer to the type of instruction in which the subject matter stands like an iron curtain between pupil and teacher. The task of the teacher is, first of all, to transfer the external legacy of our people. And for that legacy to be expressed and accepted, the transfer itself must be a significant happening. The idea that remains timeless will bypass the mind and heart of man. Man lives in time, in a particular situation, and only an idea that happens is capable of being conveyed. For an idea to happen, the teacher must relive its significance, he must become one with what he says. Only deep calls to deep.

The task of the teacher is to be a midwife to the student and a midwife to our tradition. At the hands of a clumsy practitioner, ideas will be still-born, the outcome may be a monster. At the hands of a master, a new life will be born.

The secret of effective teaching lies in making a pupil a contemporary of the living moment of teaching. The outcome is not only the retention of the content of teaching but also of the moment of teaching. It is not enough for the pupil to appropriate the subject matter; the pupil and the teacher must go through significant moments, sharing insight and appreciation.

I know it is not easy. I am aware of the difficulty. I know how hard it is to teach. The first moment in each class is like the hour in which the Jews stood at the Red Sea. But when the reward comes, it is a song. Everybody faces in his own life the trial and fleeing from the slavery and the fleshpots of Egypt, and of being pursued by Pharaoh.

The trouble is that the Bible itself has become to our people like the Red Sea, and we are called upon to perform the miracle of splitting the waters and leading them through. Yet miracles do happen, and to this experience we are committed, and we thank God three times a day for miracles that happen to us daily.

The failure of religious education has its root in the *decline of faith in religious education,* and ultimately in the lack of faith in value education.

Our premise is the certainty of being able to educate the inner man; to form as well as to inform the personality; to develop not only memory but also the capacity for insight; not only information but also appreciation; not only proficiency but also reverence; not only learning but also faith; not only skills but also inner attitudes.

Abstaining from cultivating inner attitudes is an abdication of responsibility. It means turning over the child to other agencies of our mass culture that powerfully affect attitudes and value judgments, such as television or comic books, Hollywood and Madison Avenue, the impact of which represents a major threat to the independence, sensitivity, inner balance, and freedom of the individual.

Constant danger requires constant vigilance, constant guidance. What is needed is defense in depth, in the depth of every person. But the tragedy of our civilization is the liquidation of the inner man. We are doing our utmost to flatten man. Spiritual resources are being depleted.

Judaism is committed to the notion that education can and must reach the inner man, that its goal is to refine and to exalt the nature of man.

Supremely sensitive as the prophets are to the wickedness of man and deeply conscious of his stubbornness and callousness, they also insist upon the ability of man to change, to repent, to return to God and live by justice and compassion. Prophecy may be defined as a formidable effort to change any spiritual *status quo,* as an everlasting protest against any fatalistic conception of life, against those who teach that human nature will never change. The belief in the possibility to affect and to ennoble human beings is the rock upon which all of Judaism is built. Denial of this belief would render all of Torah innocuous. The Torah is not description but guidance; not an acceptance but a challenge; not reminiscence but commandment. It is not a portraiture of that which is but a vision, an anticipation of that which ought to be.

The essential value of the intellectual experience is the experience itself; its value is not to be looked for in the external gain that may and should ensue, but in the intrinsic insight that will endure. The study of Torah is a challenge to the mind as well as an act of being involved in the dialogue of God and man, an act of sanctification of time. True learning is a way of relating oneself to something which is both holy and universal (see "Religion in a Free Society," p. 57).

Learning, study is more than preparation of young people for good citizenship. Study is a form of worship, an act of inner purification.

The test of achievement is in the ability of the teacher to let an idea happen. Teaching is the communication of an event. A thought comes to pass in the teacher and continues in the pupil. The failure of teaching is assured when teacher and pupil are like parallel lines that meet only in infinity.

No idea can come about in a vacuum. For a word of the Bible to happen it must permeate the soul, relate to one's problems, dreams, and emotions. Detached from the living issues of the human situation, our commitment becomes dim, inane. In other words, to teach religion means to teach a way of dealing with living problems of human existence (see "Religion in a Free Society," p. 4; "Depth Theology," pp. 115 ff.), with the problems of the student who sits in front of us. Otherwise, it remains trivial. And religion cannot survive as a triviality.

We superimpose beliefs and demands derived from prophetic experiences and insights upon minds conditioned by a set of assumptions and opinions to which those prophetic insights are both alien and irrelevant. Unless we open the minds to a dimension of reality the prophets were sensitive to, to the challenge, problems, and enigmas which we and the prophets have in common, their beliefs and demands will fall on deaf ears.

Thus religious education involves not only subject matter, but also a unique way of thinking, a view about man and his destiny, about nature and history. Taught in an intellectual vacuum, our curriculum is meaningless; taught in the context of a philosophy derived from nonbiblical assumptions, it must remain either innocuous or self-defeating. Every educational act involves an attitude to values. An understanding of values lies, therefore, at the root of education.

We must not underestimate the difficulties of moral living. It takes great courage, wisdom, defiance, and depth of faith to remain moral. We have been guilty of oversimplification. We maintain that virtue pays, we forget that vice pays more. In many of our textbooks the words "sin" or "evil inclination" do not occur. One may gain the impression that the evil inclination does not exist any more or has gone up to the moon.

Do we prepare the student for years of going through tensions, of facing ordeals and tribulations?

Man is born to face temptations and to make decisions. He is born to insist as well as to resist. There is neither faith nor integrity without awareness of the difficulty of faith and the arduousness of integrity. The task is to develop convictions as well as spiritual audacity.

It is useless *to teach moral values*. Of all disciplines within the field of philosophy, ethics is the least advanced, the most insecure.

Character education cannot be taught as only character education. Nor can the moral problem be dealt with detached from the total problem of being human.

It is the antecedents of moral commitment, acts that happen within the depth of a person, moments that bring about the attachment to faith, upon which commitment to moral values depends.

You can affect a person only if you reach his inner life, the level where every human being is insecure and feels his incompleteness, the level of awareness that lies beyond articulation.

Character education can only be carried out in depth, as *cultivation of total sensitivity*. There is no compassion without a sense of wonder and reverence for the mystery of being. Character education must begin by involving man's innate sense of wonder and continue to cultivate man's capacity for radical amazement, by raising issues which the individual is called upon to answer inwardly, personally.

To educate means to cultivate the soul, not only the mind.

You cultivate the soul by cultivating empathy and reverence for others, by calling attention to the grandeur, the mystery of all being, to the holy dimension of human existence by teaching how to relate the common to the spiritual. The soul is discovered in response, in acts of transcending the self, in the awareness of ends that surpass one's interest and needs.

Every one of us is sooner or later confronted with ultimate problems. How can I relate my life to the source of ultimate meaning? Why am I here at all, and what is my purpose? My life is very precious to me. Is my life nothing but a statistical symbol? a scientific fact? Or is life a symbol for God? a dramatic opportunity?

We have discovered in our own days the terrifying seriousness of human history; the profound earnestness of human history. The problem of man is more grave than we were able to realize generations ago.

The religious mind did not have to wait for the atomic bomb to learn that life is an extremely serious business.

Verbally, we seem to be committed to the idea that man is created in the likeness of God. But are we committed to it intellectually? If the divine likeness is our premise, then the question arises: How should a being created in the likeness of God act, think, feel? How should we live in a way which is compatible with our being a likeness of God?

What do I see when I see a man? What do I see when I face an audience such as this? How to retain a sensitivity to the wonder and mystery of this very moment? How not to profane the act of holding the attention of so many human beings?

Religion in America is inclined to follow rather than to challenge the general trends of opinion, as if the task of religion were to serve as a handmaid of civilization. Religion begins where philosophy ends. Without religious education, general education may end in the trivialization of man himself.

Our schools must endeavor to place religious education in a system of reference to the fundamental problems of existence. How to illumine the inner chaos? How to simplify the self? We all must live in two spheres—in society and in privacy. To survive in society, we must thrive in privacy.

Faith in God presupposes an awareness of the presence of God. It involves not only an attitude to the holy but also a way of relating oneself to the common.

God's temple is a sanctuary without walls. If the sanctuary is everywhere, then we can sense the ark or the altar somewhere.

Our schools must do what nonreligious schools have failed to accomplish: to convey to the student a sense for the marvel and mystery of being alive, a sense of indebtedness as well as a sense of significant being, an awareness of holiness in time, the capacity for celebration, *the ability to hold God and man in one thought at one time.*

We must address ourselves, in education, to the fundamental problems of existence: How to illumine the inner chaos? How to simplify the self?

Most people are afflicted with false problems. They fail to be aware of what really ails them, of what is ultimately at stake in the life of man. Our most precious insights come from encountering that which is greater than ourselves. Religious education adds a new dimension to the individual, a dimension in which he is exposed and responds to divine meaning, truth, and wisdom.

What man thinks of himself, of society, of humanity, determines his way of making a decision.

Without an intimate awareness of the grandeur of living, the transcendent glory of justice and compassion, the earnestness and ultimate significance of freedom and responsibility, we will fail.

Life in its totality, the days, the weeks, the years, all of life must
have a shape, a form, color and quality. Life must be seen not piece-
meal but as a whole. To every individual his own life is unprecedented, incomparable, infinitely precious. Every life is pregnant with
beauty, and in need of a form in which to be expressed.

Immortality of the soul ought to be our central concern. By this, I
mean the immortality of the soul while the body is still alive. Some
human beings die long before their bodies do. The first task of religion is to serve as a reminder that man has a soul, that the community has a soul. Did we not witness how entire nations lost their
souls? The surest way to forfeit the soul is to ignore the spirit.

Life must be earned spiritually, not only materially. A good
conscience is the invention of the devil. Man knows more than he
understands. He senses more than he is able to say. Reducing
knowledge to the limits of understanding is to stultify our intelligence. To maintain that everything we know we are able to understand, that everything we sense we are able to say, is an invention of
idiots. *Intellectual embarrassment,* awareness of our inability to say
what we sense, is a prerequisite of intelligence.

To foster depth of awareness, sheer openness of both mind and
senses to what is given, is as vital to us as the training in the art of
explanation and expression.

It is important for our lives to explain experiences, yet it is also
important for us to know that experiences explain our lives.

Spiritual values can be experienced in acts of love and compassion,
in acts of ritual, in the search for truth, in moments of sensing the
mystery of living.

Spiritual values are, of course, delicate, precious, and intangible.
They can neither be measured nor firmly and exactly described. And
yet spiritual attitudes can be evoked and fostered, character can be
affected, generosity and reverence can be cultivated.

Reality we seek to express in terms of mathematical figures and
conceptual generalizations. The artist knows that a human face, for
example, represents an image, the complexity and uniqueness of

which cannot be captured in the language of science. What the artist conveys in the language of color, shape, light, form, or sound remains beyond the grasp of generalization and conceptualization.

The language of Judaism is that of deeds. What cannot be captured in words we try to utter in deeds.

Extremely important in Jewish tradition is the spiritual centrality of the *word*.

It is neither in color nor in plastic form, but in the word where the insights and the spiritual power of more than thirty centuries are contained. These repositories will remain locked, the thoughts they contain will remain out of range, unless we approach them with heart and soul, with intelligence and imagination. Great words in the Bible, in the Prayer Book, are jewels that must not be pawned for loss of appreciation. Words are repositories of the spirit. It is only after we kindle a light in the words that we are able to behold the riches they contain. It is only after we arrive within a word that we become aware of the riches our own souls contain.

The philosophy of educating man is determined by the philosophy of the nature of man. The prevailing philosophy of education operates upon the assumption that man and his destiny must be conceived in terms of *interests and needs*. I maintain that if we continue to entertain such a view, education will be doomed to failure.

Such a view is part of a way of thinking which tends to flatten things. We deal with human beings as if they had no depth, as if the world had only two dimensions. We have developed a sense of power, we have developed a sense of beauty; we know how to use the forces of matter, we know how to enjoy the beauty of nature. Intellectually, we know the universe is not here for our sake; it is not here to please our ego. Practically, however, we act as if the purpose of the universe were to *satisfy our interests and needs*.

However, a life without *demands* on the mind, heart, body, and soul, a life without constant intellectual effort, spells the doom of culture. We must not remain the errand-boys of yesteryear's fashions; we must not embalm notorious clichés.

An adequate philosophy of education must seek to understand its goals *in terms of ends as well as in terms of needs,* in terms of values as well as in terms of interests and desires. Our tradition insists that we must neither defy desire nor vilify it. Far from defying legitimate needs, it regards authentic needs as spiritual opportunities. It tries to teach us not only to satisfy needs, but also to surpass them. The error or idolatry is to idolize needs, to convert needs into ends. As I have said elsewhere, the goal *is to convert ends into needs.* To develop a need for that which we may not feel the need of, to desire what is commanded.

Satisfying a need is part of the continuum of the psyche, serving an end, doing a *mitzvah,* is a *breakthrough.* However, the goal remains to integrate the end into the psychological structure of needs, for action to generate motivation.

Ultimate ends, as seen by our tradition, are not timeless values, metaphysical entities, frozen absolutes. Ultimate ends are *mitzvoth, demands.*

All needs are one-sided. When hungry we are in need of food, yet food is not in need of being consumed. Things of beauty attract our minds, we feel the need of perceiving them, yet they are not in need of being perceived by us. It is in such one-sidedness that most of living is imprisoned. Examine an average mind, and you will find that it is dominated by an effort to cut reality to the measure of the ego, as if the world existed for the sake of pleasing one's ego. Religion begins with the certainty that something is asked of us, that there are ends which are in need of us. Unlike all other values, moral and religious ends evoke in us a sense of obligation. They present themselves as tasks rather than as objects of perception. Thus religious living consists in serving ends or "values" which are in need of us.

For several generations philosophers have wrestled with the problem of values. In our own time the conclusion has been reached that we cannot in correct language formulate an answer to the question, *"What is value?"*

Those of us who try to think about human existence in terms of the biblical tradition will be careful not to detach the concept of values from the concept of deeds. Values taken by themselves are timeless, disembodied, detached from both God and man. Yet values do not float about in a vacuum, they are capable of being thought of only in terms of something that happens or is being done, carried out; not an object for reflection, but a challenge to which we respond.

There never was a time in which the need for self-expression was so much stressed. Yet there was never a time in which self-expression was so rarely achieved. If self-expression is the only goal, it can never be achieved. The self gains when losing itself in the contemplation of the nonself, in the contemplation of the world, for example. Self-expression depends upon self-attachment to what is greater than the self.

There is neither freedom nor genuine self-expression without quiet inner preparation. We must cultivate moments of silence to bring about one moment of genuine expression. We must bear many burdens to have the strength to carry out one act of freedom.

What is the ideal of religious education? One of its goals is to give norm, purpose, meaning, direction, and depth to what may be regarded as one of the ideals of general education, namely, the fullest possible development of the individual.

This ideal of the fullest possible development of the individual must be placed within the context of religious values. The individual is not seen in isolation but in relation to God and is subject to the norms which such a relation implies.

We maintain that just as it is important for a person to select a particular objective for his own life, such as a career, it is important for him to live in the awareness of a meaning which transcends all particular objectives, the loyalty to which is ultimately even more important than the success and failure in the pursuit of his particular objective.

To regard the ideal of the development of the personality as the exclusive goal of education is both an oversimplification and a distortion. Every individual has many personalities, as William James pointed out.

The individual is a child to his mother, a student to his teacher, a lover to his wife, an employee to his employer, and a boss to those who work for him. It remains a question whether the full development of the personality is either desirable or possible. There may be aspects of one's personality which do not deserve to be fully developed.

Just as a major end of scientific and professional training is to confer control over nature and to offer vocational proficiency, so it is a major end of religious training to convey the meaning of self-control and to offer a sense of personal vocation.

To help an individual to satisfy the urge and compulsion of personal development is to act according to the law of life. Yet such help must not be given blindly, but rather in full consideration of a direction and greater meaning.

Personal meaning is meaningless, unless it is related to a transpersonal meaning. Thus religious education assumes that there are other goals besides that of the development of the individual, some of which are personal, while others point beyond personal existence.

Religious education must recognize the dialectic of a human situation, pay attention to both the individual and the people, to discipline and spontaneity, to principle and example, to the pattern and the poetry, to inwardness and outwardness, to ideas and events.

There is no knowledge without reverence. No understanding without love. Thought without a concern, an idea without the verification of living it is a half truth.

The truth is to cultivate intellectual piety as well as ritual observance, stillness as well as discipline, the importance of patience as a way of listening, rejection of complacency and conceit, the vital necessity of inner growth, the building of responsibility, the active involvement in aiding our fellow men, as well as a sense of authenticity.

I have serious doubts whether every one of us suffers from an *Oedipus complex.* I am inclined to believe that many of us are afflicted with an *Abraham complex*. Of Abraham the Lord says, "For I have singled him out, that he may instruct his children and his posterity to keep the way of the Lord by doing what is just and right" (Genesis 18:19).

To keep our Abraham complex alive in our children remains our responsibility. The fear lest we fail to be sensitive to the situation of a poor man—and all men are poor—is the most important test of whether we have fear of God. Reverence for God involves reverence for man.

We are living through one of the great hours of history. The false gods are crumbling, and the hearts are hungry for the voice of God. But the voice has been stifled. To recapture the echo, we must be honest in our willingness to listen, unprejudiced in our readiness to understand.

Faith in the sense of being involved in the mystery of God and man is not the same as acceptance of definitive formulations of articles of belief. Even he who merely strives for faith in the living God is on the threshold of faith. The test is honesty and stillness.

Our error is in the failure to understand that creed without faith is like a body without a heart. Just as faith may become blind, cruel, and fierce, creed may become shoddy, sterile, and deaf. Let us insist that alienation from dogma does not necessarily mean the loss of faith.

Jewish faith, I repeat, is not a formula. It is an attitude, the joy of living a life in which God has a stake, or being involved with God. Such faith is neither an easy nor a secure achievement. Nor is it an attitude acquired all at once or once and for all. It takes an instant to trust an idol; it takes ages to achieve attachment to him. It requires effort, stirring, strain, preparation. It grows in awareness of mystery, in prayer, in deeds which transcend selfish needs. It grows a lifetime to burst forth for single moments. Faith implies striving for faith. It is never an arrival; it is always being on the way, man's effort to come out of his callousness. Faith comes with the discovery of being needed, of having a vocation, of being commanded.

Faith is not born by way of logical succession: first the idea of

God, second the proposition that he is, and third the assent to the proposition. Nor is it true that we must settle all doubts before we can attain faith. Abraham, Moses, the prophets, Ezra the Scribe, as well as Job were faced with implacable perplexities.

Faith begins in embarrassment, in being overwhelmed, in being silenced.

That is what we must do: to carve out a moment in insight in the dark catacombs of everyday routine.

He who seeks a God to suit his astuteness, to appease his vanity, to satisfy his curiosity, will find at the end a figment of his imagination. He who goes out to seek God on a bridge of abstract demonstrations will arrive at a castle in the air. Only a bridge made of life itself, of deeds of compassion, of instants of wonder, of moments of reverence, will lead us to an understanding of what faith has to say.

The great problem in the life of man is whether to trust, to have faith in God. The great problem in the life of God is whether to trust, to have faith in man.

The central issue is not man's decision to extend formal recognition to God, to furnish God with a certificate that he exists, but the realization of our importance to God's design; not to prove that God is alive, but to prove that man is not dead; not to prove him, but to prove ourselves.

The purpose of faith is not to satisfy curiosity or to fulfill a human need, but to confront man with a sublime challenge, to satisfy a divine need.

What will make us worthy of faith? What will give us the strength to pray? This is how the religion of Abraham begins. "The Lord said to Abraham, 'Go forth from your native land and from your father's house to the land that I will show you'" (Genesis 12:1).

Religion begins as a breaking off, as a going away. It continues in acts of nonconformity to idolatry.

There is still another aspect of Jewish faith. A Jew does not believe alone; he believes with the Community of Israel; he shares an insight of three thousand years of sacred Jewish history. Religious living is not only a private concern. Our own life is a movement in the symphony of ages. We are taught to pray as well as to live in the first person plural, to do the good "in the name of all Israel." All generations are present in every generation. The community of Israel lives in every Jew. Every Jew, and the individual Jew, can survive only through intimate attachment to involvement in the community.

Something basic could and should be done for the development of spiritual sensitivity. There are certain prerequisites for spiritual existence, certain insights, attitudes, and emotions upon which spiritual existence is contingent and which are insignia of human dignity.

By way of simplification the two major goals of Jewish education may be described as *learning* and *sensitivity*. He who is devoid of sensitivity is incapable of self-denial; he who is devoid of learning is incapable of piety.

Faith does not come out of nothing. There are antecedents of religious commitment, acts that happen within the depth of the person, moments that necessitate groping for faith: the sense of wonder and mystery, reverence and radical amazement, the sense of indebtedness and embarrassment, the fallacy of absolute expedience, the demonic nature of man's false sense of sovereignty, openness to history, concern for ultimate meaning of existence, the vital importance of inwardness, the awareness of man's ultimate accountability before God.

What is religious about religious education? The spirit in which the word is taught, the awareness of learning as an act of shaping the mind in the image of the word of God.

Let me conclude with a story recorded in an eighteenth-century Hebrew book. A young man once wanted to become a blacksmith. So he became an apprentice to a blacksmith, and he learned all the necessary techniques of the trade: how to hold the tongs, how to lift the sledge, how to smite the anvil, even how to blow the fire with the bellows. Having finished his apprenticeship, he was chosen to be employed at the smithy of the royal palace. However, the young man's delight soon came to an end, when he discovered that he had failed to learn how to kindle a spark. All his skill and knowledge in handling the tools were of no avail.

I am often embarrassed when I discover that I am myself like that apprentice—that I know facts and I know techniques, but I have failed to learn how to kindle a spark. I conclude, therefore, with the hope that you who work in the royal smithy of Jewish education will each of you be able to kindle a spark.

5 / To Grow
in Wisdom

I see the sick and the despised, the defeated and the bitter, the rejected and the lonely. I see them clustered together and alone, clinging to a hope for somebody's affection that does not come to pass. I hear them pray for the release that comes with death. I see them deprived and forgotten, masters yesterday, outcasts today.

What we owe the old is reverence, but all they ask for is consideration, attention, not to be discarded and forgotten. What they deserve is preference, yet we do not even grant them equality. One father finds it possible to sustain a dozen children, yet a dozen children find it impossible to sustain one father.

Perhaps this is the most distressing aspect of the situation. The care for the old is regarded as an act of charity rather than as a supreme privilege. In the never dying utterance of the Ten Commandments, the God of Israel did not proclaim: Honor Me, Revere Me. He proclaimed instead: Revere your father and your mother. There is no reverence for God without reverence for father and mother.

In Jewish tradition the honor for father and mother is a commandment, the perfect fulfillment of which surpasses the power of man. There is no limit to what one ought to do in carrying out this privilege of devotion (see "Children and Youth," p. 39). God is invisible, but my mother is His presence. . . .

Father and mother are always older, more advanced in years. But is being advanced in years to be considered an advance or a retreat?

Ours is a twin problem: the attitude of society to the old and old age as well as the attitude of the old to being old.

The typical attitude to old age is characterized by fear, confusion, absurdity, self-deception, and dishonesty. It is painful and bizarre. Old age is something we are all anxious to attain. However, once attained we consider it a defeat, a form of capital punishment. In enabling us to reach old age, medical science may think that it gave us a blessing; however, we continue to act as if it were a disease.

More money and time are spent on the art of concealing the signs of old age than on the art of dealing with heart disease or cancer. You find more patients in the beauty parlors than in the hospitals. We would rather be bald than gray. A white hair is an abomination. Being old is a defeat, something to be ashamed of. Authenticity and honesty of existence are readily exchanged for false luster, for camouflage, sham, and deception.

A gray hair may destroy the chance for promotion, may cost a salesman his job, and inwardly alienate a son from his father. The fear of being considered old has become a traumatic obsession. Only very few people are endowed with the rare and supreme courage to admit their true age without embarrassment. With the rest of us, courage and honesty go underground when the question of age is discussed. The most delightful resolution the White House Conference on Aging could pass would be to eliminate from now on any mention of the date of birth from the birth certificate.

A vast amount of human misery, as well as enormous cultural and spiritual damage, is due to these twin phenomena of our civilization: the contempt for the old and the traumatic fear of getting old. Monotheism has acquired a new meaning: the one and only thing that counts is being young. Youth is our god, and being young is divine. To be sure, youth is a very marvelous thing. However, the cult of youth is idolatry. Abraham is the grand old man, but the legend of Faust is pagan.

A revision of attitudes and conceptions is necessary. Old age is not a defeat but a victory, not a punishment but a privilege. In education we stress the importance of the adjustment of the young to society. Our task is to call for the adjustment of society to the old.

By what standards do we measure culture? It is customary to evaluate a nation by the magnitude of its scientific contributions or the quality of its artistic achievements. However, the true standard by which to gauge a culture is the extent to which reverence, compassion, justice are to be found in the daily lives of a whole people, not only in the acts of isolated individuals. Culture is *a style of living compatible with the grandeur of being human.*

The test of a people is how it behaves toward the old. It is easy to love children. Even tyrants and dictators make a point of being fond of children. But the affection and care for the old, the incurable, the helpless are the true gold mines of a culture.

We maintain that all men are created equal, including the old. What is extraordinary is that we feel called upon to plead for such equality, in contrast to other civilizations in which the superiority of the old is maintained.

In our own days, a new type of fear has evolved in the hearts of men: the fear of medical bills. In the spirit of the principle that reverence for the old takes precedence over reverence for God, we are compelled to confess that a nation should be ready to sell, if necessary, the treasures from its art collection and the sacred objects from its houses of worship in order to help one sick man.

Is there anything as holy, as urgent, as noble, as the effort of the whole nation to provide medical care for the old?

This is one of the great biblical insights: the needs of suffering humanity are a matter of personal as well as public responsibility. The representatives of the community are held responsible for the neglect of human life if they have failed to provide properly for those in need. The ancient sages realized that it was not enough to rely upon individual benevolence, and that care for the sick was a responsibility of the community.

It is in accord with this tradition that all major religious organizations have endorsed the principle of government responsibility and the use of the Social Security mechanism as the most effective medium for dealing with the problem of medical care for the aged.

It is marvelous indeed that for the first time in history, our society is able to provide for the material needs of its senior citizens. Yet, in addition to the problem of material security, we must face the problem of psychological and spiritual security.

How to save the old from despondency, despair? How to lend beauty to being old? How to regain the authenticity of old age?

Old age is a major challenge to the inner life; it takes both wisdom and strength not to succumb to it. According to all the standards we employ socially as well as privately, the aged person is condemned as inferior. In terms of manpower he is a liability, a burden, a drain on our resources. Conditioned to operate as a machine for making and spending money, with all other relationships dependent upon its efficiency, the moment the machine is out of order and beyond repair, one begins to feel like a ghost without a sense of reality. The aged may be described as a person *who does not dream anymore,* devoid of ambition, and living in fear of losing his status. Regarding himself as a person who has outlived his usefulness, he feels as if he had to apologize for being alive.

The tragedy is that old age comes upon us as a shock for which we are unprepared. If life is defined exclusively in terms of functions and activities, is it still worth living when these functions and activities are sharply curtailed?

The tragedy, I repeat, is that most of us are unprepared for old age. We know a great deal about what to do with things, even what to do with other people; we hardly know what to do with ourselves. We know how to act in public; we do not know what to do in privacy. Old age involves the problem of what to do with privacy.

Among some primitive peoples the old were generally neglected and when helpless exposed to die. Today one can even be placed in a luxury hotel and be left to die.

While we do not officially define old age as a second childhood, some of the programs we devise are highly effective in helping the aged to become children. The popular approach is: "Keep alive a zest for living in the elderly, by encouraging them to continue old hobbies, or to develop new ones." Now preoccupation with games and hobbies, the overemphasis on recreation, while certainly conducive to eliminating boredom temporarily, hardly contribute to inner strength. The effect is, rather, a pickled existence, preserved in brine with spices.

Is this the way and goal of existence: to study, grow, toil, mature, and to reach the age of retirement in order to live like a child? After all, *to be retired does not mean to be retarded.*

What is the role of recreation in the life of the aged? Is it merely to serve as a substitute for work one has done in earlier years? It seems to me that recreation is serving a different purpose, and that an overindulgence in recreational activities aggravates rather than ameliorates a condition it is trying to deal with, namely *the trivialization of existence.* In the past it was ritual and prayer that staved off that danger.

For thousands of years human existence was not simply confined to the satisfaction of trivial needs. Through prayer and ritual man was able to remain open to the wonder and mystery of existence, to lend a tinge of glory to daily deeds.

Modern man has discarded ritual, failed to learn the art of prayer, but found a substitute for both in occupational routine. He severed relations to God, to the cosmos, even to his people, but became engrossed in the search for success. The excitement of success took the place of inspiration. Upon his retirement from labor or business, games and hobbies, the country club or golf take the place of church, synagogue, ritual, and prayer. This, then, is the fact: hobbies have become *a substitute for ritual,* not only for work. Should we not clearly distinguish between recreation as a substitution and recreation as a solution?

Authentic human existence includes both work and worship, utilization and celebration. We have a right to consume because we have the power to celebrate. The man of our time is losing the power to celebrate; instead of participating in spiritual celebration, he seeks to be amused or entertained (see "Children and Youth," p.

40). Upon reaching the summit of his years, man discovers that entertainment is no substitute for celebration.

What are the basic spiritual ills of old age?

(1) The sense of being useless to, and rejected by, family and society; (2) the sense of inner emptiness and boredom; (3) loneliness and the fear of time. Let us analyze the root as well as the cure of these three ills.

1. The sense of being useless to, and rejected by, family and society

While it is vitally important to see man in his relation to society, we must not forget that society is *not* man's only and ultimate referent. In spite of the fact that our ideologies and institutions continue to imply that the worth of a person is equivalent to his usefulness to society, every one of us entertains the keen expectation that other people will not regard him merely because of what he is worth to them, because he is capable of satisfying other people's needs, but will regard him as a being significant and valuable in himself. Just as the grandeur of the sun or an oak tree is not reducible to the functions it fulfills, so is the grandeur of a human life not reducible to the needs it is capable of satisfying. Even he who does not regard himself as an absolute end, rebels against being treated as a means to an end, as subservient to other men. The rich, the men of the world, want to be loved for their own sake, for their essence, whatever it may mean, not for their achievements or possessions. Nor do the old and sick expect help because of what they may give us in return. Who needs the handicapped, the incurably sick, the maintenance of whom is a drain on the treasury of the state? It is, moreover, obvious that a person's service to society does not claim all of his life and can therefore not be the ultimate answer to his quest of meaning for life as a whole. Man has more to give than what other men are able or willing to accept. To say that life could consist of care for others, of incessant service to the world, would be a vulgar boast. What we are able to bestow upon others is usually less and rarely more than a tithe.

There are alleys in the soul where man walks alone, ways that do not lead to society, a world of privacy that shrinks from the public eye. Life comprises not only arable, productive land, but also mountains of dreams, an underground of sorrow, towers of yearning, which can hardly be utilized to the last for the good of society, unless man be converted into a machine in which every screw must serve a function or be removed. It is a profiteering state which, trying to exploit the individual, asks all of man for itself.

And if society as embodied in the state should prove to be corrupt and my effort to cure its evils unavailing, would my life as an individual have been totally devoid of meaning? If society should decide to reject my services and even place me in solitary confinement, so that I would surely die without being able to bequeath any influence to the world I love, would I then feel compelled to end my life?

Human existence cannot derive its ultimate meaning from society, because society itself is in need of meaning. It is as legitimate to ask: Is mankind needed? as it is to ask: Am I needed?

Humanity begins in the individual man, just as history takes its rise from a singular event. It is always one man at a time whom we keep in mind when we pledge: "With malice toward none, with charity for all," or when we try to fulfill: "Love thy neighbor as thyself." The term "mankind," which in biology denotes the human species, has an entirely different meaning in the realm of ethics and religion. Here mankind is not conceived as a species, as an abstract concept, stripped from its concrete reality, but as an abundance of specific individuals; as a community of persons rather than as a herd or a multitude of nondescripts.

While it is true that the good of all counts more than the good of one, it is the concrete individual who lends meaning to the human race. We do not think that a human being is valuable because he is a member of the race; it is rather the opposite: the human race is valuable because it is composed of human beings.

While dependent on society as well as on the air that sustains us, and while other men compose the system of relations in which the curve of our actions takes its course, it is as individuals that we are beset with desires, fears and hopes, challenged, called upon and endowed with the power of will and a spark of responsibility.

2. THE SENSE OF INNER
EMPTINESS AND BOREDOM

Old age often is an age of anguish and boredom. The only answer to such anguish is *a sense of significant being.*

The sense of significant being is a thing of the spirit. Stunts, butters, games, hobbies, slogans—all are evasions. What is necessary is an approach, a getting close to the sources of the spirit. Not the suppression of the sense of futility, but its solution; not reading material to while away one's time, but learning to exalt one's faculties is the answer; not entertainment but celebration.

To attain a sense of significant being we must learn to be involved in thoughts that are ahead of what we already comprehend, to be involved in deeds that will generate higher motivations.

There is a level of existence where one cannot think anymore in terms of self-centered needs and satisfactions, where the problem that cannot be silenced is: Who needs me? Who needs mankind? How does one relate himself to a source of ultimate meaning? The cry for such relatedness which gains intensity with old age is a cry for a referent that transcends personal existence. It is not experienced as a need from within but as a situation of being exposed to a demand from without.

Significant being is not measured by the amount of needs that agitate a person but by the intensity and depth of the response to a wisdom in relation to which *my* mind is an afterthought, by the discovery that the moment to come is an anticipation, an expectation, waiting to receive *my* existence. Significant being means experiencing moments of time as a comprehension which embraces *me*.

What a person lives by is not only a sense of belonging but also a *sense of indebtedness*. The need to be needed corresponds to a fact: something is asked of man, of every man. Advancing in years must not be taken to mean a process of suspending the requirements and commitments under which a person lives. To be is to obey. A person must never cease to be.[1]

Our work for the advanced in years is handicapped by our clinging to the dogmatic belief in the immutability of man. We conceive of his inner life as a closed system, as an automatic, unilinear, irreversible process which cannot be altered, and of old age as a stage of stagnation into which a person enters with his habits, follies, and prejudices. To be good to the old is to cater to their prejudices and eccentricities.

May I suggest that man's potential for change and growth is much greater than we are willing to admit and that old age be regarded not as the age of stagnation but as *the age of opportunities for inner growth?* The old person must not be treated as a patient, nor regard his retirement as a prolonged state of resignation.

The years of old age may enable us to attain the high values we failed to sense, the insights we have missed, the wisdom we ignored. They are indeed formative years, rich in possibilities to unlearn the follies of a lifetime, to see through inbred self-deceptions, to deepen understanding and compassion, to widen the horizon of honesty, to refine the sense of fairness.

One ought to enter old age the way one enters the senior year at a university, in exciting anticipation of consummation. Rich in perspective, experienced in failure, the person advanced in years is capable of shedding prejudices and the fever of vested interests. He does not see anymore in every fellow man a person who stands in his way, and competitiveness may cease to be his way of thinking.

At every home for the aged there is a director of recreation in charge of physical activities; there ought to be also a director of learning in charge of intellectual activities. We insist upon minimum standards for physical well being, what about minimum standards for intellectual well being?

What the nation needs is senior universities, universities for the advanced in years where wise men should teach the potentially wise, where the purpose of learning is not a career, but where the purpose of learning is learning itself.

Education for Retirement. The goal is not to keep the old man busy, but to remind him that every moment is an opportunity for greatness. Inner purification is at least as important as hobbies and recreation. The elimination of resentments, of residues of bitterness, of jealousies and wrangling is certainly a goal for which one must strive.

Only very few people realize that it is in the days of our youth that we prepare ourselves for old age.

This is an imperative we must be conscious of even in youth. Prepare spiritually for old age and learn how to cultivate it. The ancient equation of old age and wisdom is far from being a misconception. However, age is no guarantee for wisdom. A Hebrew proverb maintains: "A wise old man the older he gets the wiser he becomes, a vulgar old man the older he gets the less wise he becomes." People are anxious to save up financial means for old age; they should also be anxious to prepare a spiritual income for old age. That ancient principle—listen to the voice of the old—becomes meaningless when the old have nothing meaningful to say. Wisdom, maturity, tranquillity do not come all of a sudden when we retire from business. We must begin teaching in public schools about the virtues that come to fruition with the advance in years, about the wisdom and peace that arrive in old age. Reverence for the old must be an essential part of elementary education at school, and particularly at home. *Education for retirement* is a life-long process.

3. LONELINESS AND THE FEAR OF TIME

One of the major ills of old age as well as one of the roots of the general fear of old age is *the fear of time*. It is like living on a craggy ridge over a wide abyss. Time is the only aspect of existence which is completely beyond man's control. He may succeed in conquering space, in sending satellites around the moon, but time remains immune to his power; a moment gone by not even General Motors can bring back. Being used to dealing with things he can manage, the encounter with time is the most stunning shock that comes to man. In his younger years, he is too busy to react to it; it is in old age that time may become a nightmare. We are all infatuated with the splendor of space, with the grandeur of things of space. *Thing* is a category that lies heavy on our minds, tyrannizing all our thoughts. Our imagination tends to mold all concepts in its image. In our daily lives we attend primarily to that which the senses are spelling out for us; to what the eyes perceive, to what the fingers touch. Reality to us is thinghood, consisting of substances that occupy space; even God is conceived by most of us as a thing.

The result of our thingness is our blindness to all reality that fails to identify itself as a thing, as a matter of fact. This is obvious in our understanding of time, which being thingless and insubstantial, appears to us as if it has no reality.

Indeed, we know what to do with space but do not know what to do about time, except to make it subservient to space, or to while it away, *to kill time.* However, *time is life,* and to kill time is to murder (cf. "Religion in a Free Society," p. 19). Most of us seem to labor for the sake of things of space. As a result we suffer from a deeply rooted dread of time and stand aghast when compelled to look into its face. Time to us is sarcasm, a slick treacherous monster with a jaw like a furnace incinerating every moment of our lives. Shrinking, therefore, from facing time, we escape for shelter to things of space. The intentions we are unable to carry out we deposit in space; possessions become symbols of our repressions, jubilees of frustrations. But things of space are not fireproof; they only add fuel to the flames. Is the joy of possession an antidote to the terror of time which grows to be a dread of the inevitable death? Things, when magnified, are forgeries of happiness, they are a threat to our very lives; we are more harassed than supported by the Frankensteins of spatial things.

Most of us do not live in time but run away from it; we do not see its face, but its make-up. The past is either forgotten or preserved as a cliché, and the present moment is either bartered for a silly trinket or beclouded by false anticipations. The present moment is a zero, and so is the next moment, and a vast stretch of life turns out to be a series of zeros, with no real number in front.

Blind to the marvel of the present moment, we live with memories of moments missed, in anxiety about an emptiness that lies ahead. We are totally unprepared when the problem strikes us in unmitigated form.

It is impossible for man to shirk the problem of time. The more we think the more we realize that we cannot conquer time through space. We can only master time in time.

Time is man's most important frontier, the advance region of significant being, a region where man's true freedom lies. Space divides us, time unites us. We wage wars over things of space; the treasures of time lie open to every man.

Time has independent ultimate significance; it is of more majesty and more evocative of awe than even a sky studded with stars. Gliding gently in the most ancient of all splendors, it tells so much more than space can say in its broken language of things, playing symphonies upon the instruments of isolated beings, unlocking the earth and making it happen. Time is the process of creation, and things of space are results of creation. When looking at space we see the products of creation; when intuiting time we hear the process of creation. Things of space exhibit a deceptive independence. They show off a veneer of limited permanence. Things created conceal the Creator. It is the dimension of time wherein man meets God, wherein man becomes aware that every instant is an act of creation, a Beginning, opening up new roads for ultimate realizations. *Time is the presence of God in the world of space,* and it is within time that we are able to sense the unity of all beings.

Time is perpetual presence, perpetual novelty. Every moment is a new arrival, a new bestowal. *Just to be is a blessing, just to live is holy. The moment is the marvel;* it is in evading the marvel of the moment that boredom begins which ends in despair.

Old age has the vicious tendency of depriving a person of the present. The aged thinks of himself as belonging to the past. But it is precisely the openness to the present that he must strive for. The marvel is discovered in celebration.

He who lives with a sense for the Presence knows that to get older does not mean to lose time but rather to gain time. And, he also knows that in all his deeds, the chief task of man is to sanctify time. All it takes to sanctify time is *God, a soul, and a moment. And the three are always here.*

It is still considered proper to expect that the first responsibility in planning for the senior citizen rests with the family. Such expectation presupposes the concept of a family which is not only an economic unit but also an interplay of profoundly personal relations. It thinks of the family not only as a process of living together but also of a series of decisive acts and events in which all members are involved and by which they are inwardly affected.

What is characteristic of the modern family is that on the level of profound personal experience, parents and children live apart. The experiences shared at home are perfunctory rather than creative. In the past, it was the role of the father to lead the children through moments of exaltation. Whatever stood out as venerable and lofty was associated with the father. Now we are entering a social structure in which the father is becoming obsolete, and in which there are only three ages: childhood, adolescence, and old age. The husband of the mother is not a father, he is a regular guy, a playmate for the boys, engaged in the same foibles and subject to similar impulses. Since he neither represents the legacy of the past nor is capable of keeping pace with the boys in the pursuit of the future, his status is rather precarious.

Children today experience their highest moments of exaltation in a children's world, in which there is no room for parents. But unless a fellowship of spiritual experience is re-established, the parent will remain an outsider to the child's soul. This is one of the beauties of the human spirit. We appreciate *what we share,* we do not appreciate *what we receive.* Friendship, affection is not acquired by giving presents. Friendship, affection comes about by two people sharing a significant moment, by having an experience in common. You do not attain the affection of your teen-age son by giving him an expensive car.

It is not necessary for man to submit to the constant corrosion of his finest sensibilities and to accept as inevitable the liquidation of the inner man. It is within the power of man to save the secret substance that holds the world of man together. The way to overcome loneliness is not by waiting to receive a donation of companionship but rather by offering and giving companionship and meaning to others.

The real bond between two generations is the insights they share, the appreciation they have in common, the moments of inner experience in which they meet. A parent is not only an economic provider, playmate, shelter, and affection. A human being is in need of security, he is also in need of inspiration, of exaltation and a transcendent meaning of existence. And to a child, the parent represents the inspiration, the exaltation, and the meaning. To my child, I am either the embodiment of the spirit or its caricature. No book, no image, no symbol can replace my role in the imagination and the recesses of my child's soul.

It is easy to speak about the things we are committed to; it is hard to communicate *the commitment itself.* It is easy to convey the resentments we harbor; it is hard to communicate the praise, the worship, the sense of the ineffable.

We have nearly lost the art of conveying to our children our power to praise, our ability to cherish the things that cannot be quantified.

This, then is a most urgent problem: How to convey the inexpressible legacy, the moments of insight, how to invoke unconditional commitment to justice and compassion, a sensitivity to the stillness of the holy, attachment to sacred words.

There is no human being who does not carry a treasure in his soul; a moment of insight, a memory of love, a dream of excellence, a call to worship.

In order to be a master one must learn how to be an apprentice. Reverence for the old, dialogue between generations, is as important to the dignity of the young as it is for the well-being of the old. We deprive ourselves by disparaging the old.

We must seek ways to overcome the traumatic fear of being old, the prejudice, the discrimination against those advanced in years. All men are created equal, including those advanced in years. Being old is not necessarily the same as being stale. The effort to restore the dignity of old age will depend upon our ability to revive the equation of old age and wisdom. Wisdom is the substance upon which the inner security of the old will forever depend. But the attainment of wisdom is the work of a life time.

Old men need a vision, not only recreation.

Old men need a dream, not only a memory.

It takes three things to attain a sense of significant being:

  God

  A Soul

  And a Moment.

And the three are always here.

Just to be is a blessing. Just to live is holy.

NOTE

1. For discussion of these ideas see Heschel, *Who Is Man?* (Stanford: Stanford University Press, 1965); cf. also "Idols in the Temples," pp. 107 f.

6 / Religion
and Race

I

At the first conference on religion and race, the main participants
were Pharaoh and Moses. Moses' words were: "Thus says the Lord,
the God of Israel, let My people go that they may celebrate a feast to
Me." While Pharaoh retorted: "Who is the Lord, that I should heed
this voice and let Israel go? I do not know the Lord, and moreover I
will not let Israel go."

The outcome of that summit meeting has not come to an end.
Pharaoh is not ready to capitulate. The exodus began, but is far
from having been completed. In fact, it was easier for the children of
Israel to cross the Red Sea than for a Negro to cross certain university campuses.

Let us dodge no issues. Let us yield no inch to bigotry, let us make
no compromise with callousness.

In the words of William Lloyd Garrison, "I will be as harsh as
truth, and as uncompromising as justice. On this subject [slavery] I
do not wish to think, to speak, or to write with moderation. I am in
earnest—I will not equivocate—I will not excuse—I will not retreat
a sincle inch—and I will be heard."

Religion and race. How can the two be uttered together? To act
in the spirit of religion is to unite what lies apart, to remember that
humanity as a whole is God's beloved child. To act in the spirit of

race is to sunder, to slash, to dismember the flesh of living humanity. Is this the way to honor a father: to torture his child? How can we hear the word "race" and feel no self-reproach?

Race as a *normative* legal or political concept is capable of expanding to formidable dimensions. A mere thought, it extends to become a way of thinking, a highway of insolence, as well as a standard of values, overriding truth, justice, beauty. As a standard of values and behavior, race operates as a comprehensive doctrine, as racism. And racism is worse than idolatry. *Racism is satanism,* unmitigated evil.

Few of us seem to realize how insidious, how radical, how universal an evil racism is. Few of us realize that racism is man's gravest threat to man, the maximum of hatred for a mimimum of reason, the maximum of cruelty for a minimum of thinking.

Perhaps this Conference should have been called "Religion *or* Race." You cannot worship God and at the same time look at man as if he were a horse.

Shortly before he died, Moses spoke to his people. "I call heaven and earth to witness against you this day: I have put before you life and death, blessing and curse. *Choose life"* (Deuteronomy 30:19). The aim of this conference is first of all to state clearly the stark alternative. I call heaven and earth to witness against you this day: I have set before you religion and race, life and death, blessing and curse. Choose life.

"Race prejudice, a universal human ailment, is the most recalcitrant aspect of the evil in man" (Reinhold Niebuhr), a treacherous denial of the existence of God.

What is an idol? *Any god who is mine but not yours,* any god concerned with me but not with you, *is an idol.*

Faith in God is not simply *an afterlife-insurance policy. Racial or religious bigotry* must be recognized for what it is: *satanism, blasphemy.*

In several ways man is set apart from all beings created in six days. The Bible does not say, God created the plant or the animal; it says, God created *different* kinds of plants, *different kinds* of animals (Genesis 1: 11–12, 21–25). In striking contrast, it does not say, God created different kinds of man, men of different colors and races; it proclaims, God created one single man. From one single man all men are descended.

To think of man in terms of white, black, or yellow is more than an error. It is *an eye disease, a cancer of the soul.*

The redeeming quality of man lies in his ability to sense his kinship with all men. Yet there is a deadly poison that inflames the eye, making us see the generality of race but not the uniqueness of the human face. Pigmentation is what counts. The Negro is a stranger to many souls. There are people in our country whose moral sensitivity suffers a blackout when confronted with the black man's predicament.

How many disasters do we have to go through in order to realize that all of humanity has a stake in the liberty of one person; whenever one person is offended, we are all hurt. What begins as inequality of some inevitably ends as inequality of all.

In referring to the Negro in this paper we must, of course, always keep equally in mind the plight of all individuals belonging to a racial, religious, ethnic, or cultural minority.

This Conference should dedicate itself not only to the problem of the Negro but also to the problem of the white man, not only to the plight of the colored but also to the situation of the white people, to the cure of a disease affecting the spiritual substance and condition of every one of us. What we need is an NAAAP, a National Association for the Advancement of All People. Prayer and prejudice cannot dwell in the same heart. Worship without compassion is worse than self-deception; it is an abomination.

Thus the problem is not only how to do justice to the colored people, it is also how to stop the profanation of God's name by dishonoring the Negro's name.

One hundred years ago the emancipation was proclaimed. It is time for the white man to strive for *self-emancipation,* to set himself free of bigotry, to stop being a slave to wholesale contempt, a passive recipient of slander.

II

"Again I saw all the oppressions that are practiced under the sun. And behold, the tears of the oppressed, and they had no one to comfort them!" (Ecclesiastes 4:1.)

There is a form of oppression which is more painful and more scathing than physical injury or economic privation. It is *public humiliation*. What afflicts my conscience is that my face, whose skin happens not to be dark, instead of radiating the likeness of God, has come to be taken as an image of haughty assumption and overbearance. Whether justified or not, I, the white man, have become in the eyes of others a symbol of arrogance and pretension, giving offense to other human beings, hurting their pride, even without intending it. My very presence inflicting insult!

My heart is sick when I think of the anguish and the sighs, of the quiet tears shed in the nights in the overcrowded dwellings in the slums of our great cities, of the pangs of despair, of the cup of humiliation that is running over.

The crime of murder is tangible and punishable by law. The sin of insult is imponderable, invisible. When blood is shed, human eyes see red; when a heart is crushed, it is only God who shares the pain.

In the Hebrew language one word denotes both crimes. "Bloodshed," in Hebrew, is the word that denotes both murder and humiliation. The law demands: one should rather be killed than commit murder. Piety demands: one should rather commit suicide than offend a person publicly. It is better, the Talmud insists, to throw oneself alive into a burning furnace than to humiliate a human being publicly.

He who commits a major sin may repent and be forgiven. But he who offends a person publicly will have no share in the life to come.

It is not within the power of God to forgive the sins committed toward men. We must first ask for forgiveness of those whom our society has wronged before asking for the forgiveness of God.

Daily we patronize institutions which are visible manifestations of arrogance toward those whose skin differs from ours. Daily we cooperate with people who are guilty of active discrimination.

How long will *I* continue to be tolerant of, even a participant in, acts of embarrassing and humiliating human beings, in restaurants, hotels, buses, or parks, employment agencies, public schools and universities? One ought rather be shamed than put others to shame.

Our rabbis taught: "Those who are insulted but do not insult, hear themselves reviled without answering, act through love and rejoice in suffering, of them Scripture says: 'They who love the Lord are as the sun when rising in full splendor' (Judges 5:31)."

Let us cease to be apologetic, cautious, timid. Racial tension and strife is both sin and punishment. *The Negro's plight,* the blighted areas in the large cities, are they not the fruit of our sins?

By negligence and silence we have all become accessory before the God of mercy to the injustice committed against the Negroes by men of our nation. Our derelictions are many. We have failed to demand, to insist, to challenge, to chastise.

In the words of Thomas Jefferson, "I tremble for my country when I reflect that God is just."

III

There are several ways of dealing with our bad conscience. (1) We can extenuate our responsibility; (2) we can keep the Negro out of our sight; (3) we can alleviate our qualms by pointing to the progress made; (4) we can delegate the responsibility to the courts; (5) we can silence our conscience by cultivating indifference; (6) we can dedicate our minds to issues of a far more sublime nature.

(1) Modern thought has a tendency to extenuate personal responsibility. Understanding the complexity of human nature, the inter-relationship of individual and society, of consciousness and the

subconscious, we find it difficult to isolate the deed from the circumstances in which it was done. Our enthusiasm is easily stunned by realizing the ramifications and complexity of the problem we face and the enormous obstacles we encounter in trying to implement the philosophy affirmed in the 13th and 14th Amendments as well as in the 1954 decision of the Supreme Court. Yet this general tendency, for all its important correctives and insights, has often had the effect of obscuring our essential vision, aiding our conscience to grow scales: excuses, pretense, self-pity. The sense of guilt may disappear; no crime is absolute, no sin devoid of apology. Within the limits of the human mind, relativity may be true and merciful. Yet the mind's scope embraces but a fragment of society, a few instants of history; it thinks of what has happened, it is unable to imagine what might have happened. The qualms of my conscience are easily cured—even while the agony for which I am accountable continues unabated.

(2) Another way of dealing with a bad conscience is to keep the Negro out of sight.

The Word proclaims: Love thy neighbor! *So we make it impossible for him to be a neighbor.* Let a Negro move into our neighborhood and madness overtakes the residents. To quote an editorial in the *Christian Century* of Dec. 26, 1962:

> The ghettoization of the Negro in American society is increasing. Three million Negroes—roughly one-sixth of the nation's Negro population—are now congested in five of the greatest metropolitan centers of the north. The alienation of the Negro from the mainstream of American life proceeds apace. The Negro is discovering to his sorrow that the mobility which he gained in the Emancipation Proclamation and the 13th and 14th Amendments to the Constitution nearly a hundred years ago merely enables him to move from one ghetto to another. A partial apartheid—economic, social, political and religious—continues to be enforced by the white people of the U.S. They use various pressures—some open, some covert—to keep the Negro isolated from the nation's social, cultural and

religious community, the result being black islands surrounded by a vast white sea. Such enclaves in American society not only destroy the cohesiveness of the nation but also offend the Negro's dignity and restrict his opportunity. These segregated islands are also an embarrassment to white people who want an open society but are trapped by a system they despise. Restricted housing is the chief offender. So long as the racially exclusive patterns of suburban America continue, the Negro will remain an exile in his own land.

(3) To some Americans the situation of the Negro, for all its stains and spots, seems fair and trim. So many revolutionary changes have taken place in the field of civil rights, so many deeds of charity are being done; so much decency radiates day and night. Our standards are modest; our sense of injustice tolerable, timid; our moral indignation impermanent; yet human violence is interminable, unbearable, permanent. The conscience builds its confines, is subject to fatigue, longs for comfort. Yet those who are hurt, and He who inhabits eternity, neither slumber nor sleep.

(4) Most of us are content to delegate the problem to the courts, as if justice were a matter for professionals or specialists. But to do justice is what God demands of every man: it is the supreme commandment, and one that cannot be fulfilled vicariously.

Righteousness must dwell not only in the places where justice is judicially administered. There are many ways of evading the law and escaping the arm of justice. Only a few acts of violence are brought to the attention of the courts. As a rule, those who know how to exploit are endowed with the skill to justify their acts, while those who are easily exploited possess no skill in pleading their own cause. Those who neither exploit nor are exploited are ready to fight when their own interests are harmed; they will not be involved when not personally affected. Who shall plead for the helpless? Who shall prevent the epidemic of injustice that no court of justice is capable of stopping?

In a sense, the calling of the prophet may be described as that of an advocate or champion, speaking for those who are too weak to plead their own cause.[1] Indeed, the major activity of the prophets was *interference,* remonstrating about wrongs inflicted on other people, meddling in affairs which were seemingly neither their concern nor their responsibility. A prudent man is he who minds his own business, staying away from questions which do not involve his own interests, particularly when not authorized to step in—and prophets were given no mandate by the widows and orphans to plead their cause. The prophet is a person who is not tolerant of wrongs done to others, who resents other people's injuries. He even calls upon others to be the champions of the poor. It is to every member of the community, not alone to the judges, that Isaiah directs his plea:

> Seek justice, relieve the oppressed,
> Judge the fatherless, plead for the widow.
>   Isaiah 1:17

(5) There is an evil which most of us condone and are even guilty of: *indifference to evil.* We remain neutral, impartial, and not easily moved by the wrongs done unto other people. Indifference to evil is more insidious than evil itself; it is more universal, more contagious, more dangerous. A silent justification, it makes possible an evil erupting as an exception becoming the rule and being in turn accepted.

The prophets' great contribution to humanity was the discovery of *the evil of indifference.* One may be decent and sinister, pious and sinful.

The prophet is a person who suffers the harms done to others. Wherever a crime is committed, it is as if the prophet were the victim and the prey. The prophet's angry words cry. The wrath of God is a lamentation. All prophecy is one great exclamation: God is not indifferent to evil! He is always concerned, He is personally affected by what man does to man. He is a God of pathos.

(6) In condemning the clergymen who joined Dr. Martin Luther

King, Jr., in protesting against local statutes and practices which denied constitutional liberties to groups of citizens on account of race, a white preacher declared: "The job of the minister is to lend the souls of men to God, not to bring about confusion by getting tangled up in transitory social problems."

In contrast to this definition, the prophets passionately proclaim that God himself is concerned with "the transitory social problems," with the blights of society, with the affairs of the market place.

What is the essence of being a prophet? *A prophet is a person who holds God and men in one thought at one time, at all times.* Our tragedy begins with *the segregation of God,* with the bifurcation of the secular and sacred. We worry more about the purity of dogma than about the *integrity of love. We think of God in the past tense* and refuse to realize that *God is always present* and *never, never past;* that God may be more intimately *present in slums than in mansions, with those who are smarting under the abuse of the callous.*

There are, of course, many among us whose record in dealing with the Negroes and other minority groups is unspotted. However, an honest estimation of the moral state of our society will disclose: *Some are guilty, but all are responsible.* If we admit that the individual is in some measure conditioned or affected by the public climate of opinion, an individual's crime discloses society's corruption. In a community not indifferent to suffering, uncompromisingly impatient with cruelty and falsehood, racial discrimination would be infrequent rather than common.

IV

That equality is a good thing, a fine goal, may be generally accepted. What is lacking is a sense of the *monstrosity of inequality.* Seen from the perspective of prophetic faith, the predicament of justice is the predicament of God.

Of course, more and more people are becoming aware of the Negro problem, but they fail to grasp its being a personal problem.

People are increasingly fearful of social tension and disturbance. However, so long as our society is more concerned to prevent racial strife than to prevent humiliation, the cause of strife, its moral status will be depressing, indeed.

The history of interracial relations is a nightmare. Equality of all men, a platitude to some minds, remains a scandal to many hearts. Inequality is the ideal setting for the abuse of power, a perfect justification for man's cruelty to man. Equality is an obstacle to callousness, setting a limit to power. Indeed, the history of mankind may be described as the history of the tension between power and equality.

Equality is an interpersonal relationship, involving both a claim and a recognition. My claim to equality has its logical basis in the recognition of my fellow men's identical claim. Do I not forfeit my own rights by denying to my fellow men the rights I claim for myself?

It is not humanity that endows the sky with inalienable stars. It is not society that bestows upon every man his inalienable rights. Equality of all men is not due to man's innocence or virtue. Equality of man is due to *God's love and commitment to all men.*

The ultimate worth of man is due neither to his virtue nor to his faith. *It is due to God's virtue, to God's faith. Wherever you see a trace of man, there is the presence of God.* From the perspective of eternity our recognition of equality of all men seems as generous an act as the acknowledgment that stars and planets have a right to be.

How can I withhold from others what does not belong to me?

Equality as a religious commandment goes beyond the principle of equality before the law. Equality as a religious commandment means *personal involvement,* fellowship, mutual reverence and concern. It means my being hurt when a Negro is offended. It means that I am bereaved whenever a Negro is *disfranchised.*

The shotgun blasts that have been fired at the house of James Meredith's father in Kosciusko, Mississippi, make us cry for shame wherever we are.

There is no insight more disclosing: *God is One, and humanity is one.* There is no possibility more frightening: God's name may be desecrated.

God is every man's pedigree. He is either the Father of all men or of no man. The image of God is either in every man or in no man.

From the point of view of moral philosophy it is our duty to have regard for every man. Yet such regard is contingent upon the moral merit of the particular man. From the point of view of religious philosophy it is our duty to have regard and compassion for every man regardless of his moral merit. God's covenant is with all men, and we must never be oblivious of *the equality of the divine dignity* of all men. The image of God is in the criminal as well as in the saint. How can my regard for man be contingent upon his merit, if I know that in the eyes of God I myself may be without merit!

You shall not make yourself a graven image or any likeness of God. The making and worshiping of images is considered an abomination, vehemently condemned in the Bible. The world and God are not of the same essence. There can be no man-made symbols of God.

And yet there is something in the world that the Bible does regard as a symbol of God. It is not a temple or a tree, it is not a statue or a star. *The symbol of God is man,* every man. How significant is the fact that the term *tselem,* which is frequently used in a damnatory sense for a man-made image of God, as well as the term *demuth,* likeness—of which Isaiah claims (40:18), no *demuth* can be applied to God—are employed in denoting man as an image and likeness of God. Man, every man, must be treated with the honor due to a likeness representing the King of kings.

There are many motivations by which prejudice is nourished, many reasons for despising the poor, for keeping the underprivileged in his place. However, the Bible insists that the interests of the poor have precedence over the interests of the rich. The prophets have a bias in favor of the poor.

God seeks out him who is pursued (Ecclesiastes 3:15), even if the pursuer is righteous and the pursued is wicked, because man's condition is God's concern. To discriminate against man is to despise what God demands.

> He who oppresses a poor man insults his Maker;
> But he who is kind to the needy honors Him.
> Proverbs 14:31; cf. 17:15

V

The way we act, the way we fail to act is a disgrace which must not go on forever. This is not a white man's world. This is not a colored man's world. It is God's world. No man has a place in this world who tries to keep another man in his place. It is time for the white man to repent. We have failed to use the avenues open to us to educate the hearts and minds of men, to identify ourselves with those who are underprivileged. But repentance is more than contrition and remose for sins, for harms done. Repentance means a new insight, a new spirit. It also means a course of action.

Racism is an evil of tremendous power, but God's will transcends all powers. Surrender to despair is surrender to evil. It is important to feel anxiety, it is sinful to wallow in despair.

What we need is a total mobilization of heart, intelligence, and wealth for the purpose of love and justice. God is in search of man, waiting, hoping for man to do His will.

The most practical thing is not to weep but to act and to have faith in God's assistance and grace in our trying to do His will.

This world, this society can be redeemed. God has a stake in our moral predicament. I cannot believe that God will be defeated.

What we face is a human emergency. It will require much devotion, wisdom, and divine grace to eliminate that massive sense of inferiority, the creeping bitterness. It will require a high quality of imaginative sympathy, sustained cooperation both in thought and in action, by individuals as well as by institutions, to weed out memories of frustration, roots of resentment.

We must act even when inclination and vested interests would militate against equality. Human self-interest is often our Nemesis! It is the audacity of faith that redeems us. To have faith is to be ahead of one's normal thoughts, to transcend confused motivations, to lift oneself by one's bootstraps. Mere knowledge or belief is too feeble to be a cure of man's hostility to man, of man's tendency to fratricide. The only remedy is *personal sacrifice:* to abandon, to reject what seems dear and even plausible for the sake of the greater truth; to do more than one is ready to understand for the sake of God. Required is a breakthrough, a *leap of action.* It is the deed that will purify the heart. It is the deed that will sanctify the mind. The deed is the test, the trial, and the risk.

The plight of the Negro must become our most important concern. Seen in the light of our religious tradition, *the Negro problem is God's gift to America,* the test of our integrity, a magnificent spiritual opportunity.

Humanity can thrive only when challenged, when called upon to answer new demands, to reach out for new heights. Imagine how smug, complacent, vapid, and foolish we would be, if we had to subsist on prosperity alone. It is for us to understand that religion is not sentimentality, that God is not a patron. Religion is a demand, God is a challenge, speaking to us in the language of human situations. His voice is in the dimension of history.

The universe is done. The greater masterpiece still undone, still in the process of being created, is history. For accomplishing His grand design, God needs the help of man. Man is and has the instrument of God, which he may or may not use in consonance with the grand design. Life is clay, and righteousness the mold in which God wants history to be shaped. But human beings, instead of fashioning the clay, deform the shape. God needs mercy, righteousness; His needs cannot be satisfied in space, by sitting in pews, by visiting temples, but in history, in time. It is within the realm of history that man is charged with God's mission.[2]

There are those who maintain that the situation is too grave for us to do much about it, that whatever we might do would be "too little and too late," that the most practical thing we can do is "to weep" and to despair. If such a message is true, then God has spoken in vain.

Such a message is four thousand years too late. It is good Babylonian theology. In the meantime, certain things have happened: Abraham, Moses, the Prophets, the Christian Gospel.

History is not all darkness. It was good that Moses did not study theology under the teachers of that message; otherwise, I would still be in Egypt building pyramids. Abraham was all alone in a world of paganism; the difficulties he faced were hardly less grave than ours.

The greatest heresy is despair, despair of men's power for goodness, men's power for love.

It is not enough for us to exhort the Government. What we must do is to set an example, not merely to acknowledge the Negro but to welcome him, not grudgingly but joyously, to take delight in enabling him to enjoy what is due to him. We are all *Pharaohs* or *slaves of Pharaohs*. It is sad to be a slave of Pharaoh. *It is horrible to be a Pharaoh.*

Daily we should take account and ask: What have I done today *to alleviate the anguish, to mitigate the evil, to prevent humiliation?*

Let there be a grain of prophet in every man!

Our concern must be expressed not symbolically, but literally; not only publicly, but also *privately;* not only occasionally, but regularly.

What we need is the involvement of every one of us as individuals. What we need is *restlessness,* a constant awareness of the monstrosity of injustice.

The concern for the dignity of the Negro must be an explicit tenet of our creeds. He who offends a Negro, whether as a landowner or employer, whether as waiter or salesgirl, is guilty of offending the majesty of God. No minister or layman has a right to question the principle that reverence for God is shown in reverence for man, that the fear we must feel lest we hurt or humiliate a human being must be as unconditional as fear of God. An act of violence is an act of desecration. To be arrogant toward man is to be blasphemous toward God.

In the words of Pope John XXIII, when opening the Twenty-first Ecumenical Council, "divine Providence is leading us to a new order of human relations." History has made us all neighbors. The age of moral mediocrity and complacency has run out. This is a time for radical commitment, for radical action.

Let us not forget the story of the sons of Jacob. Joseph, the dreamer of dreams, was sold into slavery by his own brothers. But at the end it was Joseph who rose to be the savior of those who had sold him into captivity.

Mankind lies groaning, afflicted by fear, frustration, and despair. Perhaps it is the will of God that among the Josephs of the future there will be many who have once been slaves and whose skin is dark. The great spiritual resources of the Negroes, their capacity for joy, their quiet nobility, their attachment to the Bible, their power of worship and enthusiasm, may prove a blessing to all mankind.

In the words of the prophet Amos (5:24):

> Let justice roll down like waters,
> and righteousness like a mighty stream.

A mighty stream, expressive of the vehemence of a never-ending, surging, fighting movement—as if obstacles had to be washed away for justice to be done. No rock is so hard that water cannot pierce it. "But the mountain falls and crumbles away, and the rock is removed from its place; the waters wear away the stones" (Job 14:18 f.). Justice is not a mere norm, but a fighting challenge, a restless drive.

Righteousness as a mere tributary, feeding the immense stream of human interests, is easily exhausted and more easily abused. But righteousness is not a trickle; it is God's power in the world, a torrent, an impetuous drive, full of grandeur and majesty. The surge is choked, the sweep is blocked. Yet the mighty stream will break all dikes.

Justice, people seem to agree, is a principle, a norm, an ideal of the highest importance. We all insist that it ought to be—but it may not be. In the eyes of the prophets, justice is more than an idea or a norm: justice is charged with the omnipotence of God. What ought to be, shall be![3]

NOTES

1. See Heschel, *The Prophets* (New York: Harper & Row, 1962), pp. 204–205.
2. See Heschel, *The Prophets,* p. 198.
3. See Heschel, *The Prophets,* pp. 212–213.

7 / The White Man on Trial

The decisive event in the story of the exodus of the children of Israel from Egypt was the crossing of the Red Sea. The sea became a dry land and the waters divided. It was a moment of supreme spiritual exaltation, of sublime joy, and prophetic elevation for the entire people. Every Israelite beheld the *Glory* with a clarity which even a prophet like Ezekiel did not experience.

Then Moses led Israel onward from the Red Sea, and they went three days in the Wilderness and found no water. When they came to Marah, they could not drink the water in Marah because it was bitter. And they murmured against Moses, saying. "What shall we drink?"

This episode seems shocking. What a comedown! Only three days earlier they had reached the highest peak of prophetic and spiritual exaltation, and now they complain about such a prosaic and un-spiritual item as water. . . .

The Negroes of America behave just like the children of Israel. Only in 1963 they experienced the miracle of having turned the tide of history, the joy of finding millions of Americans involved in the struggle for civil rights, the exaltation of fellowship, the March to Washington. Now only a few months later they have the audacity to murmur: "What shall we drink? We want adequate education, decent housing, proper employment." How ordinary, how unpoetic, how annoying!

Life could be so pleasant. The Beatles have just paid us a visit. The AT&T is about to split its stock. Dividends are higher than ever. Castro is quiet and well-mannered. Russia is purchasing grain from us. Only the Negroes continue to disturb us: What shall we drink?

We are ready to applaud dramatic struggles once a year in Washington. For the sake of lofty principles we will spend a day or two in jail somewhere in Alabama.

But that prosaic demand for housing without vermin, for adequate schools, for adequate employment—right here in the vicinity of Park Avenue in New York City—sounds so trite, so drab, so banal, so devoid of magnificence.

"Human affairs are hardly worth considering in earnest, and yet we must be in earnest about them—a sad necessity constrains us," says Plato in a mood of melancholy. He apologizes later for his "low opinion of mankind" which, he explains, emerges from comparing men with the gods. "Let us grant, if you wish, that the human race is not to be despised, but is worthy of some consideration."

"The gods attend to great matters; they neglect small ones," Cicero maintains. According to Aristotle, the gods are not concerned at all with the dispensation of good and bad fortune or external things. To the Hebrew prophet, however, no subject is as worthy of consideration as the plight of man, Indeed, God Himself is described as reflecting over the plight of man rather than as contemplating eternal ideas. His mind is preoccupied with man, with the concrete actualities of history rather than with the timeless issues of thought. In the prophet's message, nothing that has bearing upon good and evil is small or trite in the eyes of God.[1]

The teaching of Judaism is the *theology of the common deed*. The Bible insists that God is *concerned with everydayness, with the trivialities of life*. The great challenge does not lie in organizing solemn demonstrations, but in how we manage the commonplace. The prophet's field of concern is not the mysteries of heaven, the glories of eternity, but the blights of society, the affairs of the market place. He addresses himself to those who trample upon the needy, who increase the price of grain, use dishonest scales, and sell the refuse of corn (Amos 8:4-6). The predominant feature of the biblical pattern of life is unassuming, unheroic, inconspicuous piety, the sanctification of trifles, attentiveness to details.

"The wages of a hired servant shall not abide with thee all night until the morning" (Leviticus 19:13). Don't delay the payment due to him. "If you meet your enemy's ox or his ass going astray, you shall bring it back to him. If you see the ass of one who hates you lying under its burden . . . help him to lift it up" (Exodus 23:4-5). "When you build a new house, you shall make a parapet for your roof," to prevent anyone from falling from it (Deuteronomy 22:8).

May I, however, qualify a statement I made before. Most of us, Negro and white, have not yet completed the crossing of the Red Sea. There is still a long way to go. In fact, it was easier for the children of Israel to cross the Red Sea than for the Civil Rights legislation to pass the floor of the United States Senate.

When at the Burning Bush, Moses was called by the Lord to go to Pharaoh and lead Israel out of Egypt, he hesitated, saying: "Please, Oh Lord, I am not eloquent . . . I am slow of speech and slow of tongue." How marvelous it would be if some of our Senators who are preparing for a filibuster would share this quality of Moses.

Pharaoh was a lover of distinctions. In discussing the public accommodation bill, he suggested: "I will let some of you go, and let the rest of you stay." Yet Moses insisted: "We will go with our young and our old; we will go with our sons and our daughters, with our flocks and our herds."

Efforts must be exerted on two levels; on the level of principles and attitudes as well as on the level of practical application. We must continue to dedicate ourselves not only to the problem of the Negro, but also to the problem of the white man.

The tragedy of Pharaoh was the failure to realize that the exodus from slavery could have spelled redemption for both Israel and Egypt. Would that Pharaoh and the Egyptians had joined the Israelites in the desert and together stood at the foot of Sinai!

The Negro problem adds a spiritual purpose to our lives as Americans: No person can be kept apart. All men are involved in the predicament of one man.

Ideas have *power,* ideas have *life.* But no idea has *self-perpetuating* power, no idea is assured of *immortal* life. The life of an idea depends upon the commitment of a people to it. Let this commitment be reduced to lip-service, and the idea will die.

The validity of the idea of equality, so dear, so precious to all of us, must not be taken for granted. Unless we continue to be fighting witnesses, unless we live it, it might die on our lips. Let us remember that equality of all men, regardless of race, culture, and religion, is still not accepted universally in our own day nor was it widely accepted in years gone by.

Hailed by Thomas Jefferson as a self-evident truth, it has been denounced by William Sumner as a flagrant falsehood. Recalled by Abraham Lincoln as the proposition to which this nation was dedicated, it has been branded by Calhoun as an absurd hypothesis. Seen by De Tocqueville as synonymous with democracy, it has been equated by Dr. Nicholas Murray Butler with a democracy that is spurious. Claimed by Laski to be the necessary condition for liberty, it has been cited by Lord Acton as the "deepest cause which made the French Revolution so disastrous to liberty." It has been dubbed by Rufus Choate as a "glittering generality," and assailed by Emile Faguet as the "democratic tarantula."[2]

The challenge we face is a test of our integrity. We are all on trial, we are all under judgment. The issue is not political or social expediency. The issue is whether we are morally strong, whether we are spiritually worthy to answer God's demand. Shall we continue to be deaf, shall we continue to be sensitive only when our own needs and interests are involved?

We have attained a high standard of living. We must seek to attain a high standard of thinking.

The problem we face is to be or not to be human. The situation of the Negro is the test, the trial, and the risk.

It is not only how we worry about the Negroes in America that is our test. It is also how we are concerned for the spiritual plight of the Jews in Russia who are denied the right of religious equality, how we are concerned for the people of Tibet, the hungry masses in India and Brazil, for the sick and the poor, the wetbacks, the Braceros in our own country.

The plight of the Negro is a living reminder of our failure, a melancholy example of our dereliction. I cannot speak about the Negro without a sense of embarrassment at the fact that it was not the authority of the religious institutions that proclaimed once and for all the evil of segregation, that the religious institutions had to be prodded into action by the decision of the Supreme Court of 1954.

Yet it is not the skin alone that serves as an excuse for indifference or prejudice. We are involved in a major legal and social revolution, but we fail to realize that we also face a spiritual emergency, the need for all of us to change our image of the Negro as well as the need of the Negro to enhance his own proper image. There is a disrespect for the Negro in the hearts of many white people. It is a psychological law that people will only respect a person who has self-respect and entertain contempt for a person who has self-contempt. The important challenge therefore is: to stop that oppressive sense of inferiority, to instill courage, to create a vision.

No man is a fortress, no heart is made of stone. It will take much love and wisdom to cure the hearts of millions who have endured humiliation, experiences of insult, of being rebuffed for so many decades. There is nothing in the world that may be regarded as holy as eliminating anguish, as alleviating pain.

The solution will not be achieved by the elimination of prejudice. It will be achieved by the inspiration of fellowship, by their assuming equal responsibility for the cultural and spiritual advancement of our nation.

The problem is not only what the white man will do for the Negro, but above all the regeneration of the moral vigor of the Negro. Great spiritual resources of the Negro lie still untapped. A new source of spiritual strength will be opened to all of us by the integration of the Negro.

What is needed is not toleration but justice, not admission but acceptance.

There are no administrative solutions to spiritual problems. The United States Senate, the courts, and the laws will only enable us to embark upon the task; it will remain a challenge to our wisdom, to our power of love to complete the task.

Equality must not be equated with enforcement of conformity. The demand for equal dignity must not be confused with a demand for general leveling. Equality is not a mechanical concept. It implies the right to be a conformist as well as the right to be different.

What is the meaning of integration? To integrate means to unite, to form into a whole. Integration means fellowship, mutual respect, and concern.

True fellowship is not attained by going to the race-tracks together. True fellowship is attained by the reverence we share, by the commitments we cherish, by going through moments of insight together. It will not be attained by riding on the same bus, by the mere placing of children together in the same room. It will be attained by sharing moments of joy, cultural values, insights, commitments.

Let us not reduce the great idea of integration to an empty togetherness. Our vision is not of white and Negro in integrated saloons. Our vision is of a day when the problem of color and race will be irrelevant. It is not the admissions office that will do it—it is the inspired teacher and the power of a great faith that will accomplish it.

The primary issue is not to integrate the schools, important as it is. The primary issue is to improve and to democratize the school. Integration is implied in democratization. The primary issue is to revolutionize education.

What exacerbates the situation is the fact that the entire system of our civilization finds itself in a grave crisis. The goal we have in mind is integration. But is it significant to speak of integration into a disintegrating society? Integration means relating and adjusting

individuals to a society and to a system of values. Yet our values are
in a state of dissolution, and our society betrays its own commitments. There is a continual corrosion of our moral and spiritual
sensitivities. Is it possible to achieve the desegregation of the Negro
while promoting the dehumanization of man? Togetherness in
emptiness?

Are we in a strong position to preach to the Negro about family
morality while the breakdown of standards is treated casually by the
entire society—abetted, fostered, and exploited by vast commercial
interests?

Will it be a gain if the Negro churches, many of which are rich in
simplicity of faith, in discipline and devotion, will be dissolved and
integrated into the more sophisticated bourgeois institutions, into
churches with a swimming pool?

Integration of the Negro is an opportunity to examine the integrity of our entire society, our standards of thinking, our modes of
living. If integration is not to be a move from the ghetto of Harlem
to spiritual slums, if integration is to be more than mechanical and
formal, we have to transform the fabric of our society.

What is needed is a spiritual revolution. We must rise to a higher
plane of thinking.

We have recently gone through a period of profound grief and
dreadful consternation: the death of Pope John XXIII, and the
assassination of John F. Kennedy. Men all over the world felt
suddenly deprived of a magnificence, bereaved of a living promise
and a hope which illumined our lives for a few brief years. The
world in which these two men lived will never be the same.

And yet the year in which these events occurred—1963—contained
another message as well. Our world which is full of cynicism,
frustration, and despair, received in 1963 a flash of inspiration; 1963
was a noble year, a triumph of conscience, a triumph of faith. It will
depend upon us whether 1963 will remain a chapter in sacred
history.

Callousness is sovereign and smug; it clings to the soul and will not give in. The exponents of despair continue to stress that those who are guilty are devoid of contrition, deaf to argument, that the only way to end oppression is violence, brute force.

No one who entered the year 1963 with uncertainty and apprehension could fail to sense that this was a great year in the spiritual history of man.

Who would have believed what we have seen? Who would have expected what we have witnessed? The overwhelming majority of the American people stood up and gave witness to the proposition that all men are created equal and accepted, without reservation, the demands of justice, the commitment to end discrimination, to bring about complete desegregation. A new image of the humanity of the Negro dominates the mind. This is a triumph of conscience!

This major revolution took place with a minimum of bloodshed, in complete disavowal of the use of violence. It is important for us to remember that the credit for this victory of the spirit goes above all to the Negroes. In spite of the pressure of groups on both sides insisting that violence alone can solve the racial problem, the Negro with his admirable patience adhered to his faith in justice, to his faith in the conscience of the white man. This is a triumph of faith.

Can we match that patience with our concern, with our involvement? The white man is on trial. Can we match the spiritual dignity of this great revolution with devotion and incessant activity? Shall the triumph of faith be defeated by a premature sense of accomplishment? We have achieved a consensus of conscience, we must now strive for incessant action.

In a world full of absurdity and repeated failures, the advancement in this cause was an outburst of righteousness, a veritable revelation of what is strong and good in our nation.

The children of Israel were slaves in Egypt. Yet their full redemption was not on the day they left Egypt. Their full redemption was on the day on which they stood before Sinai and heard the voice: I am the Lord your God Who took you out of the land of slavery. . . .

The exodus from Egypt found its purpose and meaning in the revelation at Sinai. Sinai remained a triumph that goes on forever.

The exodus from segregation will, and this we know, bring all the benefits and blessings of a free society to all its members. Its grandeur will endure if this great movement will continue to be inspired by the sense that its deep meaning is a triumph of conscience and a triumph of faith.

In this hour of spiritual scarcity, dominated as we are by powers of pompous vulgarity, we must hope and pray that the precious spiritual qualities of the Negro people, their deep religious faith, their love of the Bible, their power to pray, their commitment to nonviolence may continue to live on. Integration must not mean liquidation of the treasures of the soul.

Let the white people, however, realize that the strength of reliance on nonviolence may not stand the test of long and bitter humiliation. Unless the Negroes come to realize that their struggle is a struggle for all Americans, unless they are joined in this struggle by white people, the spiritual gains of 1963 may be lost.

Let us beware of oversimplification. What will be required is both wisdom and perseverance. Only generosity may atone for the callousness and the greed of generations. In many a crisis it will be necessary for us to have the power to feel the Negro's grief in our hearts, the Negro's tear in our throat.

At this moment, the issue is not only prejudice and discrimination. Underneath the struggle for civil rights is a call for social change, automation, the crisis and failure of education, the abuse of freedom, callousness, and a massive sense of absurdity.

What is at stake is a social movement, a call for social change in social theory and practice. Technology is transforming our society continuously, industry is recklessly dynamic, yet our thinking is static. Prosperity and comfort have made us listless; smug, indifferent. We enjoy our privileges, we detest any dislocation in our intellectual habits. But automation is with us, and so is poverty, and unemployment.

The Negro is a group in motion while most segments of our society prefer to be at ease.

The Negro movement is an outcry of pain in which a sickness of our total society comes to expression: supersonic planes and sub-standard housing; esoteric science and vulgar ethics; an elite of highly specialized experts, and a mass of unprepared, unskilled laborers. The apex of the pyramid ascends most rapidly, while the basis expands with equal rapidity. It is the Negro movement that sounds the alarm at a time when the rest of society seems content and unprepared to face a social emergency. It is the problem of jobs for the disemployed, dignity for those who are on relief, employment for the unskilled, the threat of automation, the curse of poverty, the blighted slums in our cities.

When the legislative or executive branch of the Government fails to satisfy the just claims of minority groups, these groups have traditionally been forced to resort to unconventional, dramatic methods, for example, the suffragist movement, the drive to organize labor into unions.

It is true that errors have been made in the strategy and tactics of the civil rights movement. But where a minority of the society has to carry the total burden for social change (because that minority is the only segment of society in motion) it must use tactics commensurate with its strength. Therefore, while Negroes know that you can't get many jobs by lying in front of trucks or hanging on cranes, they must engage in such tactics to call people's attention to the problem.

For example, how tragic that it is left to A. Philip Randolph of the Brotherhood of Sleeping Car Porters to organize a committee for a $1.50 minimum hourly wage. For the fact remains that if the labor movement were in motion—truly in motion, in defense of the poor—then it would not be left to Negroes alone to organize such a committee.

If at some point Negroes become so desperate economically that they stage a sit-in, in the State Legislature, they will be called extremist by the very segments of society which have abdicated their responsibility to create the kind of movement which could be broader and therefore capable of using more conventional tactics.

White people—church people, liberals—have to understand this: You push a man into a corner. He behaves desperately. Then you ask, Why does he behave desperately?

Religion becomes a mockery if we remain callous to the irony of sending satellites to the sky and failing to find employment for our fellow citizens, of a highly publicized World's Fair and insufficient funds for the extermination of vermin in the slums.

Is religion to be a mockery?

NOTES

1. See Heschel, *The Prophets* (New York: Harper & Row, 1962), p. 5.
2. J. F. Ferguson, *The Philosophy of Equality* (Washington, 1943), p. xi.

II

8 / Depth Theology

Where is religion to be found? What sort of entity is it? What is its mode of being?

He who is in search of art will find it in works of art as preserved, for example, in art collections. He who is in search of literature will find it in books as preserved in libraries. But where is the place of religion? Do visible symbols as preserved in temples, doctrines and dogmas as contained in books, contain the totality of religion?

It seems preposterous to regard religion as an isolated, self subsisting entity, as a *Ding an sich*. Indeed, there is an inherent weakness of religion not to take offense at the segregation of God, to forget that the true sanctuary has no walls. Religion has often suffered from the tendency to become an end in itself, to seclude the holy, to become parochial, self-indulgent, self-seeking; as if the task were not to ennoble human nature, but to enhance the power and beauty of its institutions or to enlarge the body of doctrines. It has often done more to canonize prejudices than to wrestle for truth; to petrify the sacred than to sanctify the secular. Yet the task of religion is to be a challenge to the stabilization of values.

Religion has been reduced to institution, symbol, theology. It does not affect the pretheological situation, the presymbolic depth of existence. To redirect the trend, we must lay bare what is involved in religious existence; we must recover the situations which both precede and correspond to the theological formulations; we must recall the questions which religious doctrines are trying to answer, *the antecedents of religious commitment,* the presuppositions of faith. A major task of philosophy of religion is, as said above, to rediscover the questions to which religion is an answer. The inquiry must proceed both by delving into the consciousness of man and by delving into the teachings and attitudes of the religious tradition.

The urgent problem is not only the truth of religion, but man's capacity to sense the truth of religion, the authenticity of religious concern. Religious truth does not shine in a vacuum. It is certainly not comprehensible when the antecedents of religious insight and commitment are wasted away; when the mind is dazzled by ideologies which either obscure or misrepresent man's ultimate questions; when life is lived in a way which tends to abuse and to squander the gold mines, the challenging resources of human existence. The primary issue of theology is *pretheological;* it is the total situation of man and his attitudes toward life and the world. It is from this point of view that we must realize that there are four dimensions in religion.

What are the four dimensions of religious existence? To the eye of the spectator, religion seems to consist exclusively of two components: of ritual and myth, of sacrament and dogma, of deed and scripture. The importance of these components is beyond dispute; the emphasis in different systems upon either of the two only indicates the indispensability of both. To some the truth of religion is in its ritual,[1] to others the essence of religion is in its dogma.[2]

There is another component, however, which may be regarded as the vital ingredient, and yet because of its imponderable nature it often escapes the eye of the observer. It is that which goes on within the person: the innerness of religion. Vague and often indescribable, it is the heart of religious existence. Ritual and myth, dogma and deed remain externals unless there is a response from within the person, a moment of identification and penetration to make them internals. We must distinguish between four dimensions of religious existence, four necessary components of man's relationships to God: a) the teaching, the essentials of which are summarized in the form of a creed; it is the creed that contains norms and principles about matters sacred or eternal, the dimension of the doctrine; b) faith, inwardness, the direction of one's heart, the intimacy of religion, the dimension of privacy; c) the law, or the sacred act to be carried out in the sanctuary, in society or at home, the dimension of the deed; d) the context in which creed, faith and ritual come to pass, such as the community or the covenant, history, tradition, the dimension of transcendence. Are these dimensions always present? There are situations in which the dimension of depth is missing: the word is proclaimed, the deed is done, but the soul is silent. There are also situations in which nothing is happening to the sense, but the whole soul is aflame. Some consider the objective performance to be so sacred and effective that the inner component is of little account. What is the worth of one individual's evanescent response compared with the majesty of a revealed word, the preciousness of a ritual? Others regard the inner moment as the vital principle or the culmination of existence. The study of ritual is like phonetics, the science of sounds; the study of dogma is like grammar, the science of the inflections of language; while the study of inner acts is like semantics, the science of meanings.[3]

We do not have a word for the understanding of these moments, for the events that make up the secret history of religion, or for the records in which these instants are captured. Theology is the doctrine of God, but these moments are neither doctrine nor exclusively divine. They are human as well as divine. The Psalms are not records of theology. The Psalms are the birthpangs of theology; their words plummet-lines reaching into the depth of the divine-human situation out of which genuine theology arises.

Theology has often suffered from a preoccupation with the dogma, the content of believing. The act of believing; the questions, What happens within the person to bring about faith? What does it mean to believe?—all this is the concern of a special type of inquiry which may be called "depth theology."

The theme of theology is the content of believing; the theme of depth theology is the act of believing, its purpose being to explore the depth of faith, the substratum out of which belief arises. It deals with acts which precede articulation and defy definition.

Thus many issues of religious existence may be looked upon in two ways: from the perspective of depth theology and from the perspective of theology.

The principle of the Mosaic authorship of the Pentateuch rests upon two premises: One, that Moses was a prophet, that is, inspired by God, the recipient of divine revelation; two, that Moses wrote the Pentateuch. The first premise refers to a mystery which we can neither imagine nor define; the second premise refers to an act that can be described in categories of time and space. Theology would stress the second premise; depth theology would stress the first premise.

Miracles happen simultaneously in two realms: in the realm of time and space, and in the realm of the soul. Is only an event in the physical world to be considered a marvel, while man's marvel at the miracle, the illumination of the soul, is to be considered inferior in importance?

When the people Israel crossed the Red Sea, two things happened: the waters split, and between man and God all distance was gone. There was no veil, no vagueness. There was only His presence: This is my God, the Israelite exclaimed. Most miracles that happen in space are lost in the heart; the miracle of the Red Sea became a song, "The Song of the Red Sea."

Theology declares: depth theology evokes; theology demands believing and obedience: depth theology hopes for responding and appreciation.

Theology deals with permanent facts; depth theology deals with moments. Dogma and ritual are permanent possessions of religion; moments come and go. Theology abstracts and generalizes. It subsists apart from all that goes on in the world. It preserves the legacy; it perpetuates traditions. Yet without the spontaneity of the person, response and inner identification, without the sympathy of understanding, the body of tradition crumbles between the fingers. What is the ultimate nature of the sacred words which tradition preserves?

These words are not made of paper but of life. The task is not to reproduce in sound what is preserved in graphic signs; the task is to resurrect its life, to feel its pulse, so that the life within the words should reproduce its kind within our lives. Indeed, there is a heritage of insight as there is a tradition of words and rituals. It is a heritage easily forfeited, easily forgotten.

We stay away from depth theology because its themes are not easily captured in words, because we are afraid of vagueness. There is no casuistry of the inner life, no codification of innerness. Yet a life made explicit, a soul efficiently organized, would be devoid of its resources.

Theology speaks for the people; depth theology speaks for the individual. Theology strives for communication, for universality; depth theology strives for insight, for uniqueness.

Theology is like sculpture, depth theology like music. Theology is in the books; depth theology is in the hearts. The former is doctrine, the latter an event. Theologies divide us; depth theology unites us.

Depth theology seeks to meet the person in moments in which the whole person is involved, in moments which are affected by all a person thinks, feels, and acts. It draws upon that which happens to man in moments of confrontation with ultimate reality. It is in such moments that decisive insights are born. Some of these insights lend themselves to conceptualization, while others seem to overflow the vessels of our conceptual powers.

To convey these insights, man must use a language which is compatible with his sense of the ineffable, the terms of which do not pretend to describe, but to indicate; to point to, rather than to capture. These terms are not always imaginative; they are often paradoxical, radical, or negative. The chief danger to philosophy of religion lies in the temptation to generalize what is essentially unique, to explicate what is intrinsically inexplicable, to adjust the uncommon to our common sense.

Depth theology warns us against intellectual self-righteousness, against self-certainty and smugness. It insists upon the inadequacy of our faith, upon *the incongruity of dogma and mystery*. The depth of insight is never fathomed, never expressed. Who can be sure of his own faith? Or who can find Him in the mirror of his concepts?

A story is told of a Hasid who was listening to an expert in medieval Jewish scholasticism, holding forth upon the attributes of God, setting forth with logical exactness which statements may be predicted of God. After the discourse came to an end, the Hasid remarked: "If God were the way you described Him, I would not believe in Him. . . ."

Speculative theology, concerned as it is with achieving final formulations of the ideas of faith, is always in danger of taking itself too seriously, of believing to have found adequate expression in an area in which no words are ever adequate.

By the standards of speculative theology, the image and language of Psalm 19 appear to be objectionable. Surely terms such as "King," "Creator," "Master" are more acceptable, since they convey the supremacy and majesty of God as well as man's dependence on Him. In contrast the term "Shepherd" implies not only man's dependence on God but also God's need for man. The sheep look to the shepherd for shelter, food, and protection. At the same time the well-being of the shepherd is bound up with the well-being of the sheep. They are to him milk, meat, clothing, and material wealth.

As said above, the theme of theology is the content of believing; the theme of depth theology is the act of believing. The first we call faith, the second creed or dogma. Creed and faith, theology and depth theology depend upon each other.

Why are dogmas necessary? We cannot be in rapport with the reality of the divine except for rare, fugitive moments. How can these moments be saved for the long hours of functional living, when the thoughts that feed like bees on the inscrutable desert us, and we lose both the sight and the drive? Dogmas are like the amber in which bees, once alive, are embalmed, and which are capable of being electrified when our minds become exposed to the power of the ineffable. For the problems with which we must always grapple are: How to communicate those rare moments of insight to all hours of our life. How to commit intuition to concepts, the ineffable to words, communion to rational understand. How to convey our insights to others and to unite in a fellowship of faith. It is the creed that attempts to answer these problems.

The insights of depth theology are vague; they often defy formulation and expression. It is the task of theology to establish the doctrines, to bring about coherence, and to find words compatible with the insights. On the other hand, theological doctrines tend to move on their own momentum, to become a substitute for insight, informative rather than evocative. We must see to it that each has an independent status, a power and efficacy of its own which enables it to contribute something in the cooperation.

And yet man has often made a god out of a dogma, a graven image which he worshiped, to which he prayed. He would rather believe in dogmas than in God, serving them not for the sake of heaven but for the sake of a creed, the diminutive of faith.

Dogmas are the poor mind's share in the divine. A creed is almost all a poor man has. Skin for skin, he will give his life for all that he has. Yea, he may be ready to take other people's lives, if they refuse to share his tenets.

Depth theology may become an impasse, the catacomb of subjectivism. To be a passageway leading from man to man, from generation to generation, it must be crystallized and assume the form of a doctrine or principle. Theology is the crystallization of the insights of depth theology.

However, crystallization may result in petrification. Indeed, the stability of the dogma or the institution has often taken precedence over the spontaneity of the person.

The vitality of religion depends upon keeping alive the polarity of doctrine and insight, of dogma and faith, of ritual and response, of institution and the individual. Religion degenerates when the spectacle becomes a substitute for spontaneity, when demonstration takes the place of penetration.

Innerness is not autonomous. Whatever happens within the person is affected by thoughts and facts that come from without. Without the content of theology, innerness is a void or turns to spiritual narcissism.

The two realms act upon each other. Theology must teach us, for example, whether the world is of God, an emanation of His being, or whether the world is by God, a creation of His will.

Whether there is a disjunctive relationship between God and man, or whether there is a dimension where God and man meet—and above all: What does God demand of man? Depth theology must guide us in experiencing our own selves as well as the world in the light of the teaching we receive, in translating a thought into prayer, a doctrine into a personal response, to perceive a mystery as a challenge, a problem as a call addressed to our innermost selves.

Outward action may take place in isolation. Inward action never happens in isolation; there are no walls in the inner life. All forces and motivations act upon each other; righteousness and wickedness reflect each other.

Psalm 23, the Shepherd Psalm, which adds almost nothing to a conceptual theology, is one of the most significant expressions of depth theology.

The truly great events are never recorded. The dates of the Turco-Greek war and of the battle of Jena have been preserved. But the moment in which the line was born, "The Lord is my shepherd, I shall not want" is not contained in the annals of history. Yet that moment has never ceased.

What are the antecedents of religious commitment? What are some of the acts that happen within the depths of a person, the moments that necessitate our groping for faith in the living God?

Not speculation, but the sense of mystery precipitated the problem of all problems. Not the apparent, but the hidden within the apparent; not the design of the universe, but the mystery of the design of the universe; not the definable issues, but the indefinable enigmas, the questions we do not know how to ask, have always poured oil on the flames of man's anxiety. Religion begins with the sense of the ineffable, with the awareness of a reality that discredits our pride.

The world seems to have two faces. Living in one realm, it seems that the face of the world is open to us; living in another realm, it is as if the world stood with its back to us. Citizens of two realms, we must all sustain a dual allegiance: we sense the ineffable in one realm; we name and exploit reality in another. To maintain the right balance of mystery and meaning, of stillness and utterance, of reverence and action seems to be the goal of religious existence. It is not only the sight of the pale populace of heaven, but also the galaxy of blades of grass that deprives us of intellectual levity. Our wisdom becomes cobweb, our understanding obsolete. The experience of the sublime is a humiliation as well as an exaltation.

The delicate balance of mystery and meaning, of reverence and action, has been perilously upset. Our knowledge has been flattened. We see the world in one dimension and treat all problems on the same level. From the fact that we learned how to replace the kerosene lamp, we have deduced that we can replace the mystery of existence. We may be able to experiment with mice and still be unable to experiment with prayer.

By the mystery I do not mean the fact that the world in which we live is not exhausted by those properties which can be measured, added, subtracted, multiplied. By the mystery I mean a dimension of all beings, including the measurable aspects of beings and the act of measuring itself. It is given with and within experience.

The mystery is not a matter pertaining to the things *not yet* known, but something that will never be known. It is something we face but to which we cannot relate ourselves. We stand in its presence, yet unable to grasp its essence. We are like deaf people who see the sounds but are unable to hear them.

The sense of mystery gives grandeur to the mind and fertility to the soul. We cripple man's character, we injure his soul, by pretending that there are no depths in reality and no abysses in human thought.

Sensitivity to the mystery of living is the essence of human dignity. It is the soil in which our consciousness has its roots, and out of which a sense of meaning is derived. Man does not live by explana-

tions alone, but by the sense of wonder and mystery. Without it
there is neither religion nor morality, neither sacrifice nor creativity.

You will not enter the gates of religion through the door of
speech. The way to God is through the depths of the self. The soul
is a key; the depth is the door. In the depth of the soul there is a
prayer, an invocation, a cry for meaning, a craving for justification.

There is only one legitimate form of religious expression: prayer.
All other forms are commentaries: descriptions, discourses tend to
become diversions.

The elements of depth theology are those situations in which the
door to ultimate significance is not locked, in which the mystery is
not obscured. These elements are acts of wonder and awe, a sense of
indebtedness, moments of embarrassment and moments of being
that are pregnant with meaning, acts of yearning and luminous
moments of insight.

The purpose of depth theology, we have said, is not to establish a
doctrine but to lay bare some of the roots of our being, stirred by the
Ultimate Question. Its theme is faith in *status nascendi,* the birthpangs of insight.

One of the most precious gifts which mankind received from the
Bible is a *bad conscience*. The Bible requires the utmost— "Ye shall
be holy"; "Thou shalt love thy God with all thy heart, with all thy
soul, with all thy might"; "Thou shalt love thy neighbor as thyself."
Who could be pleased with his accomplishments? No voice is more
authentic than the prophet's rebuke to complacency, the prophet's
call to repentance. "I am before Thee like a vessel full of shame."

We realize our true plight in discovering that we care very little
for our fellow man or for God; what is ultimately important is of no
ultimate concern to us.

At the root of our sense of embarrassment and indebtedness[4] is a
sense of appreciation. There is no ultimate embarrassment without
an intuition of greatness, without an awareness of the grandeur and
mystery of ultimate meaning.

Indebtedness is a sign of worthiness, of being a recipient of something precious and of holding it in trust. Our ultimate embarrass-

ment is a sign of being involved in a mysterious design. Man is abashed because his destiny is to reflect a divine image rather than a caricature. To exist as a human means to assist the divine. For the divine to be done, the human part must be present.

No man is sterile. Every soul is pregnant with a seed of insight. It is vague and hidden. No mother has ever seen the life she carries under her heart. In some people the seed grows, in others it decays. Some give birth to life. Others miscarry it. Some know how to bear, to nurse, and to rear an insight that comes into being. Others do not know how to cherish the burden of a child, and others again do not see the child to which they give birth; the child may die at birth or may be taken away.

Such pregnancy is a sense of the fullness of time, of being with meaning. Things are marvels, moments are tokens of grace. There is abundance of love in God's concealment. No shadows can deceive a heart drunk with joy. Stillness is His witness. All noise is gone.

There is power in the seed. At times it lifts us up high, and it is as if we walked from one mountaintop to another; at other times you feel like hiding in a corner, like vanishing in shame. It is a singing in the heart as well as a distress. You recognize the pregnant ones by the sign in the song.

We are pregnant with a thought for which we have no image. We are endowed with a song which we cannot utter, with a word we do not know how to spell. Then we open a Psalm, and there is the song and the word. Only that the song within us grows. We pour it into a deed; we fashion it into words, but the song is never exhausted.

What we must do is to nurse the song in the recesses of the soul.

Over and above all frustrations, there is a certainty that we are never alone in doing the good. We love with Him Who loves the world.

NOTES

1. Emile Durkheim and Robertson Smith stress the priority of ritual over belief.

2. "From the age of fifteen, dogma has been the fundamental principle

of my religion. I know of no other religion; I cannot enter into the idea of any other sort of religion; religion, as a mere sentiment, is to me a dream and a mockery." (J. H. Newman, *Apologia Pro Vita Sua,* Chap. 2.)

3. See Heschel, *Man Is Not Alone* (New York: Farrar, Straus, 1951), pp. 167 ff.

4. See Heschel, *Who Is Man?* (Stanford: Stanford University Press, 1965).

9 / Confusion of Good and Evil

Once upon a time a king received a shocking report about the new harvest: Whoever eats of the crop becomes mad. So he called together his counselors. Since no other food was available, the alternative was clear. Not to eat of the new harvest would be to die of starvation, to eat would be to become mad. The decision reached by the king was: We will all have to eat, but let at least a few of us continue to keep in mind that we are mad. This parable by Rabbi Nahman of Bratslav (1772–1811) comes to my mind in opening an essay on the meaning of Reinhold Niebuhr to our generation. He reminds us what we are.

In boldness of penetration, depth of insight, fullness of vision and comprehensiveness, Reinhold Niebuhr's system excels everything which the whole of American theology has hitherto produced. A pioneer for his generation, he speaks of the eternal in a world of spiritual absenteeism, compelling it to listen to him. It is not easy to listen to him because he not only plants new truths but also roots out old errors, even the most comfortable and satisfying ones. Yet the degree to which Niebuhr does influence American thinking is one of the most significant facts of contemporary American history.

In an age that "has no vantage point from which to understand the predicament of modern man,"[1] Niebuhr not only helps many of his contemporaries to see through their delusions, deceptions, and pretensions; he also succeeds in recovering some of the insights of prophetic thinking that are of tremendous aid in understanding the central issues of existence from a religious perspective.[2]

In the following pages an attempt is made to examine some of Niebuhr's views in the light of Jewish thinking. We shall confine ourselves to a few aspects of his doctrine of evil, particularly those of common conviction and concern.

I

Niebuhr reminds us that "there is a mystery of evil in human life to which modern culture has been completely oblivious."[3]

It may have been possible prior to 1914 to believe with Herbert Spencer, who in his *Evanescence of Evil* asserted that "evil perpetually tends to disappear."[4] The certainty of evil's gradual extinction through the growth of culture and education was a part of the belief in the steady progress of mankind, of the belief in "redemption through progress." But the horrors through which we have lived in the past forty years have totally discredited such simple, easy-going optimism.

"Therefore he who is prudent will keep silent in such a time; for it is an evil time" (Amos 5:13). But Niebuhr is not prudent. The road to disaster is paved with pleasant illusions, and the way to deal with evil is not to ignore it. Indeed, the effort to minimize the power of evil has had fateful results in the past. It has not only weakened our alertness to the dangers of existence but also impaired our sense of guilt, our ability to repent, and our power to pray, "Forgive us for we have sinned."

Niebuhr's distinctive contribution to contemporary thinking lies in his comprehension of "the dimension of depth in life," in his tracing every problem with which he deals "to some ultimate origin." He stresses the antinomies and ambiguities of man's historic existence and denies that they can be overcome in history itself. He has shown that the tragic aspect of man cannot be reduced either to a psychological or to a biological quality; that it is rather an aspect of history, of the structure of existence. The question that is going to occupy us is to what degree Niebuhr's thought is within the biblical and prophetic tradition.

Many modern theologians have consistently maintained that the Bible stands for optimism, that pessimism is alien to its spirit.[5] There is, however, very little evidence to support such a view. With the exception of the first chapter of the Book of Genesis, the rest of the Bible does not cease to refer to the sorrow, sins, and evils of this world. As Maimonides pointed out (in a different context and order), the ideas that apply to the world in the state of its coming into being do not apply to the world that is in being. The design of the Creator was for a world that was to be good, very good; but then something mysterious happened, to which Jewish tradition alludes in many ways, and the picture of the world profoundly changed. When the prophets look at the world, they behold "distress and darkness, the gloom of anguish" (Isaiah 8:22). When they look at the land, they find it "full of guilt against the Holy One of Israel" (Jeremiah 51:5). "O Lord, how long shall I cry for help, and Thou wilt not hear? Or cry to Thee 'violence!' and Thou wilt not save? Why dost Thou make me see wrongs and look upon trouble? Destruction and violence are before me; strife and contention arise. So the law is slacked and justice never goes forth. For the wicked surround the righteous, so justice goes forth perverted" (Habakkuk 1:2 4). This is a world in which the way of the wicked prosper and "all who are treacherous thrive" (Jeremiah 12:1); a world which made it possible for some people to maintain that "Everyone who does evil is good in the sight of the Lord, and He delights in them," and for others to ask, "Where is the God of justice?" (Malachi 2:17).

The psalmist did not feel that this was a happy world when he prayed: "O God, do not keep silence; do not hold peace or be still, O God. For, lo, Thy enemies are in uproar; those who hate thee have raised their heads" (Psalm 83:2-3).

The terror and anguish that came upon the psalmist were not caused by calamities in nature but by the wickedness of man, by the evils in history:

> Fearfulness and trembling come upon me,
> Honor has overwhelmed me.
> And I said, Oh that I had wings like a dove!
> Then would I fly away, and be at rest.
>
> Psalm 55:6–7.

These are the words of Moses in his last days: "I know how defiant and stiffnecked you are. . . . I know that, when I am dead, you will act wickedly, and turn aside from the path which I enjoined upon you; and in time to come misfortune will befall you, for having done evil in the sight of the Lord" (Deuteronomy 31:27–29). It is not a sweet picture of man that Isaiah paints, saying: "You have never heard, you have never known, from of old your ear has not been opened. For I knew that you would deal very treacherously, and that from birth you were called a rebel" (Isaiah 48:8).

There is one line that expresses the mood of the Jewish man throughout the ages: *"The earth is given into the hand of the wicked"* (Job 9:24).[6]

How does the world look in the eyes of God? Are we ever told that the Lord saw that the righteousness of man was great in the earth, and that He was glad to have made man on the earth? The general tone of the biblical view of history is set after the first ten generations: "The Lord saw how great was man's wickedness on earth, and how every plan devised by his mind was nothing but evil all the time. And the Lord regretted that He had made man on earth, and His heart was saddened" (Genesis 6:5–6; cf. 8:21). One great cry resounds throughout the Bible: The wickedness of man is great on the earth. It is voiced by the prophets; it is echoed by the psalmist.

> The two dominant attitudes of prophetic faith are gratitude and contrition; gratitude for creation and contrition before judgment; or, in other words, confidence that life is good in spite of its evil and that it is evil in spite of good. In such faith both sentimentality and despair are avoided.[7]

The absence of the awareness of the mystery of evil is a tragic blindness of modern man. In his vocabulary the word is missing. But without an awareness of sin, without the fear of evil, there can be no repentance.

II

A major concern of Niebuhr's thinking is the problem of realism and the lack of realism in our contemporary "nominalistic" culture. An example of the sentimentality and unreality that dominate the political opinions of the liberal world is the belief that the power of man's lust and ambitions is no more than some subrational impulse, which can be managed with more astute social engineering or more psychiatric help. In contrast, Niebuhr insists that the freedom of the self is a radical one and is not easily brought under the control of reason, just as it is not easily kept within the confines of nature's harmonies.

The utopianism and deductive thinking of the modern mentality are best illustrated in its relation to the problem of egocentricity, the universality of which is "empirically respected by all men of affairs who are charged with any responsibility in business or government."[8] Yet academic empiricism continues to insist that the universal tendency to egocentricity is due to faulty education and that it could be overcome either by adequate psychiatric technique or social reforms.

The fact that the phenomenon of self-seeking may be related, not to specific forms of insecurity, but to the insecurity of life itself, seems to be obscured in even the most sophisticated psychological theory, which is why psychological theories are so irrelevant to political theory.

Such sentimentality and unreality have often been considered a distinctly biblical attitude, while in truth the Bible constantly reminds us of man's frailty and unreliability. "All flesh is grass, and all the strength thereof is as the flower of the field. The grass withers, the flower fades . . . surely the people is grass" (Isaiah 40:6-7). "Put not your trust in princes, nor in the son of man, in whom there is no help" (Psalm 146:3). Isaiah calls upon us not to trust the world; the psalmist tells us not to rely on man.

What the rabbis thought about the nature of man may be shown in the following comment. We read in Habakkuk 1:14, *And Thou makest man as the fishes of the sea, and as the creeping things, that have no ruler over them?* "Why is man here compared to the fishes of the sea? . . . Just as among fishes of the sea, the greater swallow up the smaller ones, so with men, were it not for fear of government, men would swallow each other alive. This is just what we have learned: Rabbi Hanina, the Deputy High Priest, said, 'Pray for the welfare of the government, for were it not for fear thereof, men would swallow each other alive.' "[9]

According to Rabbi Jacob, "This world is like a vestibule before the world to come; prepare yourself in the vestibule, so that you may enter the banquet hall."[10] There is no reward for good deeds in this world.[11] The time for reward promised in the Bible is the life to come.[12] According to the Rav, "The world was created for the extremely pious or the extremely wicked, for men like Rabbi Hanina ben Dosa [a saint who lived in the first century of the common era] or for men like King Ahab; this world was created for the extremely wicked, the world to come was created for the extremely pious."[13] "In this world war and suffering, evil inclination, Satan, and the angel of death hold sway."[14]

In the Jewish mystical literature of the thirteenth century the doctrine is advanced that world history consists of seven periods (*shemitah*), each lasting seven thousand years, which in the Jubilee, the fifty thousandth year, will reach its culmination. The current period is one which is dominated by the divine quality of "stern judgment." In it the evil urge, licentiousness, arrogance, forgetfulness, and unholiness prevail.[15]

According to Rabbi Shneur Zalman of Ladi: "Anything that refuses to regard itself as nothing beside God but, on the contrary, asserts itself as an entity separate from God does not receive the light of its vitality from the inner holiness and essence of God." It receives the light of its vitality, so to speak, from the "hind-part" of his holiness, and only after it has gone through myriad channels of emanation and has been so obscured and contracted that it is capable of living "in exile," apart from God. And that is why this material world is called a *"world of shells"* (*kelipoth*), *"the other side"* (*sitra ahra*). And this is why all the things that happen in this world are harsh and evil, and this is why the wicked prevail.[16]

The pious Jews put no trust in the secular world. "They realized quite well that the world was full of ordeals and dangers, that it contained Cain's jealousy of Abel, the cold malevolence of Sodom, and the hatred of Esau, but they also knew that there was in it the charity of Abraham and the tenderness of Rachel. Harassed and oppressed, they carried deep within their hearts a contempt for the world, with its power and pomp, with its bustling and boasting. . . . They knew that the Jews were in exile, that the world was unredeemed."[17] Dazzled by the splendor of Western civilization, the modern Jew has been prone to forget that the world is unredeemed, and that God is in exile. The present generation which has witnessed the most unspeakable horrors committed by man and sponsored by an extremely civilized nation is beginning to realize how monstrous an illusion it was to substitute faith in man for faith in God.

We do not feel "at home" in the world. With the psalmist we pray, "I am a stranger on earth, hide not Thy commandments from me" (119:19). Indeed, if not for our endless power to forget and our great ability to disregard, who could be at ease even for one moment in a lifetime? In the face of so much evil and suffering, of countless examples of failure to live up to the will of God, in a world where His will is defied, where His kingship is denied, who can fail to see the discrepancy between the world and the will of God?

And yet, just because of the realization of the power of evil, life in this world assumed unique significance and worth. Evil is not only a threat; it is also a challenge. It is precisely because of the task of fighting evil that life in this world is so preciously significant. True, there is no reward for good deeds in this world; yet this does not mean that the world is a prison. It is rather a prelude, a vestibule, a place of preparation, of initiation, of apprenticeship to a future life, where the guests prepare to enter *tricilinium,* or the banquet hall.[18] Life in this world is a time for action, for good works, for worship and sanctification, as eternity is a time for retribution. It is eve of the Sabbath, on which the repast is prepared for the Lord's day; it is the season of duty and submission, as the morrow shall be that of freedom from every yoke. More precious, therefore, than all of life to come is a single hour of life on earth—an hour of repentance and good deeds. Eternity gives only in the degree that it receives. This is why the Book of Ecclesiastes pronounced the dead lion less happy than the living dog.[19]

III

Niebuhr's central problem is not the problem of sin or the problem of evil. His problem is not good *and* evil, but the evil within the good, or more accurately the *confusion* of good and evil.

More frustrating than the fact that evil is real, mighty, and tempting is the fact that it thrives so well in the disguise of the good, and that it can draw its nutriment from the life of the holy. In this world, it seems, the holy and the unholy do not exist apart but are mixed, interrelated, and confounded; it is a world where idols are at home, and where even the worship of God may be alloyed with the worship of idols.

In Jewish mysticism we often come upon the view that in this world neither good nor evil exists in purity, and that there is no good without the admixture of evil nor evil without the admixture of good. The confusion of good and evil is the central problem of history and the ultimate issue of redemption. The confusion goes back to the very process of creation.

"When God came to create the world and reveal what was hidden in the depths and disclose light out of darkness, they were all wrapped in one another, and therefore light emerged from darkness and from the impenetrable came forth the profound. So, too, from good issues evil and from mercy issues judgement, and all are intertwined, the good impulse and the evil impulse."[20]

Ezekiel saw in his great vision that "a stormy wind came out of the north, and a great cloud, with brightness [nogah] round about it, and fire flashing forth continually" (1:4). He first beheld the powers of unholiness. A *great cloud* represents "the power of destruction"; "it is called *great,* on account of its darkness, which is so intense that it hides and makes invisible all the sources of light, thus overshadowing the whole world. The *fire flashing forth* indicates the fire of rigorous judgment that never departs from it. *With brightness round about it* . . . that is, although it is the very region of defilement, yet it is surrounded by a certain brightness . . . it possesses an aspect of holiness, and hence should not be treated with contempt, but should be allowed a part in the side of holiness."[21] Even Satan contains a particle of sanctity. In doing his ugly work as the seducer of man, his intention is "for the sake of heaven," for it is for a purpose such as this that he was created.[22]

The great saint Rabbi Hirsch of Zydatschov once remarked to his disciple and nephew: "Even after I had reached the age of forty—the age of understanding—I was not sure whether my life was not immersed in that mire and confusion of good and evil [nogah]. . . . My son, every moment of my life I fear lest I am caught in that confusion."[23]

All of history is a sphere where good is mixed with evil. The supreme task of man, his share in redeeming the work of creation, consists in an effort to separate good from evil and evil from good. Since evil can only exist parasitically on good, it will cease to be when that separation will be accomplished. Redemption, therefore, is contingent upon the *separation* of good and evil.

IV

Most high religions make an effort to present the world and life as a unified whole and to regard all discord and incongruities as provisional or illusory. They seek a universal principle of meaning and are pantheistic either in the cosmic or in the acosmic sense. In contrast, the emphasis in Jewish mysticism is upon the contradictory, the paradoxical, and the unresolved mystery. The temporal world comes into existence through God's creation. "Thereby a realm of freedom and mystery is indicated beyond the capacity of reason to comprehend."[24] The final irrationality of the givenness of things is frankly accepted.

The pinnacles of faith embodying paradox and contradiction, and straining at the limits of rationality, are made plausible when understood as the keys which make the drama of human life comprehensible and without which it either is given a too simple meaning or falls into meaninglessness.

To Jewish tradition, too, paradox is an essential way of understanding the world, history, and nature. Tension, contrast, contradiction characterize all of reality. This is why, in the language of the *Zohar,* our universe is called *'alma de-peruda,* "the world of separation." Strife, tension, and contradiction afflict all of life, including the study of the Torah; even the sages of the Talmud disagree on many details of the law. "God has also set one thing against the other; the good against the evil, and the evil against the good; good from good and evil from evil; the good marks out the evil and the evil marks out the good; good is reserved for the good ones and evil is reserved for the evil ones."[25] The passage in Ecclesiastes 7:14, "God has made the one as well as the other," inspired a medieval Jewish author to compose a treatise (*Temurah*) for the purpose of proving that contrast and contradiction are necessary to existence. "All things cleave to one another, the pure and the impure. There is no pure except through impurity; a mystery which is expressed in the words: *a clean thing out of an unclean* (Job 14:4). The brain is contained in a shell, a shell which will not be broken until that time when the dead shall rise again. Then will the shell be broken and the light shine out into the world from the brain, without any covering on it."[26] However, there is a polarity in everything except God. For all tension ends in God. He is beyond all dichotomies.

But it is true that not only the world He created but even His relation to the world is characterized by the polarity of justice and mercy, of law and love. When His justice is imposed, His mercy is afflicted.[27] Yet in His own being He is One. Thus the pinnacle of Jewish truth is a mystery of divine unity. "Thou art One and none can penetrate . . . the mystery of Thy unfathomable unity" (Ibn Gabirol).

Evil, Niebuhr claims, is much more inextricably bound up with good than most psychological systems realize. There is an element of perversity in all human action; there is "the inevitability of sin in all human striving." "The corruption of evil is at the heart of human personality."[28] Thus "the supposedly objective and dispassionate ideas of the world of culture . . . are always subject to the corruption of man's spiritual pretension, to human sin."[29] This becomes manifest in the fact that "the tragedies in human history, the cruelties and fanaticisms, have not been caused by the criminals . . . but by the good people . . . by the idealists who did not understand the strange mixture of self-interest and ideals which is compounded in all human motives." Niebuhr warns, therefore, against making the cause of religion appear to be "a contest between God-fearing believers and unrighteous unbelievers." He points to the fact that biblical religion has emphasized "the *inequality of guilt just as much as the equality of sin.*" "Especially severe judgments fall upon the rich and the powerful, the mighty and the noble, the wise and the righteous."[30] Indeed, the most horrible manifestation of evil occurs when it acts in the guise of good. In dealing with the problem of evil religious living must include an effort in two directions: separation and purification. By separation is meant the detachment of good from evil; by purification is meant the elimination of evil from good.

Judaism is also aware of the danger of evil's intrusion into the instrument of good. Therefore at the great ritual on the Day of Atonement the high priest would cast lots upon the two goats: one lot for the Lord and the other lot for Azazel. The purpose of the ritual of the goat on which the lot fell for Azazel was *to atone for the evil.* The High Priest would lay both his hands upon the head of the goat, on which the lot fell for Azazel, "and confess over him all the iniquities of the children of Israel, all their transgressions, all their sins." While the purpose of the goat upon which the lot fell for the Lord was "to make atonement *for the holy place,* because of the uncleannesses of the children of Israel, and because of their transgressions, even all their sins; and so shall he do for the tent of meeting, that dwells with them in the midst of their uncleannesses" (Leviticus 16:16). At the most sacred day of the year the supreme task was *to atone for the holy.* It preceded the sacrifice, the purpose of which was to atone for the sins.

The ambiguity of human virtue has been a central issue in the lives of many Jewish thinkers, particularly in the history of Hasidism.

"God asks for the heart."[31] Yet our greatest failure is in the heart. "The heart is deceitful above all things, it is exceedingly weak—who can know it?" (Jeremiah 17:9). The regard for the ego permeates all our thinking. Is it ever possible to disentangle oneself from the intricate plexus of self-interests? Indeed, the demand to serve God in purity, selflessly, "for His sake," on the one hand, and the realization of our inability to detach ourselves from vested interests, represent the tragic tension in the life of piety.[32] In this sense, not only our evil deeds, but even our good deeds precipitate a problem.

What is our situation in trying to carry out the will of God? In addition to our being uncertain of whether our motivation—*prior to the act*—is pure, we are continually embarrassed *during the act* with "alien thoughts" which taint our consciousness with selfish intentions. And even following the act there is the danger of self-righteousness, vanity, and the sense of superiority, derived from what are supposed to be acts of dedication to God.

It is easier to discipline the body than to control the soul. The pious man knows that his inner life is full of pitfalls. The ego, the evil inclination, is constantly trying to enchant him. The temptations are fierce, yet his resistance is unyielding. And so he proves his spiritual strength and stands victorious, unconquerable. Does not his situation look glorious? But then the evil inclination employs a more subtle device, approaching him with congratulations: What a pious man you are! He begins to feel proud of himself. And there he is caught in the trap (Rabbi Raphael of Bersht).

"For there is not a righteous man upon this earth, that does good and sins not" (Ecclesiastes 7:20). The commentators take this verse to mean that even a righteous man sins on occasion, suggesting that his life is a mosaic of perfect deeds with a few sins strewn about. The Ba'al Shem, however, reads the verse: *For there is not a righteous man upon earth that does good and there is no sin in the good.* "It is impossible that the good should be free of self-interest."[32] Empirically, our spiritual situation looks hopeless: "We are all as an unclean thing, and all our deeds of righteousness are as filthy rags" (Isaiah 64:5).

"Even the good deeds we do are not pleasing but instead revolting. For we perform them out of the desire for self-aggrandizement and for pride, and in order to impress our neighbors."[34]

Who can be trustful of his good intention, knowing that under the cloak of *kavanah* there may hide a streak of vanity? Who can claim to have fulfilled even one *mitzvah* with perfect devotion? Said Rabbi Elimelech of Lizhensk to one of his disciples, "I am sixty years old, and I have not fulfilled one *mitzvah.*"[35] *There is not a single mitzvah which we fulfill perfectly* . . . except circumcision and the Torah that we study in our childhood,[36] for these two acts are not infringed upon by "alien thoughts" or impure motivations.

The mind is never immune to alien intentions, and there seems to be no way of ever weeding them out completely. A Hasidic Rabbi was asked by his disciples, in the last hours of his life, whom they should choose as their master after his passing away. He said, "If someone should give you the way to eradicate 'alien thoughts,' know he is not your master."

We shall not know with what we are to worship the Lord until we arrive there (Exodus 10:26). "All our service, all the good deeds we are doing in this world, we do not know whether they are of any value, whether they are really pure, honest or done for the sake of heaven—until we arrive there—in the world to come, only there shall we learn what our service was here."[37]

The human will cannot circumvent the snare of the ego nor can the mind disentangle itself from the confusion of bias in which it is trapped. It often looks as if God's search for the righteous man will end in a cul-de-sac.[38]

Should we, then, despair because of our being unable to attain perfect purity? We should if perfection were our goal. Yet we are not obliged to be perfect once for all, but only to rise again and again. Perfection is divine, and to make it a goal of man is to call on man to be divine. All we can do is to try to wring our hearts clean in contrition. Contrition begins with a feeling of shame at our being incapable of disentanglement from the self. To be contrite at our failures is holier than to be complacent in perfection.

It is a problem of supreme gravity. If an act to be good must be done exclusively for the sake of God, are we ever able to do the good? Rabbi Nahman of Kossov gave an answer in the form of a parable. A stork fell into the mud and was unable to pull out his legs until an idea occurred to him. Does he not have a long beak? So he stuck his beak into the mud, leaned upon it, and pulled out his legs. But what was the use? His legs were out, but his beak was stuck. So another idea occurred to him. He stuck his legs into the mud and pulled out his beak. But what was the use? The legs were stuck in the mud. . . .

Such is exactly the condition of man. Succeeding in one way, he fails in another. We must constantly remember: We spoil, and God restores. How ugly is the way in which we despoil, and how good and how beautiful is the way in which He restores!

And yet, Judaism insists upon the deed and hopes for the intention. Every morning a Jew prays, "Lord our God, make the words of Thy Torah pleasant in our mouth . . . so that we study Thy Torah for its own sake."

While constantly keeping the goal in mind, we are taught that for pedagogic reasons one must continue to observe the law even when one is not ready to fulfill it "for the sake of God." For the good, even though it is not done for its own sake, will teach us at the end how to act for the sake of God. We must continue to perform the sacred deeds even though we may be compelled to bribe the self with human incentives. Purity of motivation is the goal; constancy of action is the way.

The ego is redeemed by the absorbing power and the inexorable provocativeness of a just task which we face. It is the deed that carries us away, that transports the soul, proving to us that the greatest beauty grows at the greatest distance from the center of the ego.

Deeds that are set upon ideal goals, that are not performed with careless ease and routine but in exertion and submission to their ends, are stronger than the surprise and attack of caprice. Serving sacred goals may eventually change mean motives. For such deeds are exacting. Whatever our motive may be in beginning such an act, the act itself demands an undivided attention. Thus the desire for reward is not the driving force of the poet in his creative moments, and the pursuit of pleasure or profit is not the essence of a religious or moral act.

At the moment in which an artist is absorbed in playing a concerto, the thought of applause, fame, or remuneration is far from his mind. The complete attention of the artist, his whole being, is involved in the music. Should any extraneous thought enter his mind, it would arrest his concentration and mar the purity of his playing. The reward may have been on his mind when he negotiated with his agent, but during the performance it is only the music that claims his complete concentration.

Similar may be man's situation in carrying out a religious or moral act. Left alone the soul is subject to caprice. Yet there is a power in the deed that purifies desires. It is the act, life itself, that educates the will. The good motive comes into being while doing the good.

If the antecedent motive is sure of itself, the act will continue to unfold, and obtrusive intentions could even serve to invigorate the initial motive which may absorb the vigor of the intruder into its

own strength. Man may be replete with ugly motives, but a deed
and God are stronger than ugly motives. The redemptive power
discharged in carrying out the good purifies the mind. The deed is
wiser than the heart.

This, then, seems to be the attitude of Judaism. Though deeply
aware of how impure and imperfect all our deeds are, the fact of our
doing is cherished as the highest privilege, as a source of joy, as that
which endows life with ultimate preciousness. We believe that
moments lived in fellowship with God, acts fulfilled in imitation of
God's will, never perish; the validity of the good remains regardless
of all impurity.

<h2 style="text-align:center">V</h2>

Central to Niebuhr's thinking is the insight that "the possibilities
of evil grow with the possibilities of good,"[39] and that *"every higher
principle of order* to which the soul might attach itself, in the effort
to rescue meaning from chaos, *is discovered,* upon analysis, *to have
new possibilities of evil in it."*[40]

That "the possibilities of evil grow with the possibilites of good"
is an insight of which Jewish tradition was aware. The good is
presumably used both in the worldly and in the spiritual sense. In
the first sense, the idea is expressed by Hillel who used to say, "The
more flesh, the more worms [in the grave]; the more property, the
more anxiety."[41] According to rabbinic legends, the wantonness of
the antediluvian generations was due "to the ideal conditions under
which mankind lived before the Flood. They knew neither toil nor
care, and as a consequence of their extraordinary prosperity they
grew insolent. In their insolence they rose up against God."[42] In the
scriptural sense, the Talmud teaches that *the greater the man, the
greater his evil inclination,*[43] for the evil inclination is more eager to
attack "the great," "the scholars," than to attack the simple people.

However, Niebuhr speaks not only of "the possibilities of evil" in
the good; he characterizes evil as an inevitable fact of human
existence. Now, if every good action is liable to corruption, what

would be the worth and relevance of the worship and service of God? Does not the grace of God consist precisely in its guarding the sacred acts from being vitiated by evil? It is profoundly true that goodness may turn to cruelty, piety to fanaticism, faith to arrogance. Yet this, we believe, is a perpetual possibility rather than a necessity, a threat rather than an inevitable result.

Biblical history bears witness to the constant corruption of man; *it does not, however, teach the inevitable corruptibility of the ultimate in the temporal process.* The holiness of Abraham, Isaac, and Jacob, and the humility of Moses are the rock on which they rely. *There are good moments in history that no subsequent evil may obliterate.* The Lord himself testified to it. The integrity of Job proved it. Abraham could not find ten righteous men in Sodom by whose merit the city would have been saved. Yet there is not a moment in history without thirty-six righteous men, unknown and hidden, by whose merit the world survives. We believe that there are corners full of light in a vastness that is dark, that unalloyed good moments are possible. It is, therefore, difficult from the point of view of biblical theology to sustain Niebuhr's view, *plausible and profound as it is.*

If the nature of man were all we had, then surely there would be no hope for us left. But we also have the word of God, the commandment, the *mitzvah.* The central biblical fact is *Sinai,* the covenant, the word of God. Sinai was superimposed on the failure of Adam. Is not the fact that we were given the knowledge of His will a sign of some ability to carry out His will? Does the word of God always remain a challenge, a gadfly? Is not the voice of God powerful enough to shake the wilderness of the soul, to strip the ego bare, to flash forth His will like fire, so that we all cry, "Glory"?

To the Jew, Sinai is at stake in every act of man, and the supreme problem is not good and evil but God, and His commandment to love good and to hate evil. The central issue is not the sinfulness but the obligations of man.

While insisting upon the contrast between God's power and man's power, God's grace and human failure, Judaism stresses a third aspect, the *mitzvah*. It is a *mitzvah* that gives meaning to our existence. The *mitzvah,* the carrying out of a sacred deed, is given to us as a constant opportunity. Thus there are two poles of piety: the right and the wrong deed; *mitzvah* and sin. The overemphasis upon sin may lead to a deprecation of "works"; the overemphasis upon *mitzvah* may lead to self-righteousness. The first may result in a denial of the relevance of history and in an overly eschatological view; the second in a denial of messianism and a secular optimism. Against both dangers Judaism warns repeatedly.

We must never forget that we are always exposed to sin. "Be not sure of yourself till the day of your death," said Hillel.[44] We have been taught that one may be impregnated with the spirit of the holy all the days of his life, yet one moment of carelessness is sufficient to plunge into the abyss. *There is but one step between me and death* (I Samuel 20:3). On the other hand, we are taught to remember that we are always given the opportunity to serve Him. Significantly, Jewish tradition, while conscious of the possibilities of evil in the good, stresses the *possibilities of further good in the good.* Ben Azzai said, "Be eager to do a minor *mitzvah* and flee from transgression; for one *mitzvah* leads to [brings on] another *mitzvah,* and one transgression leads to another transgression; for the reward of a *mitzvah* is a *mitzvah,* and the reward of a transgression is a transgression."[45]

Judaism, in stressing the fundamental importance of the *mitzvah,* assumes that man is endowed with the ability to fulfill what God demands, at least to some degree. This may, indeed, be an article of prophetic faith: the belief in our ability to do His will. "Surely this Commandment [*mitzvah*] which I enjoin upon you this day is not too baffling for you, nor is it beyond reach. It is not in the heavens, that you should say, 'Who among us can go up to the heavens and get it for us and impart it to us, that we may observe it?' Neither is it beyond the sea that you should say, 'Who among us can cross to the other side of the sea and get it for us and impart it to us, that we may observe it?' No, the thing is very close to, in your mouth and in your heart, to observe it" (Deuteronomy 30:11–14). Man's actual failures rather than his essential inability to do the good are constantly stressed by Jewish tradition, which claims that man is able to acquire "merit" before God. The doctrine of merits implies the certainty that for all imperfection the worth of good deeds remains in all eternity.

It is true that the law of love, the demand for the impossible, and our constant failures and transgression create in us grief and a tension that may drive us to despair. Yet, is not the reality of God's love greater than the law of love? Will He not accept us in all our frailty and weakness? "For He knows our nature [*Yetszer*]; He remembers that we are dust" (Psalm 103:14).

"In liberal Christianity there is an implicit assumption that human nature has the resources to fulfill what the Gospel demands. The Kantian axiom, 'I ought, therefore I can,' is accepted as basic to all analyses of the moral situation. In classical Christianity the perfectionism of the Gospel stands in a much more difficult relation to the estimate of human resources. The love commandment stands in juxtaposition to the fact of sin. It helps, in fact, to create the consciousness of sin."[46]

Judaism, too, would reject the axiom, "I ought, therefore I can"; it would claim, instead, "Thou art commanded, therefore thou canst." It claims, as I have said, that man has the resources to fulfill what God commands, at least to some degree. On the other hand, we are continually warned lest we rely on man's own power and believe that the "indeterminate extension of human capacities would eventually alter the human situation." Our tradition does not believe that the good deeds alone will redeem history; it is the obedience to God that will make us worthy of being redeemed by God.

If Judaism had relied on the human resources for the good, on man's ability to fulfill what God demands, on man's power to achieve redemption, why did it insist upon the promise of messianic redemption? Indeed, messianism implies that any course of living, even the supreme human efforts, must fail in redeeming the world. In other words, history is not sufficient to itself.

Yet the Hebraic tradition insists upon the *mitzvah* as the instrument in dealing with evil. At the end of days, evil will be conquered by the One; in historic times evils must be conquered one by one.

This is what the prophets discovered: History is a nightmare. There are more scandals, more acts of corruption, than are dreamed of in philosophy. It would be blasphemous to believe that what we witness is the end of God's creation. It is an act of evil to accept the state of evil as either inevitable or final. Others may be satisfied with improvement; the prophets insist upon redemption. The way man acts is a disgrace, and it must not go on forever. Together with condemnation, the prophets offer a promise. The heart of stone will be taken away, a heart of flesh will be given instead (Ezekiel 11:19). Even the nature of the beasts will change to match the glory of the age. The end of days will be the end of fear, the end of war; idolatry will disappear, knowledge of God will prevail.

The inner history of Israel is a history of waiting for God, of waiting for His arrival. Just as Israel is certain of the reality of the Promised Land, so is she certain of the coming of "the promised day." She lives by a promise of "the day of the Lord," a day of judgment followed by redemption, when evil will be consumed and an age of glory will ensue.

The climax of our hopes is the establishment of the kingship of God, and a passion for its realization must permeate all our thoughts. For the ultimate concern of the Jew is not personal salvation but universal redemption. Redemption is not an event that will take place all at once at "the end of days" but a process that goes on all the time. Man's good deeds are single acts in the long drama of redemption, and every deed counts. One must live as if the redemption of all men depended upon the devotion of one's own life. Thus life, every life, we regard as an immense opportunity to enhance the good that God has placed in His creation. And the vision of a world free of hatred and war, of a world filled with understanding for God as the ocean is filled with water, the certainty of ultimate redemption must continue to inspire our thought and action.

A full appreciation of the significance of Reinhold Niebuhr will have to take into account not only his teachings but also his *religious epistemology*. It will, furthermore, turn not only to his books but also to his deeds. For all his profundity, his prophetic radicalism, his insights into the ultimate aspects of human destiny, his sense for the dimension of eternity, Niebuhr has maintained a concern for the immediate problems of justice and equity in human relations. His spirituality combines heaven and earth, as it were. It does not separate soul from body, or mind from unity of man's physical and spiritual life. His way is an example of one who does justly, loves mercy, and walks humbly with his God, an example of the unity of worship and living.

NOTES

1. *Faith and History* (New York, 1949), p. 9.
2. "I have as a Christian theologian sought to strengthen the Hebraic-prophetic content of the Christian tradition." Reinhold Niebuhr, introduction to Waldo Frank's *The Jew in Our Time* (New York, 1944).
3. *An Interpretation of Christian Ethics*, p. 119.
4. "All evil results from the non-adaptation of constitution to conditions. . . . Eventually true is it that evil perpetually tends to disappear. In virtue of an essential principle of life, this non-adaption of an organism to its conditions is ever being rectified; and modification of one or both continues until the adaption is complete. Whatever possesses vitality, from the elementary cell up to man himself, inclusive, obeys this law. . . . This universal law of physical modification is the law of mental modification also. . . . Progress, therefore, is not an accident but a necessity. Evil and immorality must surely disappear; man must surely become perfect." Herbert Spencer, *Social Statics* (New York, 1897), pp. 28–32.
5. To my knowledge Schopenhauer was one of the first to claim that the Hebrew spirit was characteristically optimistic, whereas Christianity was pessimistic. *Die Welt als Wille und Vorstellung*, II, chap. 48; *Parerga and paralipomena*, Gusbach ed., II, 397. *Sämtliche Werke*, Franenstadt ed., III, 712 f.
6. Raba, in *Baba Bathra*, 9a, referred to the end of the verse as denying divine Providence.
7. *An Interpretation of Christian Ethics*, p. 106.
8. *Christian Realism and Political Problems* (New York, 1953), pp. 7–8.
9. *Abodah Zarah*, 3b–4a; see also *Aboth*, III, 2.

10. *Aboth*, 4:21.
11. *Erubin*, 22a.
12. *Kiddushin*, 39b.
13. *Berachoth*, 61b. This world is often compared to "night"; it is even called "the world of falsehood."
14. *Midrash Vayosha, Beth Hamidrash*, ed. Jellinek (2nd ed., Jerusalem, 1938), I, 55.
15. *Temunah* (Koretz, 1784), p. 39b.
16. Rabbi Shneur Zalman of Ladi, *Tanya*, p. 10b.
17. Heschel, *The Earth Is the Lord's* (New York, 1950), p. 96.
18. *Aboth*, 4:22.
19. *Shabbat*, 30a.
20. *Zohar*, III, 80b; see also I, 156a.
21. *Ibid.*, II, 203a–203b; see pp. 69a–69b. The *kelipoth*, or the forces of the unholy, are unclean and harmful from the aspect of man. However, from the aspect of the holy, they exist because of the will of the Creator and for His sake. A spark of holiness abides in them and maintains them. Rabbi Abraham Azulai, *Or Hahamah* (Przemysl, 1897), II, 218a.
22. *Baba Bathra*, 16a.
23. Rabbi Eisik Safran, *Zohar Hai*, I.
24. *Christian Realism and Political Problems*, p. 181.
25. *Yetsirah*, vi, 6.
26. *Zohar*, II, 69b.
27. See *Sanhedrin*, 4:5.
28. *Faith and History*, pp. 205, 122.
29. *An Interpretation of Christian Ethics*, p. 123; see also p. 76.
30. *The Nature and Destiny of Man*, I, 222 ff.
31. *Sanhedrin*, 106b.
32. The essence of idolatry is to regard something as a thing in itself, separated from the holiness of God. In other words, to worship an idol does not mean to deny God; it means not to deny the self. This is why pride is idolatry. *Tanya*, 28b.
33. Rabbi Yaakob Yosef of Polnoye, *Toldoth Yaakov Yosef* (Lemburg, 1863), p. 150d.
34. Rabbi David Kimhi, *Commentary on Isaiah, ad locum*. Similarly S. D. Luzatto in his commentary. Cf. N. J. Berlin, *Commentary on Sheeltoth*, Sec. 64, p. 420. According to *Sheeltoth* the meaning of the verse is that our deeds of righteousness are as a cloth put together in patches, not woven together properly.
35. Rabbi Yaakob Aaron of Zalshin, *Beth Yaakov* (Pietrkov, 1899), p. 144; *Aboth*, 2:20.
36. *Midrash Tehillim*, 6, 1.
37. Rabbi Isaac Meir of Ger.
38. Moments of despair were known to the prophets. Elijah, fleeing

from Jezebel, fled to the wilderness, and there he sat down under a broom-tree and said, "It is enough; now, O Lord, take away my life, for I am not better than my fathers" (I Kings 19:4). Jeremiah exclaims, "Cursed be the day wherein I was born" (20:14). Cf. also Psalms 22; 39; 88; Job 9:21, 10:20f.; 14:6 f.; Ecclesiastes 4:2.

39. *An Interpretation of Christian Ethics*, p. 97.

40. *Ibid.*, p. 68.

41. *Aboth*, 2, 7.

42. Louis Ginzburg, *The Legends of the Jews*, I (Jewish Publication Society edition), 152 f.; V, 173.

43. *Sukkah* 52a; see also *Ecclesiastes Rabba* 1, 16, and *Genesis Rabba* 19, 3.

44. *Aboth*, 2:5.

45. *Ibid.*, 4:2.

46. *An Interpretation of Christian Ethics*, p. 65.

10 / Sacred Image
of Man

The biblical account of creation is couched in the language of allusion. Nothing is said about the intention or the plan that preceded the creation of heaven and earth. The Bible does not begin: And God said: Let us create heaven and earth. All we hear is an allusion to God's creative act, and not a word about intention or meaning. The same applies to the creation of all other beings. We only hear what He does, not what He thinks. "And God said: Let there be." The creation of man, however, is preceded by a forecast: "And God said: Let us make man in our image, after our likeness." The act of man's creation is preceded by an utterance of His intention, God's knowledge of man is to precede man's coming into being. God knows him before He creates him. Man's being is rooted in his being known about. It is the creation of man that opens a glimpse into the thought of God, into the meaning beyond the mystery.

"And God said: I will make man in My image (*tselem*), after My likeness (*demuth*). . . . And God created man in His image, in the image of God He created him" (Genesis 1:26 f.).

These words, which are repeated in the opening words of the fifth chapter of Genesis—*This book is the story of man.*—When God created man, He made him in the likeness (*demuth*) of God—contain, according to Jewish tradition, the fundamental statement about the nature and meaning of man.

In many religions, man is regarded as an image of a god. Yet the meaning of such regard depends on the meaning of the god whom man resembles. If the god is regarded as a man magnified, if the gods are conceived of in the image of man, then such regard tells us little about the nature and destiny of man. Where God is one among many gods, where the word "divine" is used as mere hyperbolic expression; where the difference between God and man is but a difference in degree, then an expression such as the divine image of man is equal in meaning to the idea of the supreme in man. It is only in the light of what the biblical man thinks of God, namely a Being who created heaven and earth, the God of absolute justice and compassion, the master of nature and history who transcends nature and history, that the idea of man having been created in the image of God refers to the supreme mystery of man, of his nature and existence.

Image and likeness of God. What these momentous words are trying to convey has never ceased to baffle the reader of the Bible. In the Bible, *tselem,* the word for image, is nearly always used in a derogatory sense, denoting idolatrous images.[1] The same applies to *demuth,* the word for likeness.

"To whom will ye liken Me, and make Me equal, and compare Me, that we may be alike?" (Isaiah 46:5.) "For who in the skies can be compared unto the Lord, who among the sons of might can be likened unto the Lord?" (Psalm 89:7.)

God is divine, and man is human. This contrast underlies all biblical thinking. God is never human, and man is never divine. ". . . for I am God and not man" (Hosea 11:9). "God is not man to be capricious, or mortal to change His mind" (Numbers 23:19).

Thus, the likeness of God means the likeness of Him who is unlike man. The likeness of God means the likeness of Him, compared with whom all else is like nothing.

Indeed, the words "image and likeness of God" conceal more than they reveal. They signify something which we can neither comprehend nor verify. For what is our image? What is our likeness? Is there anything about man that may be compared with God? Our eyes do not see it; our minds cannot grasp it. Taken literally, these words are absurd, if not blasphemous. And still they hold the most important truth about the meaning of man.

Obscure as the meaning of these terms is, they undoubtedly denote something *unearthly*, something that belongs to the sphere of God. *Demuth* and *tselem* are of a *higher sort of being* than the things created in the six days. This, it seems, is what the verse intends to convey: Man partakes of an unearthly divine sort of being.

An idea is relevant if it serves as an answer to a question. To understand the relevance of "the divine image and likeness," we must try to ascertain the question which it comes to answer.

Paradoxically, the problem of man arises more frequently as the problem of death than as the problem of life. It is an important fact, however, that in contrast with Babylonia and particularly Egypt, where the preoccupation with death was the central issue of religious thinking, the Bible hardly deals with death as a problem. Its central concern is not, as in the Gilgamesh Epic, how to escape death, but rather how to sanctify life. And the divine image and likeness does not serve man to attain immortality but to attain sanctity.

Man is man not because of what he has in common with the earth, but *because of what he has in common with God*. The Greek thinkers sought to understand man as *a part of the universe:* the prophets sought to understand man as *a partner of God*.

It is a concern and a task that man has in common with God.

The intention is not to identify "the image and likeness" with a particular quality or attribute of man, such as reason, speech, power, or skill. It does not refer to something which in later systems was called "the best in man," "the divine spark," "the eternal spirit," or "the immortal element" in man. It is the whole man and every man who was made in the image and likeness of God. It is both body and soul, sage and fool, saint and sinner, man in his joy and in his grief, in his righteousness and wickedness. The image is not in man; it is man.

The basic dignity of man is not made up of his achievements, virtues, or special talents. It is inherent in his very being. The commandment "Love your neighbor as yourself" (Leviticus 19:18) calls upon us to love not only the virtuous and the wise but also the vicious and the stupid man. The rabbis have, indeed, interpreted the commandment to imply that even a criminal remains our neighbor.[2]

The image-love is a love of what God loves, an act of sympathy, of participation in God's love. It is unconditional and regardless of man's merits or distinctions.

According to many thinkers, love is induced by that which delights or commands admiration. Such a view would restrict love to those worthy of receiving it and condition it upon whether a person might invoke delight or admiration. It would exclude the criminal and the corrupt members of society. In contrast, to love man, according to Judaism, is not a response to any physical, intellectual, or moral value of a person. We must love man because he is made in the image of God. Said Rabbi Akiba: *"Love thy neighbor as thyself is the supreme principle of the Torah. You must not say, since I have been put to shame (by a fellow man), let him be put to shame; since I have been slighted, let him be slighted. Said Rabbi Tanhuma: If you do so, know whom you put to shame, for in the likeness of God made He him."*[3]

Thus God loves Israel notwithstanding its backslidings (Hosea 11:1 f.). His love is a gift rather than an earning (Hosea 14:5). "It is not because you are the most numerous of peoples that the Lord set His heart on you and chose you—indeed you are the smallest of peoples, but it was because the Lord loved you . . ." (Deuteronomy 7:7–8).

Sparingly does the term "image of God" occur in the Bible. Beyond the first chapter of Genesis, it comes forth in two instances: To remind us that everything found on earth was placed under the dominion of man, except human life, and to remind us that the body of man, not only his soul, is endowed with divine dignity.

The image of God is employed in stressing the criminality of murder. "For your life-blood, too, I will require a reckoning: of every beast will I require it; of man, too, will I require a reckoning for human life, of every man for that of his fellow man! Whoever sheds the blood of man, by man shall his blood be shed; for in the image of God was man created."[4]

The image of man is also referred to in urging respect for the body of a criminal following his execution. "If a man has committed a crime punishable by death and he is put to death, and you hang him on a tree, his body shall not remain all night upon the tree, but you shall bury him the same day, for the dignity (or glory) of God is hanged (on the tree)."[5]

The intention of the verse is stressed boldly by Rabbi Meir, an outstanding authority of the second century of the common era, in the form of a parable. "To what may this be compared? To twin brothers who lived in one city; one was appointed king, and the other took to highway robbery. At the king's command they hanged him. But all who saw him exclaimed: The king is hanged! (for being twins their appearance was similar.) Whereupon the king issued a command and he was taken down."

Great, therefore, must be our esteem for every man. "Let the honour of your disciple be as dear to you as your own, let the regard for your colleague be like the reverence due to your teacher, and let the reverence for your teacher be like the reverence for God."[6] From this statement, a medieval authority concludes that our esteem for man must be as great as our esteem for God.[7]

The divine likeness of man is an idea known in many religions. It is the contribution of Judaism to have taught the tremendous implication of that idea: the metaphysical dignity of man, the divine preciousness of human life. Man is not valued in physical terms; his value is infinite. To our common sense, one human being is less than two human beings. Jewish tradition tries to teach us that for him who has caused a single soul to perish, it is as though he had caused a whole world to perish; and that for him who has saved a single soul, it is as though he has saved a whole world. This thought was conveyed in the solemn admonition to witnesses not by false testimony to be the cause of the death of an innocent man.[8]

No person may be sacrificed to save others. If an enemy said to a group of women, " 'Give us one from among you that we may defile her, and if not we will defile you all,' let the enemy defile them all, but let them not betray to them one single soul."[9]

The transcendent dignity of man implies not only inalienable rights but also incredible responsibility. Stressing the idea that one man came to be the father of all men, the Mishnah avers: "Therefore every man is bound to say, 'On account of *me* the world was created.' "[10] That is, every man is to regard himself as precious as a whole world, too precious to be wasted by sin.[11]

When the Roman government issued a decree that the Jews of Palestine should not study the Torah, should not circumcise their sons and should profane the Sabbath, the Jewish leaders went to Rome and marched through the streets at night-time, proclaiming: "Alas, in heavens' name, are we not your brothers, are we not the sons of one father and the sons of one mother? Why are we different from every nation and tongue that you issue such harsh decrees against us?"[12]

"Why was only a single man created? To teach you that for him who destroys one man, it is regarded as if he had destroyed all men, and that for him who saves one man, it is regarded as though he had saved all men. Furthermore, it was for the sake of peace, so that man might not say to his fellow man, 'My father was greater than thy father.' "[13]

The awareness of divine dignity must determine even man's relation to his own self. His soul as well as his body constitutes an image of God. This is why one is under obligation to keep his body clean. "One must wash his face, hands, and feet daily in his Maker's honour."[14] Hillel, it is said, explained this obligation by a parable. Those who are in charge of the icons of kings which are set up in their theaters and circuses scour and wash them off, and are rewarded and honored for so doing; how much more, who was created in the image and likeness of God.[15]

156   *The Insecurity of Freedom*

Indeed, Jewish piety may be expressed in the form of a supreme imperative: *Treat thyself as an image of God.* It is in the light of this imperative that we can understand the meaning of the astonishing commandment: "You shall be holy, for I, the Lord your God, am holy" (Leviticus 19:2). Holiness, an essential attribute of God, may become a quality of man. The human can become holy.

IMAGE AND DUST

There are two ways in which the Bible speaks of the creation of man. In the first chapter of the Book of Genesis, which is devoted to the creation of the physical universe, man is described as having been created in the *image and likeness* of God. In the second chapter, which tells us of the commandment not to eat of the fruit of the tree of knowledge, man is described as having been formed *out of the dust* of the earth. Together, *image* and *dust* express the polarity of the nature of man. He is formed of the most inferior stuff in the most superior image. In the language of the second chapter of Genesis, every beast of the field, and every fowl of the air, was formed of the ground. Man, however, was made not of the ground, which is the source of all vegetation and animal life, nor out of water, which is a symbol for refreshment, blessing, and wisdom. He was made of arid dust, the stuff of the desert, which is both abundant and worthless.[16]

That the end of man is dust is an indisputable fact. But so is the end of the beast. And yet, the Bible emphasizes the absolute difference between man and all other creatures. Plants and animals were brought forth by the earth, by the waters (Genesis 1:11; 20:24); they emerged from "nature" and became an "organic" part of nature. Man, on the other hand, is an artifact. The Lord both created and formed him (1:26; 2:7). He came into being by a special act of creation. He did not come forth out of dust; he did not grow out of the earth. The Lord both created and formed him (1:26).[17]

God "blew into his nostrils the breath of life; and man became a living being" (2:7). Something of His very self God placed in man, so that he owes his existence not to the forces of nature but to the Creator of all. Man is set apart from both the plants and the beasts by the fact of God being directly involved in his coming into being. It is the knowledge of this fact that inspired the psalmist's prayer: "Thy hands have made me and fashioned me; give me understanding that I may learn Thy commandments" (Psalm 119:73). Thus the statement that man was made out of dust stresses not only his fragility but also his nobility.

The polarity of man may not imply an eternal contradiction. There is dignity to dust which, just as heaven, was created by God. There is, indeed, meaning and blessing in having been formed of the dust of the earth, for it is only because he is formed of the dust of the earth that man can fulfill his destiny to cultivate the earth. Yet while the duality of human nature may not imply an eternal tension, it does imply a duality of grandeur and insignificance, a relatedness to earth and an affinity with God.

The duality is not based on the contrast of soul and body and the principles of good and evil. Unlike the Pythagoreans, the Bible does not regard the body as the sepulcher and prisonhouse of the soul or even as the seat and source of sin. The contradiction is in what man does with his soul and body. The contradiction lies in his acts rather than in his substance. As nature is not the counterwork of God but His creation and instrument, dust is not the contradiction of the image but its foil and complement. Man's sin is in his failure to live what he is. Being the master of the earth, man forgets that he is servant of God.

MAN IS DUST

For dust you are, and to dust you shall return (Genesis 3:19). These words with which the Lord addressed Adam after he sinned convey a basic part of the biblical understanding of man. The fact of man having been created "in the image and likeness of God" is mentioned as a divine secret and uttered in a divine monologue, while the fact of being dust is conveyed to man in God's dialogue with Adam. Nowhere in the Bible does man, standing before God, say, "I am thy image and likeness." Abraham, pleading with God to save the city of Sodom, knows: "Here I venture to speak to the Lord, I who am but dust and ashes" (Genesis 18:27). Job prays: "Remember, I beseech Thee, that Thou hast fashioned me as clay" (10:9). And his last words are: "I abhor my words, and repent, seeing I am dust and ashes" (42:6; see 30:19). In this spirit, the psalmist describes men as beings "that go down to the dust" (Psalm 22:30). This miserable fact, however, is also a comfort to him who discovers his failures, his spiritual feebleness. The psalmist is consoled in the knowledge that God understands our nature; He remembers that we are dust (Psalm 103:14).

Man, then, is involved in a polarity of a divine image and worthless dust. He is a duality of mysterious grandeur and pompous aridity, a vision of God and a mountain of dust. It is because of his being dust that his iniquities may be forgiven, and it is because of his being an image that his righteousness is expected.

Other expressions of the uniqueness and magnificence of man come to us from the prophets. Isaiah proclaims:

> Thus says God, the Lord,
>   Who created the heavens and stretched them out,
>   Who spread forth the earth and what comes from it,
>   Who gives breath to the people upon it and spirit
>   to those who walk in it.
>
> Isaiah 42:5

In the same way, Zechariah speaks of the Lord who stretched out the heavens and founded the earth and formed the spirit of man within him (21:1).

What is stressed about man in these passages is the forming of the spirit, the grandeur of which is made manifest by its juxtaposition with heaven and earth. The spirit in man is as much a creation of

God as heaven and earth. What is the source of human understanding? "It is a spirit in man, and the breath of the Almighty that giveth them understanding" (Job 32:8). The parallelism seems to imply that the spirit in man is a spirit of the Almighty. "The spirit of God has made me, and the breath of the Almighty gives me life," we read in the same speech (Job 33:4).

The word "spirit" in the Bible has more than one meaning. Of Bezalel it is said that he is filled with the spirit of God "with a divine spirit of skill, ability, and knowledge in every kind of craft" (Exodus 31:3). Of the prophets we hear that the spirit of God comes upon them (Isaiah 61:1; Ezekiel 11:5). Of the Messiah we are told that "the spirit of God shall rest upon him, the spirit of wisdom and understanding, the spirit of counsel and might, the spirit of knowledge and of the fear of the Lord" (Isaiah 11:2). The spirit in these passages denotes an endowment of chosen men. But, as we have seen, it is also an endowment of all men; it is that which gives them understanding.

Man holds within himself a breath of God. "The Lord God formed man from the dust of the ground, and He blew into his nostrils the breath of life; and man became a living being" (Genesis 2:7). It probably is this nonearthly aspect of human nature, the breath of God, that served as a basis for the belief in an afterlife.

"And the dust returns to the earth as it was, and the spirit returns to God who gave it" (Ecclesiastes 12:7).

SONSHIP

> Have we not all one father?
> Has not one God created us?
> > Malachi 2:10

> Did not He Who made me in the womb make him?
> Did not One fashion us in the womb?
> > Job 31:15

The idea of God as the father of man expresses not merely man's creaturely dependence on God or his personal affinity to God. It expresses the idea that man's ultimate confrontation is not with the world but with God; not only with a divine law but with *a divine concern;* not only with His wisdom and power, but also with His love and care.

Man is man because something divine is at stake in his existence. He is not an innocent bystander in the cosmic drama. There is in us more kinship with the divine than we are able to believe. The souls of men are candles of the Lord, lit on the cosmic way, rather than fireworks produced by the combustion of nature's explosive compositions, and every soul is indispensable to Him. Man is needed, he is *a need of God.*

Life is a *partnership* of God and man; God is not detached from or indifferent to our joys and griefs. Authentic, vital needs of man's body and soul are a divine concern. This is why human life is holy. God is a partner and a partisan in man's struggle for justice, peace, and holiness, and it is because of His being in need of man that He entered a *covenant* with him for all time, a mutual bond embracing God and man, a relationship to which God, not only man, is committed.

God does not judge the deeds of man impassively, in a spirit of cool detachment. His judgment is imbued with a feeling of intimate concern. He is the father of all men, not only a judge; He is a lover engaged to his people, not only a king. God stands in a passionate relationship to man. His love or anger, His mercy or disappointment is an expression of His profound participation in the history of Israel and all men.

This is the central message of the biblical prophets. God is involved in the life of man. A personal relationship, an intimate concern binds Him to mankind. Behind the various manifestations of His pathos is one motive, one need: the divine need for human righteousness.

And precious are the deeds of righteousness in the eyes of the Lord. The idea of man having been created in the image of God was interpreted, it seems, not as *an analogy of being* but as *an analogy of doing.* Man is called upon to act in the likeness of God. "As He is merciful be thou merciful."

The future of the human species depends upon our degree of reverence for the individual man. And the strength and validity of that reverence depend upon our faith in God's concern for man.

In terms of the cosmic process, all of human history counts as much as a match struck in the darkness, and the claim that there is unique and eternal value to the life of the individual must be dismissed as an absurdity. From the perspective of astronomy the extermination of millions of human beings would not be different from the extermination of insects or roaches.

Only if there is a God who cares, a God to whom the life of every individual is an event—and not only a part of an infinite process—then our sense for the sanctity and preciousness of the individual man may be maintained.

There are many questions about man which have often been raised. What is his nature? Why is he mortal? None of these issues is central biblical thinking.

The problem that challenged the biblical mind was not the obscurity of man's nature but the paradox of his existence. The starting point was not a question about man but the distinction of man; not the state of ignorance about the nature of man but rather a state of amazement at what we know about man, namely: Why is man so significant in spite of his insignificance? Not the question, Why is man mortal? But the question, Why is he so distinguished?

The problem that challenged the biblical mind was not man in and by himself. Man is never seen in isolation but always in relation to God who is the Creator, the King, and the Judge of all beings. The problem of man revolved around God's relation to man.

> Lord, what is man, that thou takest knowledge of him?
> Or the son of man, that thou makest account of him?
> Man is like unto a breath;
> His days are as a shadow that passeth away.
> Psalm 144:3-4

When I behold Thy heavens,
The work of Thy fingers,
The moon and the stars
Which Thou hast established—
What is man
That Thou shouldst be mindful of him?
And the son of man
That Thou shouldst think of him?
And make him
But a little lower than the Divine,
And crown him with glory and honour,
And make him rule over the works of Thy hands?
Thou hast put all things under his feet:
Sheep and oxen, all of them,
Yea, and the beasts of the field;
The fowl of the air, and the fish of the sea,
That pass through the paths of the seas.
                                                    Psalm 8:2–9

The insignificance of man compared with the grandeur of God underscores the paradox of God's concern for him. Neither Job nor the psalmist offers an answer to the overwhelming enigma which thus remains the central mystery of human existence. Yet the acceptance of the fact of divine concern established the biblical approach to the existence of man. It is from the perspective of that concern that the quest for an understanding of man begins.

Today the realization of the dangerous greatness of man, of his immense power and ability to destroy all life on earth, may help us to intuit man's relevance in the divine scheme. If this great world of ours is not a trifle in the eyes of God, if the creator is at all concerned with His creation, then man—who has the power to devise both culture and crime, but who is also able to be a proxy for divine justice—is important enough to be the object of divine concern.

Nowhere in Plato's Socratic dialogues do we find a direct solution to the problem, "What is man?" There is only an indirect answer,

"Man is declared to be that creature who is constantly in search of himself—a creature who in every moment of his existence must examine and scrutinize the conditions of his existence."[18] He is a being in search of meaning.

The Greek approach must be contrasted with the biblical contention that "unless the Lord builds the house, those who build it labor in vain" (Psalm 127:1). The pursuit of meaning is meaningless unless there is a meaning in pursuit of man.

To the biblical mind man is not only a creature who is constantly in search of himself but also *a creature God is constantly in search of*. Man is a creature in search of meaning because there is a meaning in search of him, because there is God's beseeching question, "Where art thou?"

Man is prone to ignore this chief question of his existence as long as he finds tranquillity in the ivory tower of petty presumption. But when the tower begins to totter, when death wipes away that which seemed mighty and independent, when in evil days the delights of success are replaced by the nightmare of futility, he becomes conscious of the peril of evasiveness, of the emptiness of small objectives. His apprehension lest in winning small prizes he would gamble his life away, throws his soul open to questions he was trying to avoid.

But what is man's answer to God's plea, "Where art thou?"

> Thus says the Lord:
> Why, when I came was there no man?
> When I called, was there no one to answer?
>   Isaiah 50:2a.

Man not only refuses to answer; he often sets out to defy and to blaspheme. Abundant are the references in the Bible not only to man's callousness, but also to his rebellion. The human species is capable of producing saints and prophets, but also scoundrels and "enemies of God." The idea of the divine image of man offers no explanation to the dreadful mystery of the evil urge in the heart of man.

The heart is deceitful above all things and desperately corrupt;
Who can understand it?

Jeremiah 17:9

Because of the tension of "the good urge" and "the evil urge,"
human life is full of perils. The only safeguard against constant
danger is constant vigilance, constant guidance. If human nature
were all we had, there would be little reason to be hopeful. Yet we
also have the word of God, the commandment, the *mitzvah*. The
central biblical fact is Sinai. Sinai was superimposed on the failure
of Adam. It initiated an order of living, an answer to the question,
How should man, a being created in the image of God, think, act
and feel?

Ugly and somber is the world to the prophetic eye; drunk with
lust for power, infatuated with war, driven by envy and greed. Man
has become a nightmare. History is being made by "guilty men,
whose own might is their god" (Habakkuk 1:11).

The meaning of having been created in the image of God is veiled
in an enigma. But perhaps we may surmise the intention was for
man to be *a witness for God,* a symbol of God. Looking at man one
should sense the presence of God. But instead of living as a witness,
he became an impostor; instead of being a symbol, he became an
idol. In his bristling presumption he developed *a false sense of
sovereignty* which fills the world with terror.

We are proud of the achievements of our technological civilization. But our pride may result in our supreme humiliation. The
pride in maintaining, "My own power and the might of my own
hand have won this wealth for me" (Deuteronomy 8:17), will cause
us to say "Our god" to the work of our hands (Hosea 14:4).

One shudders to think that involved in our civilization is a
demonic force trying to exact vengeance on God.

After having eaten the forbidden fruit, the Lord sent forth man
from Paradise, to till the ground from which he was taken. But

man, who is more subtle than any other creature that God has made, what did he do? He undertook to build a Paradise by his own might, and he is driving God from his Paradise. For generations all looked well. But now we have discovered that our Paradise is built upon the top of a volcano. The Paradise we have built may turn out to be a vast camp for the extermination of man.

This is a time to cry out. One is ashamed to be human. One is embarrassed to be called religious in the face of religion's failure to keep alive the image of God in the face of man. We see the writing on the wall but are too illiterate to understand what it says. There are no easy solutions to grave problems. All we can honestly preach is a *theology of dismay*. We have imprisoned God in our temples and slogans, and now the word of God is dying on our lips. We have ceased to be symbols. There is darkness in the East, and smugness in the West. What of the night? What of the night?

What is history?[19] Wars, victories, and wars. So many dead. So many tears. So little regret. So many fears. And who could sit in judgment over the victims of cruelty whose horror turns to hatred? Is it easy to keep the horror of wickedness from turning into a hatred of the wicked? The world is drenched in blood, and the guilt is endless. Should not all hope be abandoned?

What saved the prophets from despair was their messianic vision and the idea of man's capacity for repentance. That vision and that idea affected their understanding of history.

History is not a blind alley, and guilt is not an abyss. There is always a way that leads out of guilt: repentance or turning to God. The prophet is a person who living in dismay has the power to transcend his dismay. Over all the darkness of experience hovers the vision of a different day.

Egypt and Assyria are locked in deadly wars. Hating each other, they are both the enemies of Israel. Abominable are their idolatries, and frightful are their crimes. How does Isaiah, the son of a people which cherishes the privilege of being called by the Lord "My people," "the work of My hands" (Isaiah 60:21), feel about Egypt and Assyria?

> In that day there shall be a highway from Egypt to Assyria;
> the Assyrian will come to Egypt, and the Egyptian into
> Assyria, and the Egyptians will worship with the Assyrians.
> In that day Israel shall be a third with Egypt and Assyria, a
> blessing in the midst of the earth which the Lord of hosts has
> blessed, saying.
> Blessed be My People Egypt,
> and Assyria, the work of My hands,
> and Israel, My inheritance
>
> Isaiah 19:23-25

Our God is also the God of our enemies, without their knowing
Him and despite their defying Him. The enmity between the
nations will turn to friendship. They will live together when they
will worship together. All three will be equally God's chosen people.

NOTES

1. Numbers 33:52; I Samuel 6:5, 6, 11; II Kings 11:18, Ezekiel 7:20;
10:17; 23:14; II Chronicles 23:17.
2. *Pesahim,* 75a.
3. *Genesis Rabba,* 24, 8.
4. Genesis 9:5 f. It is not clear, however, whether the last words of
this sentence contain a condemnation of murder or a justification of
the right to pronounce the death penalty for murder.
5. The observance of this law is apparently reflected in Joshua 10:26 f.
Our translation assumes that *kelalah* is a euphemism for *kavod.* This
assumption is implied in the rabbinic interpretation of the verse and is
similar in intention to Rashi's comment: "It is a slight to the King,
because man is made in the image of God." *Kelalah* in the sense of
reproach or insult is used in Exodus 21:17. A similar interpretation is
found in Pseudo-Jonathan. Compare the rendering by Ariston of Pella:
"For he that is hanged is a reproach to God," quoted by Jerome. See
S. R. Driver, *Deuteronomy* (International Critical Commentary), Edin-
burgh, 1895, p. 248 f. However, the Septuagint as well as the Mishnah
(*Sanhedrin* 6, 4; *Tosefta Sanhedrin* 9, 7; *Talmud Sanhedrin* 46b.) take
the verse to mean "for he is hanged because of a curse against God"
. . . "as if to say why was he hanged? because he cursed the name of
God: and so (if his body be left hanging, thus reminding man of his
blasphemy) the name of God is profaned."
6. *Aboth,* IV, 15.

7. Rabbi Meir be Todros Halevi Abulafia (1180–1244), quoted by Rabbi Samuel da Uceda, Midrash Shemuel, Venice, 1579, *ad locum*.

8. *Mishnah Sanhedrin*, IV, 5.

9. *Mishnah Terumoth*, VIII, 12.

10. *Mishnah Sanhedrin*, IV, 5.

11. Rashi, *Sanhedrin*, 37a.

12. *Rosh Hashanah*, 19b.

13. *Mishnah Sanhedrin*, IV, 5.

14. *Talmud Shabbat*, 50b, and Rashi, *ad locum*.

15. *Leviticus Rabba*, 34, 3; see *Abbot de Rabbi Nathan*, version B, chap. 30, ed. Schechter, p. 66; *Midrash Tehillim*, chap. 103; *Sheeltot de Rab Ahai Gaon*, chap. 1.

16. Zephania 1:17; Zacharia 9:3; Job 22:24.

17: He was fashioned like pottery out of clay, Isaiah 45:9; Job 33:6.

18. E. Cassirer, *An Essay on Man* (New Haven: Yale University Press), p. 5.

19. See Heschel, *The Prophets* (New York: Harper & Row, 1962), pp. 185–186.

11 / Protestant Renewal: A Jewish View

The world has never yet seen a religious structure which has not at some critical moment revealed the need for repair; we see that realization radiating from the words of the prophets of Israel. It is in the spirit of reverence for what I consider to be at stake in the religious life of the Protestant community that I offer the suggestions that follow. It is an encouraging sign for renewal of the concern of Protestantism for its origins in Judaism that a Jewish scholar should be invited to write on this issue. Indeed, some of the problems I shall touch upon afflict Jews as well as Christians.

I shall write of the situation resulting from the convergence of two trends: the age-old process of dejudaization of Christianity, and the modern process of desanctification of the Hebrew Bible. Then I shall touch upon the polarity of mystery and history, and upon the issue of dedogmatization.

DEJUDAIZATION

There was early in the history of the Christian church a deliberate cultivation of differences from Judaism, a tendency to understand itself in the light not of its vast indebtedness to but rather of its divergencies from Judaism. With the emergence and expansion of Christianity in the Greco-Roman world, gentile Christians over-

168

whelmed the movement, and a continuous process of accommodation to the spirit of that world was set in motion. The result was a conscious or unconscious dejudaization of Christianity, affecting the church's way of thinking and its inner life as well as its relationship to the past and present reality of Israel—the father and mother of the very being of Christianity. The children did not arise and call the mother blessed; instead, they called the mother blind. Some theologians continue to act as if they did not know the meaning of "honor your father and your mother"; others, anxious to prove the superiority of the church, speak as if they suffer from a spiritual Oedipus complex.

The Christian message, which in its origins intended to be an affirmation and culmination of Judaism, became very early diverted into a repudiation and negation of Judaism; obsolescence and abrogation of Jewish faith became conviction and doctrine; the new covenant was conceived not as a new phase or disclosure but as abolition and replacement of the ancient one; theological thinking fashioned its terms in a spirit of antithesis to Judaism. Contrast and contradiction rather than acknowledgment of roots, relatedness and indebtedness, became the perspective. Judaism a religion of law, Christianity a religion of grace; Judaism teaches a God of wrath, Christianity a God of love; Judaism a religion of slavish obedience, Christianity the conviction of free men; Judaism is particularism, Christianity is universalism; Judaism seeks work-righteousness, Christianity preaches faith-righteousness. The teaching of the old covenant a religion of fear, the gospel of the new covenant a religion of love; a *Lohnordnung* over against a *Gnadenordnung*.

The Hebrew Bible is preparation; the gospel fulfillment. In the first is immaturity, in the second perfection; in the one you find narrow tribalism, in the other all-embracing charity.

The process of dejudaization within the church paved the way for abandonment of origins and alienation from the core of its message.

The vital issue for the church is to decide whether to look for roots in Judaism and consider itself an extension of Judaism or to look for roots in pagan Hellenism and consider itself as an antithesis to Judaism.

The spiritual alienation from Israel is most forcefully expressed in the teaching of Marcion, who affirmed the contrariety and abrupt discontinuity between the God of the Hebrew Bible and the God whom Jesus had come to reveal. Marcion wanted a Christianity free from any vestige of Judaism. He saw his task as that of showing the complete opposition between the Hebrew Bible and the Gospels. Although in the year 144 of the Christian era the church expelled the apostle of discontinuity and anathematized his doctrines, Marcion remains a formidable menace, a satanic challenge. In the modern Christian community the power of Marcionism is much more alive and widespread than is generally realized.

Notwithstanding the work of generations of dedicated scholars who have opened up new vistas in the understanding of the history and literature of ancient Israel and their relation to Christianity, there is an abiding tendency to stress the *discontinuity* between the Hebrew Bible and the New Testament. According to Rudolf Bultmann (as summarized by Bernhard W. Anderson), "for the Christian the Old Testament is not revelation, but is essentially related to God's revelation in Christ as hunger is to food and despair is to hope. . . . The God who spoke to Israel no longer speaks to us in the time of the new Covenant."[1] Here is the spiritual resurrection of Marcion. Was not the God of Israel the God of Jesus? How dare a Christian substitute his own conception of God for Jesus' understanding of God and still call himself a Christian?

What is the pedigree of the Christian gospel? These are the words with which the New Testament begins: "The book of the genealogy of Jesus Christ, the son of David, the son of Abraham" (Matthew 1:1; see also 1 Corinthians 10:1–3; 1 Peter 1:10 ff.). Yet the powerful fascination with the world of Hellenism has led many minds to look for origins of the Christian message in the world derived from Hellas. How odd of God not to have placed the cradle of Jesus in Delphi, or at least in Athens!

Despite its acceptance of *sola scriptura* which ought to have

protected it from dejudaization, Protestantism has often succumbed
to an individualistic hellenized conception of the Christian tradition,
to a romantic oversimplification of the problem of faith and inwardness, to pantheism and sentimentality. Only a conscious commitment to the roots of Christianity in Judaism could have saved it
from such distortions. To the early Christians the premise of their
belief that the word became flesh was in the certainty that the spirit
had become the word. They were alive and open to the law and the
prophets.

In modern times there is a tendency to look for the spirit everywhere except in the words of the Hebrew Bible. There is no *religio
ex nihilo*, no ultimate beginning. There is no science without presupposition and no religion without ultimate decisions. An ultimate
decision for Jew or Christian is whether to be involved in the
Hebrew Bible or to live away from it. The future of the Western
world will depend on the way in which we relate ourselves to the
Hebrew Bible.

The extent of Christianity's identification with the Hebrew Bible
is a test of its authenticity—as well as of Jewish authenticity. Lack of
such identification lies at the heart of the malaise of Protestantism
today.

THE DESANCTIFICATION OF THE BIBLE

Into his studies of the Bible the modern scholar brings his total
personality, his increased knowledge of the ancient Near East, his
power of analysis, his historic sense, his honest commitment to
truth—as well as inherent skepticism of biblical claims and tradition. In consequence, we have so much to say *about the Bible* that
we are not prepared to hear what the Bible has to say about us. We
are not in love with the Bible; we are in love with our own power
of critical acumen, with our theories about the Bible. Intellectual
narcissism is a disease to which some of us are not always immune.
The sense of the mystery and *transcendence* of what is at stake in

the Bible is lost in the process of analysis. As a result, we have brought about the desanctification of the Bible.

The basic presupposition of much modern Protestant study of Scripture, which has contributed enormously to our historical and theological discernment, is that one should treat the Bible like any other book—with objectivity and detachment. Yet objectivity is not devoid of ambiguities; it claims to be value-free, though the attitude of being value-free is itself a valuational attitude.

My mother is and is *not* like any other mother to me, and the Bible is and is *not* like any other book to me. A pianist should study musicology but remain an artist. The words of the Bible are not made of paper. In order to know them I must submit them to my judgment; in order to understand them I must stand under their judgment.

The Hebrew Bible is quoted in sermons but is absent from minds. Its intellectual relevance is ignored. Its way of thinking has not affected modern man and has remained, it seems, outside the intellectual concern of many present-day theologians. What we face is a profound alienation from the Bible. The prophets' categories have become unknown and strange. To believe, we need God, a soul, and the Word. Having rejected the notion of the Bible as a paper pope, many are left with the Bible as a collection of ill-composed records on a mass of paper.

The Bible is holiness in words. How are we to preserve within our involvement in critical studies the awareness of the holy; how are we to cultivate the understanding that the authority of the Bible is not merely an issue of either philology or chronology? More decisive than the dogmatic attempt to define the date and authorship of the biblical documents is the openness to the *presence of God* in the Bible. Such openness is not acquired offhand. It is the fruit of hard, constant care, of involvement; it is the result of praying, seeking, craving. Where and how is modern man guided to search for it today?

The words are still with us. Scripture may have vanished from our hearts. Yet the miracle of re-engagement is possible.

THE POLARITY OF MYSTERY AND HISTORY

The substance of the Christian gospel contains both proclamation and instruction: it proclaims *events*—the life, death and resurrection of Jesus—and it offers instruction—guidance, teaching full of demands. The events represent the *mystery* with which Christian existence is involved, while the teaching is concerned with this world, with the sphere of *history,* within which the commandment of love is to be fulfilled. Christianity is bound to this polarity of mystery and history. Without the mystery it would be moral teaching; without the history it would be an otherworldly movement of the spirit. Is it easy to maintain the right balance between two heterogeneous poles? It seems to me that in the history of the Christian church preoccupation with the mystery has often led to withdrawal from history and to attenuation of the demands posed by the teaching.[2]

Disregard for the supremacy of the demand has often led theologians to read an attitude of disregard for Torah in the words of the prophets. I cite a classical example:

> Behold, the days are coming, says the Lord, when I will make a new covenant with the house of Israel and the house of Judah, not like the covenant which I made with their fathers when I took them by the hand to bring them out of the land of Egypt, my covenant which they broke, though I was their husband, says the Lord. But this is the covenant which I will make with the house of Israel after those days, says the Lord: I will put my law within them, and I will write it upon their hearts; and I will be their God, and they shall be my people (Jeremiah 31: 31-33).

Is this really what the prophet meant: "the end of the previous covenant of God with his people"? Is this really what Jeremiah envisaged: "inwardness of faith," "a change in the human heart," "a personal relationship between God and people"? Let us beware of interpreting the prophets in the images of the 20th century.

"I will write it upon their hearts." Moses wrote the words of the covenant upon "tables of stone" (Exodus 34:1); now God will write the covenant upon the hearts. The heart is the person. What the prophet seems to predict is not abolition of the Torah but inner identification with it. To the biblical mind nothing in the world was as holy as the Tablets; they were placed in the Ark. Days are coming when man will become the Tables, when man will become torah.

The sharp contrast drawn between the Torah (teaching, law) and grace, between works and faith, represents a major divergence from the Hebrew way of thinking. The preoccupation with personal salvation has, it seems, a tendency to weaken one's openness to history as it unfolds in its secular and social aspects. Social ills produced in the wake of major economic, political and social revolutions seem to stir and to arouse the sensitivity of the so-called secularists sooner than they do the conscience of the pious—a situation parallel to that in Judaism when preoccupation with ritual may weaken sensitivity to social issues. In biblical days prophets were astir while the world was asleep; today the world is astir while church and synagogue are busy with trivialities.

Perhaps the demand for the "priesthood of all believers" should be supplemented by a demand for the *prophethood of all believers*.[3] Prophets make up the vanguard, standing in the first line of the battle to achieve the fulfillment of the will of God here and now. The true sanctuary has no walls; spirit and commitment must be alive in homes as well as in churches; man's total existence is the challenge.

There must be an end to the scandal of the presence of sentimentality in the face of divine grandeur, an end to the encouragement of easy assurance of salvation. God is either of extreme importance or of no importance.

The first word in God's approach to man is: "The Lord God

commanded the man . . ." (Genesis 2:16). It is the commandment we must first listen to.

Do not sell salvation too cheaply. Let us disavow easy decisions and come to realize that religious existence is arduous and full of demands, that existence as such is at the brink of the abyss. Luther had to fight against the traffic in indulgences; today he would have to fight the epidemic of self-indulgence.

The great principle of the Reformation was that knowledge of God is direct and personal. Yet ours is a civilization of indirect knowledge and of depersonalization. There is no stillness, no privacy, no cultivation of concentration or receptivity. Moreover, no person is a *tabula rasa*. The substance and the mode of religious experience are colored by and contingent upon the total direction and content of one's existence. The individual encounter may be false and idolatrous. There is the danger of false religiosity; it is not personal faith or "religious experience" alone on which we can rely. Indeed, the individual "encounter" may be an encounter with idolatry. The source of identification is the intimate union of the Word and the conscience.

DEDOGMATIZATION

The need within Protestantism for re-examination, revision and renewal is of extreme urgency. Yet renewal must not be permitted to degenerate into a trend to religion á la mode, and it must not be guided exclusively by concern for preservation of the church. The greater problem today is not how to preserve the church but how to preserve humanity, threatened not only by the possibility of nuclear explosion but also by liquidation of the inner man.

The problems we all face are both new and radical; they are religious as well as total. We have passed through the stage of social conformity and are entering that of political and intellectual automation, trapped as we are already in glittering clichés. The issue is not the incarnation; it is the elimination of God. For many people God is a forgotten myth; for many the terms in which the creeds speak seem to lie beyond the frame of modern discourse. Society and religion seem to be as remote from each other as is Cape Kennedy from the moon. On the other hand, this is a great moment for outburst and return. The absurdity of human arrogance, the deep sense of insecurity and shame, lie like dormant revelations in many souls. We have satellites in the air and a weird dread of man in our hearts.

Religion is neither a self-subsisting entity nor an end in itself. Its institutions, rituals, symbols, creeds derive their vitality from the deep roots of human existence. Detached from its roots, religion becomes irrelevant. Our predicament is due to our having forfeited the antecedents of religious faith, the prerequisites of insight and commitment. We live a life which tends to suppress rather than to cultivate the moments that precede reflection and responsiveness to ultimate demands.

The primary issue of theology is pretheological; it is the total situation of man and his attitudes toward life and the world.[4] The power to praise precedes the power of faith. Without a continuous cultivation of a sense of the ineffable, it is hard to remain open to the meaning of the holy. Each time before uttering the word "God" we must first take the mind out of the prison of platitudes and labels, must honestly sense the sheer mystery of being alive, of facing the world. The antecedents of faith include a perspective upon the world, certain ultimate questions, spiritual traditions—as well as hard-won personal insights and moments of participation in the religious life of the community. In the Western world most of these prerequisites go back to a book, the Bible.

Are dogmas unnecessary? We cannot be in rapport with the reality of the divine except for rare, fugitive moments. How can those moments be saved for the long hours of functional living, when the thoughts that feed like bees on the inscrutable desert us and we lose both the sight and the drive? Dogmas are like amber in which bees, once alive, are embalmed, and they are capable of being electrified when our minds become exposed to the power of the ineffable. For problems remain with which we must always grapple: How are we to communicate those rare moments of insight to all hours of our life? How are we to commit intuition to concepts, the ineffable to words, communion to rational understanding? How are we to convey our insights to others and unite with them in a fellowship of faith? It is the creed that attempts to answer these questions.

The adequacy of dogmas depends on whether they claim to formulate or to allude; in the first case they flaunt and fail, in the second they indicate and illumine. To be adequate they must retain a telescopic relation to the theme to which they refer, must point to the mysteries of God rather than picture them. All they can do is indicate a way, not mark an end, of thinking. Unless they serve as humble signposts on the way dogmas are obstacles. They must be allusive rather than informative or descriptive. Taken literally, they either turn flat, narrow and shallow, or become ventriloquistic myths. For example, the dogma of creation has often been reduced to a tale and robbed of its authentic meaning; but as an allusion to ultimate mystery it is of inexhaustible relevance.

There must be honest admission that the truth, the meaning, and the joy are to be found in what can be neither conceived nor achieved. The righteous lives by his faith, not by his creed. And faith is not an allegiance to a verbal formulation; on the contrary, it involves profound awareness of the inadequacy of words, concepts, deeds. Unless we realize that dogmas are tentative rather than final, that they are accommodations rather than definitions, intimations rather than descriptions; unless we learn how to share the moment and the insight to which they are trying to testify, we stand guilty of literalmindedness, of pretending to know what cannot be put into words; we are guilty of intellectual idolatry. The indispensable function of the dogmas is to make it possible for us to rise above them. The time has come to break through the bottom of theology into depth theology.

NOTES

1. B. W. Anderson, "The New Covenant and the Old" in *The Old Testament and Christian Faith* (New York: Harper & Row, 1963), p. 227.

2. See Leo Baeck, *Judaism and Christianity* (1958), pp. 171 ff.; W. D. Davies, *"The Gospel Tradition,"* in *Neotestamentica et Patristica* (1962), p. 33.

3. See Moses' exclamation: "Would that all the Lord's people were prophets, that the Lord would put His spirit upon them" (Numbers 11: 29).

4. See my book *Man Is Not Alone* (New York: Farrar, Straus, 1951), pp. 168 ff.; see also above, "Depth Theology," p. 116.

12 / The Ecumenical Movement

When Israel approached Sinai, God lifted up the mountain and held it over their heads, saying: "Either you accept the Torah or be crushed beneath the mountain."

The mountain of history is over our heads again. Shall we renew the covenant with God?

In the words of Isaiah: "The envoys of peace weep bitterly. . . . Covenants are broken, witnesses are despised, there is no regard for man" (33:7–8).

Men all over the world have a dreadful sense in common, the fear of absolute evil, the fear of total annihilation. An apocalyptic monster has descended upon the world, and there is nowhere to go, nowhere to hide.

This is an hour when even men of reason call for accommodation to absolute evil and preparation for disaster, maintaining that certain international problems are weird, demonic, beyond solution.

Dark is the world for us, for all its cities and stars. If not for Thee, O Lord, who could stand such anguish, such disgrace?

The gap between the words we preach and the lives we live threatens to become an abyss. How long will we tolerate a situation that refutes what we confess?

Is it not true that God and nuclear stockpiles cannot dwell together in one world? Is it not true that facing disaster together we must all unite to defy despair, to prevent surrender to the demonic?

The minds are sick. The hearts are mad. Humanity is drunk with a sense of absolute sovereignty. Our pride is hurt by each other's arrogance.

The dreadful predicament is not due to economic conflicts. It is due to a spiritual paralysis.

This is an age of suspicion, when most of us seem to live by the rule: Suspect thy neighbor as thyself. Such radical suspicion leads to despair of man's capacity to be free and to eventual surrender to demonic forces, surrender to idols of power, to the monsters of self-righteous ideologies.

What will save us is a revival of reverence for man, unmitigable indignation at acts of violence, burning compassion for all who are deprived, the wisdom of the heart. Before imputing guilt to others, let us examine our own failures.

What all men have in common is poverty, anguish, insecurity. What all religions have in common is power to refute the fallacy of absolute expediency, insistence that the dignity of man is in his power of compassion, in his capacity for sacrifice, self-denial.

Our era marks the end of complacency. We all face the dilemma expressed by Moses: "I have put before you life and death, blessing and curse. Choose life." Religion's task is to cultivate disgust for violence and lies, sensitivity to other people's suffering, the love of peace. God has a stake in the life of every man. He never exposes humanity to a challenge without giving humanity the power to face the challenge.

Different are the languages of prayer, but the tears are the same. We have a vision in common of Him in whose compassion all men's prayers meet.

In the words of the prophet Malachi, "From the rising of the sun to its setting My name is great among the nations, in every place incense is offered to My name, and a pure offering; for My name is great among the nations, says the Lord of hosts" (Malachi: 1:11). It seems to me that the prophet proclaims that men all over the world, though they confess different conceptions of God, are really worshiping One God, the Father of all men, though they may not even be aware of it.

What will save us? God, and our faith in man's relevance to God.

This is the agony of history: bigotry, the failure to respect each other's commitment, each other's faith. We must insist upon loyalty to the unique and holy treasures of our own tradition and at the same time acknowledge that in this aeon religious diversity may be the providence of God.

Respect for each other's commitment, respect for each other's faith, is more than a political and social imperative. It is born of the insight that God is greater than religion, that faith is deeper than dogma, that theology has its roots in depth theology.

The ecumenical perspective is the realization that religious truth does not shine in a vacuum, that the primary issue of theology is pretheological, and that religion involves the total situation of man, his attitudes and deeds, and must therefore never be kept in isolation.

It is customary to blame secular science and antireligious philosophy for the eclipse of religion in modern society. It would be more honest to blame religion for its own defeats. Religion declined not because it was refuted, but because it became irrelevant, dull, oppressive, insipid. When faith is completely replaced by creed, worship by discipline, love by habit; when the crisis of today is ignored because of the splendor of the past; when faith becomes an heirloom rather than a living fountain; when religion speaks only in the name of authority rather than with the voice of compassion—its message becomes meaningless.[1]

The great spiritual renewal within the Roman Catholic Church, inspired by Pope John XXIII, is a manifestation of the dimension of depth of religious existence. It already has opened many hearts and unlocked many precious insights.

There is a longing for peace in the hearts of man. But peace is not the same as the absence of war. Peace among men depends upon a relationship of reverence for each other.

Reverence for man means reverence for man's freedom. God has a stake in the life of man, of every man.

It was in the spirit of depth theology that Cardinal Bea announced his intention to prepare a constitution on religious liberty for presentation at the next session of the Council, in which the Fathers would be asked to come out emphatically with a public recognition of the inviolability of the human conscience as the final right of every man, no matter what his religious beliefs or ideological allegiance. Cardinal Bea stated further that the axiom "Error has no right to exist," which is used so glibly by certain Catholic apologists, is sheer nonsense, for error is an abstract concept incapable of either rights or obligations. It is persons who have rights, and even when they are in error, their right to freedom of conscience is absolute.

To quote from classic rabbinic literature: "Pious men of all nations have a share in the world to come," and are promised the reward of eternal life. "I call heaven and earth to witness that the Holy Spirit rests upon each person, Jew or gentile, man or woman, master or slave, in consonance with his deeds."

God's voice speaks in many languages, communicating itself in a diversity of intuitions.

The word of God never comes to an end. No word is God's last word.

Man's greatest task is to comprehend God's respect and regard for the freedom of man, freedom, the supreme manifestation of God's regard for man.

In the words of Pope John's Encyclical, *Pacem in Terris:* "Every human being has the right to freedom in searching for truth and in expressing and communicating his opinions. . . . Every human being has the right to honor God according to the dictates of an upright conscience."

Man's most precious thought is God, but God's most precious thought is man.

A religious man is a person who holds God and man in one thought at one time, at all times, who suffers in himself harms done to others, whose greatest passion is compassion, whose greatest strength is love and defiance of despair.

NOTE

1. See Heschel, *God in Search of Man* (New York: Farrar, Straus, 1955), p. 3.

III

13 / *The Individual Jew and His Obligations*

Disaster, deliverance, dismay—these three words mark the supreme issues of Jewish existence in our day. Yet though involving the heart and center of our existence, they remain at the periphery of our thinking. The memory of the disaster is being effaced from our minds, the deliverance we take for granted, and dismay we suppress.

Since the day the Temple was destroyed there has been no age like ours. It is as if God had rolled up all Jewish history and placed it under our heads. What is the meaning of all this? What is the import of this hour? And where is the thinking of our day?

The Torah which God gave to Moses was "white fire engraved with black fire." And this is the image of the events we experienced. The white fire of the upbuilding of Israel engraved with the black fire of ruin and disaster.

The fire conceived and bore light. Deaf to the cries out of the flames, who will understand the signs of birth? Horrible are the pangs. What will come into the world?

We have grown used to the thought that six million have been consumed. We live and think as if there had never been an Auschwitz or a Majdanek. How fast is the spread of the power to suppress! It even happens that Jewish children in America say to their teacher who mentions these martyrs in class: "You have spun the story of destruction out of your fancy!"

Six million were wiped off the face of the earth. And there is the danger that they will also be annihilated from our memories. Are they doomed to a twofold annihilation?

"The parchments are consumed but the letters soar aloft." The return to Zion we had dared to yearn for is actually taking place. This was wrought by the Almighty, and who shall say, there is nothing new under the sun? Yet the heart does not comprehend what the eyes behold. We have not grasped the marvel, we have not felt the mystery, we are powerless to speak, to illumine our lives in the light of events.

At times we feel as if a deep slumber had descended upon us; the visions appear to us like the words of a sealed, enigmatic book. Some of us shake our heads at all this and say, there is no wonder in the creation of Israel, no mystery, no marvel.

To interpret our history in the light of mere facts is to distort it. To be literal is to be ludicrous. To be sure, from the point of view of practical reason and logic the efforts of the Zionists were doomed to failure. The Zionist vision was like a fable, or a dream, and in the eyes of practical people it was absurd to be a dreamer and to build the future of a people upon the flimsy grounds of fable. Yet where practical logic failed, visionary logic succeeded.

Dark and dreadful would be our life today without the comfort and the joy that radiate out of the land of Israel. Crippled is our people, many of its limbs chopped off, some of its vital organs torn out—how strange to be alive, how great is our power to forget.

Like a flashlight in the darkness of history came the state of Israel. It is a haven of refuge for those in despair who cried for a sign that God is not forever estranged from the world of history.

Our vision must turn in four directions: What is above? What is below? What is ahead? And what is behind?

What is above? Know Who is above.

What is below? The abyss of evil.

What is ahead? Generations that shall ask: What did they say, those who lived through the disaster and the deliverance? Let us not forget: "The things that a man does in his childhood return to blacken his face in old age."

And what is behind?

The Holy One, blessed be He, took from under the throne of Glory a fiery coin, showed it to Moses, and said, "They shall give this. They shall give like this." The thought of our days will be preserved only in one form, in one coin: in a coin of fire, of white fire and of black fire.

"The letters soar aloft." Ours is the task of putting together the letters which hovered over Majdanek and Auschwitz with the letters with which Zion and Jerusalem are being built. The secret of history is concealed in our destiny. Deep within history lie the wonder and the horror, the satanic and the sublime. We have seen civilization in its depravity, and a prophetic vision in its sublimity. It behooves every Jew to say: "I am glory and ashes."

This is our tragedy. We live as if there were nothing unique about Jewish existence, as if all sufferings had been in vain, as if prophetic teachings were a misunderstanding. Our cardinal sin is that we do not grasp the sublime in our existence, that we do not know how to adjust our lives to the grandeur, our thoughts to the mystery, the single one in Israel to the Eternal One of Israel.

What is sublime in the existence of Israel? The shrieks from the gas chambers, such as have never been uttered by man, somehow resound in our depths. They are too horrible to be conveyed. Woe to the generation in whose time man could become so debased. Never has the mystery of Jewish existence been as striking as in our time. Never has a sanctuary been hallowed with so much innocent anguish. Every one of us alive is a spark of an eternal candle and a smoldering ember snatched from the fire. Without his knowing it, every one of us is crowned with the Holy. Let us learn to be aware of the majesty which hovers over our existence. Great is our sorrow, and great is our task. Let us rescue the heart of man, the heart which may reach up to the heart of heaven.

We are Jews as we are men. The alternative to our existence as

Jews is spiritual suicide, disappearance. It is not a change into something else. Judaism has allies but not substitutes. Every people has a religion that it has received from others. Only in Israel people and Torah are one. All of Israel, not only the select few, are the bearers of this unity.

Let us look at our recent history. "A servant-girl in our day has seen more than sages and prophets." The life of a Jew is sign and testimony that man hovers continually between the abyss below and the heaven above. The depravity of civilization is proof that a godless people is bound to become a satanic people. Man has become the enemy of God. The restoration of the land of Israel is a testimony to the world that the prophetic vision is not a dream, that the word of our God shall endure forever.

IF WE DO NOT BUILD A HOUSE FOR THE INDIVIDUAL

Much has been spoken and written in our midst about nation and society, about the community and its institutions. But the individual has been lost sight of. It is my task to speak about this neglected subject. It is common knowledge that Judaism is not merely concerned with the individual. He who goes his own way abandons the Jewish way. To withdraw oneself from the community is to detach oneself from the God of Israel. However, it is a fact that the Jewish people today are like a tree from which many fruits are falling off. A tree does not bear fruit every day.

What was the situation of the Jews before the time of the emancipation? As an individual he was able to preserve his spiritual privacy. His life had form, direction, inner strength, and dignity. He stood for eternity, he lived for a transcendent purpose. It was the existence of the Jews as a people that was in peril. To emphasize the distress of the people was the achievement of the Zionist movement. As an individual the Jew could live happily in Berlin and Odessa. Zionism proclaimed that the problems of the individual were secondary to those of the people, that unless a national home were built the efforts and accomplishments of the individual, however great, would be like whirling dust.

With the birth of the State of Israel, the Jews of Israel found a solution to the national problem. Meanwhile, the plight in the life of the individual, which began more than 150 years ago, has continually worsened. We are witnesses to the disintegration of Judaism in the lives of individuals, many of whom who are Jewish publicly, have ceased to be Jewish privately. "Jewish belonging" is no substitute for Jewish living.

Jewish thinking during the last three generations has had one central preoccupation. Speaking of the Jewish problem, we meant the problem of the Jewish people. The group, the community and its institutions, received all our attention. The individual and his problems were ignored. We saw the forest, but nothing else. We thought about community, we forgot the person. The time has arrived to pay heed to the forgotten individual. Judaism is a personal problem.

We have built organizations, but how Jewish is their membership? Our synagogues are beautiful, but the homes are a wilderness. We have developed forms of living socially as Jews. Jews attend Jewish meetings, belong to Jewish organizations, contribute to communal and national funds. But when left alone, or retired in our homes—they are poor in religious spirit. The American is known as a joiner. And we, too, have made a cult of belonging. The true goal includes becoming a Jew as well as belonging to a synagogue. And this is a life-long process.

If the individual is lost to Judaism in his privacy, the people are in danger of becoming a phantom. Every individual is a pillar on which the future of Judaism rests. There is no vicarious Judaism: no institution can discharge the responsibilities of the individual. Tradition is not the monopoly of an elite. Each Jew is obliged to say: "Into my hands has been given the future of the entire people." Just as every person is a microcosm, so is every Jew a miniature Jewish people. He carries within him the soul of the entire people. Most of the *mitzvoth* devolve upon the individual and are to be carried out in person. This is the audacity of Judaism: it makes the individual the mirror of the people.

The problem of the individual is the urgent issue of our time. If we do not build a house for the individual, we shall labor in vain in the building of the nation. There is nothing in the universal that is not contained in the particular. One stands aghast before the multitudes of our people: hearts without a Jewish thought, homes without a Hebrew book, books without Jewish content. A generation has arisen that knows not the Torah, that knows not how to distinguish between the Sabbath and the weekdays, between the sacred and the sensational. A grudge against Judaism rankles in the hearts of many Jews; there are individuals who hate the very fact of their having been born Jews. Many who are anxious to study any of the world's cultures have a strange lack of curiosity in regard to the sources of Jewish learning.

There are still, of course, guardians of the walls. But we are not speaking now of the faithful but of the lost sheep of the House of Israel. Horrid is the desolation, and fearful the failure. But who is to blame? The flock or the shepherds? Judaism or the Jews?

It would be a fatal distortion, I repeat, to reduce Judaism to individualism. Separation from the people Israel is detachment from the covenant with the God of Israel. At the same time, it would be suicidal to reduce Judaism to communalism, collectivism, or nationalism. Jewish existence is a personal situation. And the urgent Jewish problem today is the individual Jew.

I repeat, attachment to our people, the love of Israel, the understanding and feeling for Jews everywhere are the well-springs of our strength. But the problem is how to fulfill that attachment and that understanding in terms of individual existence.

Many of the spiritual resources of the Jewish people in America have been depleted. Socialism, Hebraism, Yiddishism, which held an earlier generation in their spell, have lost their vitality. This is the hour for the rediscovery of the grandeur of our tradition. The question is how to find the language which will reach the soul of our generation? How to retain Jewish authenticity in our contemporary civilization?

This was the Jewish dream: every table an altar, every Jew a priest. Now the Jew is losing his spiritual independence. Every rabbi is a shepherd, every Jew a part of the flock. How can we prevent Judaism from degenerating into a monopoly of rabbis? I see only one way out of the trap of institutionalism: a new emphasis upon the personal aspect of being a Jew.

By the emphasis upon the personal I mean a relatedness to the center of one's being, a relatedness to one's intimate problems, such as joy and anxiety, the sense of futility, insecurity, or the search for meaning.

There is a vital personal question which every human being is called upon to answer, day in, day out. What shall I do with my mind, my wealth, my power? The terrifying seriousness of history, the earnestness of being alive, have never been as obvious as in our own days. The problem of man is more grave than we were able to realize generations ago.

It will be said: the trouble is that faith is gone and that one cannot coerce the heart. The truth, however, is that there is a sense of embarrassment in the soul and a silent cry, a cry that may turn to prayer. The stirrings are vague. Who will lend language to the soul, direction to the mind? The satisfactions are precarious, the tongue is parched. The triumphs of agnosticism are beginning to look like defeats. There is a slow and agonizing collapse of the resistance to Judaism. Many who had strayed are trying to bring their children closer. Many parents are sending their children to all-day Hebrew schools. And even among those who desecrate the Sabbath there is a desire in some to find a way back to its observance. Many lost souls are searching for a root or an anchor. And if we do not open a way for them, many will go after strange gods. Let us not forget the danger of extinction which lies in wait for us in every country. The opportunity for a revival is glorious, and the possibilities numerous. But it is slipping through our hands.

The leaders of our people do not know *the language of the soul.*
A person goes to the synagogue. His mouth is sealed, his mind
blocked. Who shall open his heart? Who shall set his soul aright?
"The soul of every living thing praises Thy name," and shall the
soul of the Jew not know how to praise? On every Sabbath multitudes of Jews gather in the synagogues, and they depart as they have
entered. The soul does not know how to pour itself out. There is a
gulf between the soul of the individual and the atmosphere of the
synagogue. There are those who have come from afar, from the
depths of alienation, with a vague yearning in their hearts. What
they sought for was not given them, and what they already had was
taken from them.

Many are the trials and temptations of the modern Jew. The doors
of Western culture are open before him, and whenever he wishes to
enter, he finds a welcome place. Why should he not assimilate? The
worthwhileness of belonging to the Jewish people must not be taken
for granted. Why should one not detach himself from the Jewish
community and join another community? Can we expect to find
understanding on the part of every Jew: that he who separates
himself from Judaism commits spiritual suicide? Various efforts
have been made in the Diaspora to plant a vineyard of secular
culture to take the place of tradition: art, music, literature, theater,
press. With what pains has the vineyard been cultivated, how much
labor and energy have been sunk into it! And what happened? Like
the *qiqayon* of Jonah, it arose overnight and was lost overnight.

Technological civilization and secular culture are no answer to
man's ultimate questions. Literature and language are only vessels,
not the substance. This applies in particular to Jewish existence.
Compared to world culture, our secular culture will, at best, be
second rate. Is it conceivable that any secular idea will be a sufficient
motivation for the Jews scattered in the Diaspora to preserve the
bond and to take upon themselves the burden of a Jewish destiny?

Every human being is beset by personal problems. He is involved
in perplexities and embarrassments, in loneliness and frustrations.
There is a question which is uppermost in his mind: What aid,

comfort, and guidance do I derive from belonging to the Community of Israel? What does it mean to me personally? He will not affirm and appreciate that belonging, unless he is convinced that Judaism does bestow upon him the sort of guidance which no other source is capable of giving him; that living as a Jew will raise him to a plane which cannot otherwise be reached.

We who are gathered here have a concern in common: that Jews remain Jews. Every teacher of Judaism must ask himself whether he is doing the right thing in instilling loyalty to Judaism in the youth. "Thou shall not place a stumbling block before the blind." History has taught us that our existence as Jews often exacts a frightful price. Granted, no imminent danger threatens us at present. But who knows what the morrow will bring? Is our generation prepared? From the standpoint of personal security it is of course preferable for an individual to assimilate. The doors of assimilation, as I have said, are open to the multitudes of our people everywhere, and they may very well succeed in disappearing as Jews. Are we not being led astray and misleading others in our efforts to strengthen Jewish existence? To assess Judaism soberly and farsightedly is to establish it as a good to be preferred, if necessary, to any alternative which we may ever face.

FOR THE SIN WE HAVE SINNED IN DISPARAGING THE SPIRIT

We speak of the obligations of the individual to tradition. But what of the *rights* of the individual within the tradition? We have forgotten the love of God for Israel. We have forgotten that "the Holy One, blessed be He, does not ask the impossible of His creatures," that the ways of the Torah are "ways of pleasantness." "The Torah speaks in the language of men." But the sages of Israel have overlooked the man in the Jew. They gained no insight into his difficulties, and failed to understand his dilemmas. Every generation has its own problems. Every man is burdened with anxieties. But the sages remained silent; they did not guide the perplexed and showed no regard for the new problems that arose. In the past, when a Jew's education was confined to rabbinic writings, the four cubits of the Halacha, and categories of *Abbayah* and *Rabah,* shaped his thought pattern, his way of thinking and reasoning, he had but one criterion: Is it permissible or forbidden, is it kosher or not? He thought in the categories of Halacha and lived his life according to its standards. The Halacha determined not only his actions but the very mode of his thought.

A complete change has taken place in the field of education. For the most part Jews derive their knowledge not from Talmudic but from secular sources. Halachic ways of thinking and reasoning are strange to most people; they have no inkling of those concepts and values. The authors of the Halacha and the modern man do not speak the same language. A divided generation has risen. A man does not understand the language of his neighbor. Each side claims to possess all the truth. All know that Judaism is "a burden." But who knows that it is also "a joy of the spirit and the Eden of the souls," that the Sabbath is a foretaste of the world to come? Is it a sin to derive joy from Judaism? For many of us tradition has become a dried-up tree. Its taste and sap are gone. There are many who speak in the name of our people who have studied neither our history nor our literature, who have never perceived the flavor of Jewish existence, who eat the shell and discard the substance. Our fallow land is known far and wide; our rich soil is the secret of the few. We have failed in that we did not know how to convey the imponderable, how to open the eyes of the heart, how to draw forth the light of the Torah from its wrappings. We have not cultivated the eye, and the eye is dim; we have not cultivated the ear, and the ear has grown dull. We, the teachers, are of little faith. We skirt the problems; we do not reach the core.

The basic Jewish problem today is not "negation of the Diaspora" but the disparagement of the spirit, the disregard for Jewish thought. The eye of the heart is dim.

Jewish thought is neglected and cast aside like unwanted vessels. There is no intellectual movement, no reflection, no introspection.

There is much noise, but the still, small voice is not heard; much promotion but little instruction. We busy ourselves exclusively with communal affairs and forget the life of the individual. We seem to believe that propaganda and promotion are the panacea, that beautiful edifices or public demonstrations can alleviate or cure the sickness of our generation. But spiritual problems cannot be solved by administrative techniques.

We have fought for political rights, established institutions, organized conventions and political parties. But institutions and parties alone will not save the people. Jewish survival is a spiritual, and not only a political problem. An anti-intellectual climate, neglect of thought, evasion of the problems of the spirit may be our undoing.

We are all committed to the idea of the modern Jew. By modern Jew I mean a person who lives within the language and culture of a twentieth-century nation, is exposed to its challenge, its doubts and its allurements, and at the same time insists upon the preservation of Jewish authenticity in religious and even cultural terms. But let us not forget that the modern Jew is but an experiment, and who can be sure that the experiment will succeed?

The avenues of communication between Judaism and the Jew, the channels of thought and understanding, are obstructed. There is no intellectual contact between them.

THERE IS NO FAITH WITHOUT EFFORT

Judaism is an answer to man's ultimate questions. The moment we become oblivious to ultimate questions, religion becomes irrelevant, and its crisis sets in. The primary task of religious thinking is to rediscover the questions to which religion is an answer. Without an intellectual effort, without an understanding of the questions, Judaism and its answers are like stale bread to a sated man, like a solution without the riddle.

Individuals detached themselves from the tradition when they ceased to perceive the connection between the problems which agi-

tate the heart and the Torah and the Commandments, between the
landscape and the synagogue, between the setting sun and the
evening prayers, between the Sabbath and the riddle of time. A
Judaism confined to the limits of the Halacha, with all due respect
be it said, is not exactly one of the happiest products of the Diaspora. Such condensation and parochialism has little of the sweep
and power of the prophets. He who would restrict Judaism to
Halacha will distort its image and deprive it of its grandeur. Those
who cite the words of our sages: "Since the day of the destruction of
the Temple, God had no more than four cubits of the *Halacha* in
His world," forget that these words are not an expression of
triumph but, on the contrary, an expression of pain and sorrow that
the *Shechinah* was expelled from the wide world of history and
nature. The roots of religion lie in the depths of thought, in reflection that surpasses our power of expression, in awe and amazement
before the wonder and the mystery beyond all comprehension or
utterance. A religious revival will come only from inner embarrassment, from the agony of the intellect as it stands overwhelmed in
the face of the mystery which lies hidden in all things and the
inscrutable mystery of the mind itself. From the despair that goes
hand in hand with hope, from tribulation and perplexity, from
yearning and song, the faith in God bursts forth.

Authentic faith is more than an echo of a tradition. It is a creative
situation, an event. It is an act of the whole person, of mind, will,
and heart. It is *sensitivity, understanding, engagement,* and *attachment;* not something achieved once and for all, but an attitude one
may gain and lose, a flash of insight in isolated moments. But such
experiences or inspirations are rare events, may come and go, penetrate and retreat. To some people they are like shooting stars,
passing and unremembered. In others they kindle a light that is
never quenched. The remembrance of that experience and the
loyalty to the response of that moment are the forces that sustain
our faith. In this sense, *faith is faithfulness,* loyalty to an event,
loyalty to our response.

Faith comes out of awe, out of an awareness that we are exposed to His presence, out of anxiety to answer the challenge of God, out of an awareness of our being called upon. *Religion consists of God's question and man's answer*. The way to faith is the way of faith. The way to God is a way of God. Unless God asks the question, all our inquiries are in vain.

Faith in the living God is, we repeat, not easily attained. Had it been possible to prove His existence beyond dispute, atheism would have been refuted as an error long ago. Had it been possible to awaken in every man the power to answer His ultimate question, the great prophets would have achieved it long ago. Tragic is the embarrassment of the man of faith. "My tears have been my food day and night, while they say unto me all the day, where is thy God?" (Psalm 42:4). "Where are all His marvelous deeds which our father told us of?" (Judges 6:13; see Psalm 44:2). "How long, O Lord, wilt Thou hide Thyself forever?" (Psalm 89:46). "My God, my God, why has Thou forsaken me?" (Psalm 22:2).

There is no faith at first sight. A faith that comes into being like a butterfly is ephemeral. He who is swift to believe is swift to forget. Faith does not come into being out of nothing, inadvertently, unprepared, as an unearned surprise. Faith is preceded by awe, by acts of amazement at things that we apprehend but cannot comprehend.

I am not speaking of complete, unimpeachable, or opinionated faith. There are few incontestable, unambiguous dogmas. Nor is genuine faith a safe deposit box of ideas. Faith is not a system but an ongoing striving for faith, involving acceptance of perplexity, joy of devotion as well as the agony of doubts, moments of illumination as well as groping in the darkness of vapidity.

We must never cease to question our own faith and to ask what God means to us. Is He an alibi for ignorance? The white flag of surrender to the Unknown? Is He a pretext for comfort, a substitute for prestige and intellectual search?

Ezra the Scribe, the great renovator of Judaism, of whom the rabbis said that he was worthy of receiving the Torah had it not been already given through Moses (*Sanhedrin* 21b), confessed his lack of perfect faith. He tells us that after he received a royal firman from King Artaxerxes, granting him permission to lead a group of exiles from Babylonia: "I proclaimed a fast there, at the river Ahava, that we might humble ourselves before our God, to seek of Him a straight way for us, and for our little ones, and for all our substance. For I was ashamed to ask of the king a band of soldiers and horsemen to help us against the enemy in the way: because we had spoken unto the king, saying, 'The hand of our God is upon all them that seek Him for good' " (Ezra 8:21–22).

Many people will say: "Happy are those who have faith. As for us, we were not born with the capacity for it." Rejecting the idea that faith is a universal attitude, correlated to our situation as human beings, many maintain faith is a matter of luck, an innate psychological disposition. The paradox is that in rejecting religious faith they manifest an unquestioned faith in fatalism, as well as a disregard for the inner dynamics of religious existence. Such fatalism breeds, what may be called, *religious bashfulness*. The modern Jew is ashamed to live up to what is in his heart. It would look sanctimonious, if not hypocritical. He is too sophisticated; he is ashamed to pray; he is ashamed to confess that at times he is overpowered by an awe and a sense for the trace of God in the world. Bashfulness, in return, leads to a further alienation.

In the meantime a new religion is emerging throughout the world, a religion in which the body is the supreme object of worship to the exclusion of all other aspects of existence. The pursuit of its pleasures has grown into a cult; its masters are the venerated priests; for its ritual no efforts are spared. We have bartered holiness for convenience, loyalty for success, wisdom for information, joy for pleasure, tradition for fashion.

There is no faith except in the cultivation of the heart, in the depths of the soul, in the ennoblement of the mind.

And this cannot be attained amid the vulgarization of life, or without sensitivity and strain, discipline, effort, and contemplation.

There is no human being without faith. But some worship idols and others the God of Israel. We are free to choose. An idol is what man creates for himself, in his own image, in the image of his concepts, for the satisfaction of his needs and desires. "Dwell in the land and cherish faith" (Psalm 37:3)—"*Lig in der erd, un pasha dich mit emunah*" (Rabbi Mandel of Kotsk). God must not be described as a human need. On the contrary, man must be understood as a need of God. God is either of no importance or of supreme importance. Without Him all is vain: the state, civilization, the life of the individual and of society. What God means is expressed in the words: "For Thy steadfast love is better than life" (Psalm 63:3). God is He whose regard for me I value more than life.

Are we not the ones who spread the idea throughout the world that there is a God who judges the earth, who created heaven and earth, and who chose the prophets of Israel? If there is no God, it is not worthwhile to be a Jew. If there is no God, the work of the prophets of Israel is a scandal of world history.

I repeat: there is no faith without strenuous effort, effort in thought and in deed. Faith is not something snatched from mid-air, *creatio ex nihilo,* something absorbed in a fit of distraction. Awe precedes faith; the sense of wonder, amazement, and embarrassment precedes faith. "Hidden are the things we have seen; we do not know what we see." We must free ourselves from glib phrases, from superficial explanation and ideologies, and learn to behold "the miracles daily wrought for us, the wonders and the goodness, at all times, morning and noon." The way of Judaism is not to adjust God to our understanding but to adjust our understanding to God. The truth is that our religious problem is not a matter of faith but a matter of dread and fear before the awesome grandeur of Jewish existence; not a matter of sentiments or stirrings of the heart. On the contrary, the heart is opaque. "Do not be led astray by your hearts." It is a matter beyond feeling, even beyond understanding. *God is in search of man.*

MAN IN HIS GREATNESS

We are in the habit of saying that the greatest contribution of the Jew is that he was found worthy to know God. Perhaps his contribution is that he was found worthy to know man in his greatness. Only he who grasps the grandeur of man knows the glory that is in Judaism. What is his greatness? His bold attachment to God; his unconditional loyalty to the covenant with God, despite the confusion, disappointments, and God's hiding his face from us; the attachment in the acts of daily life.

It is an axiom with us that a Jew who abandons the people of Israel detaches himself from the God of Israel. But we are prone to forget that he who objects to the God of Israel, betrays the destiny of the people of Israel. Just as there is not a Jew without the people, so there is no people without God. Let us not withhold from our children the knowledge that we shall only endure in the covenant with God. The fate of God is bound up with the fate of Israel. "Ye are My witnesses, and I am God." "When you are My witnesses, I am God; and when you are not witnesses I am not God." We are witnesses, and we sin if we do not bear witness. It is impossible to utter the word "Jew" without recalling His name. There are two Hebrew names for Jew: *Yehudi,* the first three letters of which are the first three letters of the Ineffable Name, and *Israel,* the end of which, *el,* means God.

Judaism is not a matter of blood or race but a spiritual dimension of existence, a dimension of holiness. This dimension comes to expression in events and in teachings, in thoughts and deeds. Israel's strength lies in the knowledge that it is the people of the God of Abraham.

We are proud of the achievements of our technological civilization. But our pride may result in our supreme humiliation. The pride in maintaining, "My own power and the might of my own hand have won this wealth for me" (Deuteronomy 8:17), will cause us to call "the work of our hands our gods" (Hosea 14:4).

We are the bearers of the vision for all men. Shall we extinguish the vision? Habakkuk summarized all of the *mitzvoth* in one verse: "The righteous man shall live by his faith." Jewish belonging entails the love of Israel, love of the present generation and love of all the generations. The past and the present are interlocked. Love of Israel is inconceivable without including those who fashioned our heritage; without love for our generation, we shall never succeed in relating ourselves to Israel of the past. It is incumbent upon us to walk with Moses and Isaiah, Rabbi Jochanan ben Zachai, Maimonides and the Baal Shem, just as it is incumbent upon us to enter into fellowship with our contemporaries. This does not mean that everything which bears the stamp of antiquity is necessarily the best. We have outworn many a garment and many a girdle. But by and large we are inclined to deny the relevance of the past and to exchange the old for what is up-to-date. We forget that it is not in the power of the individual or of a single generation to erect the bridge that leads to truth.

If we agree that the existence of the people depends on the spiritual existence of the individual, then together with our concern for building and strengthening the State of Israel and Jewish communal institutions everywhere we have the important concern for the individual and his problems. To the individuals we say: "Do not detach yourself from the community," and to the institutions we say: "Do not detach yourself from the individual." A Jew without commitment to the spirit, a Jew without faith, without a sense of the importance of Judaism, a Jew without any observance is without Jewish substance. The attachment of the individual to the people is not of lip-service or financial contribution but a commitment in thoughts and deeds.

We have no power to issue decrees. But it is our duty to teach and to proclaim: "Guard the legacy of ages! Without the study of the Torah, without the Sabbath, without festivals, prayer, and attachment to God—there is no Jewish existence."

We succeeded in establishing the State of Israel. The time has come to establish the House of Israel. The State is in the Holy Land; the House of Israel is to be found wherever Jews have settled, a house whose windows are open toward the land of Israel. The consciousness of the people's unity is important for us. But this abstract thought alone is not sufficient to nourish our lives. Unity becomes reality only when translated into a way of living, Judaism is a historical reality, not only an idea in the mind or a sentiment of the heart. It is not a concept which hovers between heaven and earth but a fabric of living thoughts, deeds, and sentiments, and hence neither static nor unchanging. It derives its glow and substance from the sparks of light in the soul of the Jew. Every Jew is bound to bear the eternal light. The soul of man is called a light. Thus do we live in every generation. We derive our sustenance from one another. Just as one candle lights another and suffers no loss, so does a Jew draw renewed power from his fellow men and teachers.

Even if the common man in Israel performs one *mitzvah*, it is as if he had rebuilt one of the desolations of the House of Israel. We must not underestimate the value of modest attachments, even of a moment of reverence or an episode of dedication.

The renewal of the intellectual bond between Jew and Judaism, between the people and its Torah, is the call of the hour. There is no joy except in the understanding. We would do well to realize that the negation of Judaism in the life of the individual has robbed him of his glory. The trouble is that the soul is in exile, that even the Torah is in exile. There is glory in our tradition, but so much has been done to hide it. Modern man is lonely. We cannot force everything upon him. But we must attain the power to reveal to him a life in which there is glory, and say to him: "In this shall you rejoice."

THE GATES OF HALACHA ARE CLOSED

The gates of halacha are closed. No one departs and no one enters. Those inside are not concerned with those on the outside. Those on the outside do not understand those who are within. The door has been locked to those who knock, and those who are anxious to enter grow weary looking for an opening.

There are certain widespread notions which cry for revision. The depersonalization of Jewish thinking has inflicted upon us a negativist conception of halacha. Jewish law has become *"lo* with an *aleph."* We speak of it as if it were only endowed with negative attributes. Even celebrations are regarded as restrictions, as if the primary function of halacha were to restrict, to confine, to deny, and to deprive. Forgotten is the joy and the guidance, the sense of divine relevance of human deeds, the affirmation of man's kinship with God to be experienced in Jewish observance. One does not have to be a scholar in order to experience the eternal majesty of the biblical words. One does not have to be a saint in order to sense that the Sabbath is a delight. "Eternal Life He planted within us." Judaism is an *anchor of ultimate significance* to a tottering world.

There is also the notion that you observe *everything or nothing;* all the rules are of equal importance; and if one brick is removed, the whole edifice must collapse. Such intransigence, laudable as it may be as an expression of devoutness, is neither historically nor theologically justified. There were ages in Jewish history when some aspects of Jewish ritual observance were not adhered to by people who otherwise lived according to the Law. And where is the man who could claim that he has been able to fulfill literally the *mitzvah* of "Love thy neighbor as thyself"?

Intransigence is not the way to this generation. For since only a small minority of those who have forsaken the traditional way of living is prepared to accept the maximum, this notion drives away the overwhelming majority. The intransigent refuse to surrender a single iota, yet are ready to surrender the multitudes of Israel. Is it the way of Torah to say to the majority of our people: "Put the idea out of your minds that you have a share in the God of Israel"? Let us not trample on the heads of the people. We must not write off those who have left, those who are sunk in ignorance. Saving a soul sets aside the Sabbath, and the word "soul" has a double meaning.

Let us bring in the estranged. Even those who have only a minimum of attachment have the capacity for greatness.

Torah as *a total way of living* has been abandoned by the multitudes of our people, and we cannot force it upon them. We must evolve *a pedagogy of return;* we must devise *a ladder of observance.* We have no right to abrogate the Halacha, but we have also no right to abandon the Jewish people. Extremism, maximalism is not the way. Elasticity, flexibility is the way.

Ben Azzai used to say: "Do not despise any man, and do not consider anything as impossible; for there is not a man who has not his hour, and there is not a thing that has not its place." Even those who seem frivolous have moments of sensitivity, moments in which they will respond to those who combine *ahavat torah* with *ahavat Israel,* depth of appreciation with the power of thinking. Both wisdom and love are necessary to show a way how to return.

"Blessed is he who considereth the poor" (Psalm 41:2). One must have understanding and sympathy for those who are poor in spirit. Rabbi Isaac Luria said to his disciple, Rabbi Hayim Vital: " 'Sing, O barren one, who did not bear' . . . for the children of the desolate one will be more than the children of her that is married' (Isaiah 54:1). In our generation even a modest effort a person makes with *kavanah* for the sake of God is much more precious in the eyes of the Lord than the great deeds done in the generations of the past. 'Sing, O barren one'—though the generation looks barren, and its spirit continues to abate. Yet 'the children of the desolate one will be more than the children of her that is married.' "

What is the spiritual level of the multitudes of Israel? It is not on the heights of Torah but in the lowlands, in the valley. Like Ezekiel in his time, we also see the valley full of bones, and they are very dry. It is God who asks: "Son of Man, shall these bones be revived?" The answer is in our hands. Often we say in resignation: "Our bones have dried up." Now despair means paralysis. Indeed, we are spiritually poor. Instead of indulging in the sorrow and admission of our failures, let us undertake a new effort to revive the dry bones.

The mountain of full Jewish living is very high, and few are the men who know how to leap out of the valley to the top of the mountain. If we assert that a Jew has no status unless he lives at the top of the mount and fulfills all the details of all the Commandments, the masses will remain in the valley. Rabbi Judah Ben Baba said: "Not all men or all places or all times are equal."

"The Torah spoke in the language of men." "Come and see how the Voice goes forth to all Israel. Each one hears according to his ability. The old men, the young men, the women, and even Moses— each in the measure of his ability."

There is a way of Shammai of whom it is said: "He pushed him away with the builder's measure he held in his hand," and there is a way of Hillel who said, "Love peace, pursue peace, love man and bring him closer to Torah."

If a man wrongfully takes a beam that belongs to someone else and uses it in building a house or a palace and then the owner of the beam demands that it be returned to him, what is the law? The House of Shammai says: He must demolish the whole palace and restore the beam to its owner. The House of Hillel, however, says that since demolishing the palace would entail too great a loss and prevent the owner from repenting, the owner of the beam can claim only the money value of the beam, instead of the actual beam being restored, so as not to place obstacles in the way of those who wish to repent. For if they had to destroy the whole building they would not offer to make restitution. For the benefit of those who are able to return, we should set up a *ladder* in the valley, *a ladder of learning, a ladder of observance*. To each individual our advice should be: "Observe as much as you are able to, and a little more than you are able to. And this is essential: *A little more than you are able to*."

For such a pedagogy to be effective, it will be necessary to prevent the *tendency to minimalism*. The level of Jewish living must never be stationary. It is the task of religious pedagogy to instill an awareness that there is no standstill in the life of the spirit. We either *ascend* or *go down*.

The law of Hanukkah requires that every man should light one lamp for himself and one for his household. Those who seek to fulfill the law in the best possible manner should, according to the House of Shammai, light eight flames the first night, and every following night one flame less. According to the House of Hillel, the reverse is right: the first night one lamp, to be increased by one on each succeeding night.

Most of us follow the path of regression. The right way is that of the House of Hillel.

The layman will have the strength to ascend if the leader himself continues to rise, if the leader himself retains his position at the top of the ladder.

Many of our people can afford to sanctify the Seventh Day. Many people can afford to set aside times for study, for prayer. One obstacle lies in the soul, and the other obstacle is due to the maximalist conceptions.

Mitzvah goreret mitzvah. He who knows *how to begin* will also learn how to continue, *how to advance.* Provided he begins in the right spirit, provided he begins in reverence for God.

"Thy word is a lamp unto my feet, and a light unto my path" (Psalm 119:105). Why is the word compared both to a lamp and to a light? The psalmist, say the rabbis, intends to say: When I begin to study the words of the Torah, my attainment is modest. But once I enter the words, many gates open up before me.

We are told that the Holy One, blessed be He, prefers the oil of the olive tree to all other oils. So also the sages of Israel. They yearn for the Jew to become pure olive oil. Nevertheless, we have no right to depreciate the other oils. What oils may be used to kindle the Sabbath light? And what oils may not be used? Rabbi Tarfon said: "Only olive oil is to be used." Upon hearing this opinion, Rabbi Jochanan ben Nuri arose to his feet and said: "What shall the Jews of Babylon do who have only sesame oil? What shall the Jews of Persia do who have only peanut oil? What shall the Jews of Alexandria do who have only radish oil? And what shall the Jews of Cappadocia do who have no oil but naphtha?"

The people of Israel are accustomed to miracles and know: "He who commanded the oil to burn will also command the vinegar to burn."

The ladder will be flimsy unless its rungs consist of action as well as insight, of acceptance as well as appreciation. Without a return to reverence, without a revival of the sensitivity of faith, the call to discipline will sound hollow.

"We will make you ornaments of gold studded with silver" (Song of Songs 1:11). It all depends upon the spark of longing for honesty, for meaning, for sanctity.

We must initiate the Sabbath, we must learn how to initiate Jewish acts by kindling a light in the home and a light in the soul, by evoking an insight into the great love story between God and the Community of Israel.

There is a way of conveying not only information but also appreciation. The Lord said to Moses: "This is what everyone who is entered in the records shall pay: a half-shekel by the sanctuary weight" (Exodus 30:13). Moses may have found it difficult to find a way of setting forth to the people what God demands of man. Indeed, it is sometimes more difficult to ask for a half-shekel than for the whole shekel. So Rabbi Meir said: "It was as if the Lord had taken a coin of fire from under His throne of glory and, showing it to Moses, said: They shall give this. They shall give like this."

The Torah is written without vowels. Yet the vowels are the soul of the words. The Torah consists of consonants; we are called upon to supply the vowels. What we need is a way of hearing the vowels while reading the consonants.

The duties of Israel and of the Diaspora

Let us confess: there is no wholeness in the Diaspora. There are sparks but no flame, individuals but no community, schools, synagogues but no Jewish spiritual atmosphere. Only he who has been in the land of Israel knows what the Diaspora lacks.

With the establishment of the State of Israel the whole Jewish world was filled with light. But we have still not learned how to use that light. It has not influenced the way of life in the Diaspora. The heart of the Jew everywhere is bound to the land of Israel with strong, deep ties. In times of crisis he feels that whenever any one touches Israel, it is as if he touched the apple of his eye.

The question of dual loyalty will soon be outmoded. A drastic change in political thinking is bound to bring about new concepts of international relations. We must think not in terms of "dual loyalty" but in terms of "dual residence." Technological developments will do away with geographical distance and separation. A Jew will say his morning prayers in New York and walk in the streets of Jerusalem at sundown. The Jews of the Diaspora yearn to hear a spiritual message from the mouths of the people living in the land of Israel. They have felt the dangers of assimilation in their own flesh, but they are also concerned with the dangers of assimilation in the land of Israel. The settlement of Israel was not a natural thing but a gift of God.

We shall not succeed in repairing our house in the Diaspora without close relations with Israel, without the air of the land of Israel.

The Diaspora Jew has not only a duty to give but a right to receive as well: inspiration from Zion, faith from Zion.

Judaism stands on four pillars: God, the Torah, the people of Israel, and the land of Israel. The loss of any one of these entails the loss of the others; one depends upon the other. And hence every Jew, wherever he may be found, is precious.

The people of Israel is a tree whose roots are in Israel and whose branches are in the Diaspora. A tree cannot flourish without roots. But how can it bear fruit without branches? Be careful with the branches!

Just as there are *mitzvoth* in relation to the land of Israel, so are there *mitzvoth* in relation to the people of Israel. We are bound to Israel with every fiber of our being and we desire to have a share in its upbuilding. In the near future these Jews will begin to look upon the State of Israel in the light of their own problems.

What does the Jew in the Diaspora lack? An additional measure of faith in his Judaism. The Lord made the sea a sea and the dry land, dry land. Moses came and made the sea dry land. So is the life of Israel in the world: they walk on dry land in the midst of the sea. The survival of the Jew is as difficult as the splitting of the Red Sea. But the faith of the children of Israel that God will split the sea for them bore fruit. The Jew of the Diaspora has but a glimmer of awe for the generations, a seed of faith.

What will become of the seed?

14 / *Israel and Diaspora*

A mysterious relationship obtains between the Jewish people and the Jewish land, which remained throughout the ages a challenge to the Jews. It is an integral part of our destiny, and of God's vision of the Messianic kingdom. One cannot detach himself from the land without forfeiting one's position within the covenant. The political and economic realities of the State must not be allowed to obscure that mysterious relationship.[1]

The roots of our attachment to Israel lie in the spiritual depth of our existence, in the depth of prayer, of memory, of involvement in the Jewish tradition. What will be the relationship of the future generations of American Jews to Israel the land? How will Israel the land remain vital and precious to the American Jew a hundred years from now?

One cannot be a Jew except as a part of the Jewish people. But there is no Jewish people without God and Torah. Judaism is neither an experience nor a creed, neither the possession of psychic traits nor the acceptance of a theological doctrine, but the living in a holy dimension, in a spiritual order, living in the covenant with God. It comes to expression in ideas and events, in deeds and thoughts, in moments of prayer and insight, in the study of Torah, in doing the commandments.

Love of Israel embraces not only the Jews of the present but also those of the past and those of the future.

It is not flag-waving. It is the ability to listen to the voice of the prophets. It is our being involved in the wrestling of the great sages for the right understanding of the will of God.

There are three ways of aiding the State of Israel: First, to lend financial and political help to the utmost of our ability. Second, to dwell in the land of Israel. The State of Israel is not only an inspiration but also an embarrassment. One feels abashed at the thought of being a distant spectator while the most dramatic act of building and defending the land is being enacted by others. We have the fleshpots, they watch the borders. The shame of being absent is a new and urgent theme for Jewish apologetics.

How can the Jews of America resist the glory of living in Israel? How is it possible for us to stay away from the great and sacred drama being enacted in the land of Israel?

There is a third way of aiding the State of Israel, which is, in a sense, an answer to the embarrassment I just mentioned: To bring about an inner spiritual and cultural *aliyah* on the soil of America. It is the third form of aid that I should like to dwell upon. What are some of the major problems we face here in America? My answer is: the Jewish home and the Jewish individual.

There are various ailments with which we must deal. Some are part of the general climate of our society. Others are specifically Jewish.

Religion in contemporary society has become an impersonal affair, an institutional loyalty. It survives on the level of activities rather than in the stillness of commitment. It has fallen victim to the belief that real is only that which is capable of being registered by fact-finding surveys.

Inwardness is ignored. The spirit has become a myth. Having lost his awareness of his sacred image, man became deaf to the command to live in a way which is compatible with his image.

Judaism, too, has become an impersonal affair. By Judaism is meant what is done publicly rather than that which comes about in privacy. The chief virtue is social affiliation rather than conviction. Engaged as we have been in building institutions and calling for affiliation, we have neglected to deal with the personal, the private, the intimate.

Judaism without a soul is as viable as a man without a heart. Social dynamics is no substitute for meaning. Yet the failure to realize the fallacy of such substitution seems to be common in our days.

The soul is ignored. Man's form of worship is organization. Instead of examining premises, he is making surveys.

Perhaps this is the most urgent task: to save the inner man from oblivion, to remind ourselves that we are a duality of mysterious grandeur and pompous dust. Our future depends upon our appreciation of the reality of the inner life, of the splendor of thought, of the dignity of wonder and reverence. This is the most important thought: God has a stake in the life of man, of every man. But this idea cannot be imposed from without; it must be discovered by every man. It cannot be preached, it must be experienced.

But there is also the inner Jewish ailment. The detachment from tradition, the loss of memory was, in many cases, not due to a theoretical refutation of the dogmas of Judaism. It was due to the collapse of communication between the realm of tradition and the inner world of the individual. It was due, to a considerable degree, to the loss of understanding for the relevance of the tradition. The daily observance of countless rituals ceased to convey any meaning; they ceased to hold any answer to the countless problems of the individual soul, just as the ancient teachings seemed to be totally unrelated to the modern situation. Ritual had become a routine. There was too much discipline and too little delicacy; many demands, but little development. There was much empathy and not enough self-expression, much acumen and not enough music. Study was super-intellectualized. The energies of the mind were channeled to produce sharpness rather than to appreciate gentleness. Piety was separated from poetry, discipline from delight, obedience from joy. The result was not only abandonment of ritual but also loss of wisdom, loss of inwardness, privation of faith. We have sold insights of three thousand years for the price of iconoclastic and fashionable theories. We have sold our sense of authenticity for opportunities of adjustment. The greatest resistance to the insights and principles of the prophets did not come from wisdom, but from spiritual illiteracy. We have too often regarded the thinking of the prophets as a misunderstanding of reality, as attitudes which derive from such primitive concepts as totem and taboo. As a result, our prophetic past has been lost in our thinking and has gone from our books and our categories.

The crisis of our age has enabled the common man to realize that we are done without God. The possibility of a spiritual regeneration is real. Even those who cannot pray, are craving to pray. Many who cannot revere, feel reverence for reverence.

Our people are ready for a reorientation. The smugness that hovers over the yawning void of many of us can be broken. And when self-contentment will begin to decay, the seed-time for a new flower will have arrived.

We cannot come to the Jews and merely say, "Continue!" The wells that our fathers had digged have been stopped. We have to bore new wells. We have to appeal to what is deepest in man, to awaken and to foster in him the will to be more than he is. The heritage of holiness, accumulated in three thousand years of living, is hidden in the souls of this Jewish generation. It is being suppressed by phobias. Piety is in bad odor. Our work should be *education for reverence*. We should produce some immunity in the soul to the prejudices and imbue the Jew with the courage to fear God.

There is a time for organization, and there is a time for meditation. The task we face now is to build in depth, to endow our people with the ability to pray, with sensitivity, and with the awareness that we are God's stake in human history.

The chief difficulty is that a layman who enters the synagogue will make no effort. He expects the rabbi to give him everything—inspiration, instruction, excitement. Unless a person knows how to pray alone, he is incapable of praying within the congregation. The future of congregational prayer depends on whether the Jews will learn how to pray when they are alone.

I should like to advance a practical suggestion. But first, I must propose a revision of the term "practical." The term "practical" is usually associated with activities capable of being described by statistics, provided they have a mass appeal and require no sacrifice, no reorientation. I should like to stress that acts which happen in the inner life of man, a thought, a moment of prayer, the acquisition of spiritual insight, these too, are practical. External acts are empty shells, if a sense of meaning is not alive in the mind. The most practical problem we face is how to revive the spirit within the Jew. To sit still and to think of the mystery of God, to attach one's inner being to God's concern for human integrity, is just as practical as to attend a congregational meeting. It is vitally important for us to seek a way of opening our minds to the words of the Psalmist, to seek a way of discovering the meaning of the exhortations of Moses.

We have prevailed upon many people to attend a Seder. Now we must teach them how to be personally affected by the spiritual implications of the Seder. The Seder is more than a banquet; it is the actualization of an eternal hope. It is not a ceremony but a vital experience. We must learn how to be personally involved in the acts of Jewish tradition. The miracle of redemption is a daily necessity. It is not only as a people but also as individuals that we must go out of the land of bondage.

The discovery I made in Israel was that, preoccupied as the people are with political and economic problems, there is a great searching and groping for a way of returning to God. It is present among the uncommitted, and the official representatives of religion are unable to cope with it. Soldiers complain that the chaplains are concerned with the problems of dietary laws in the kitchen rather than with the questions of the mind and the longings of the heart. A wide gulf separates the guardians and the uncommitted.

A major root of the tragedy in our living by halacha lies in our detachment from the intellectual, moral, and spiritual teachings of Judaism. Unless we learn how to think as Jews, we will never be able to find meaning in the observance of halacha, whether all or only parts of it.

If our ultimate approach to life is in terms of secularism, all our talking and preaching about halacha, will remain ineffective. We must learn to understand God, man, nature, and society in terms of the prophets and the psalmist. There is a way of conveying to the modern Jew that a sense of contrition is as vital as peace of mind, that humility is not a luxury, that man without a sense for the presence of God is meaningless.

But in order to grasp that Judaism consists not only of rules and regulations, but also offers a cosmos of inner meaning, one must study the great insights into that spiritual cosmos as set forth in our literature throughout the ages which reached its highest flowering in Hasidism.

Some of the most vital books, some of the most inspiring thinkers who have the world of spirit to convey, are hardly a name to most of us.

In his effort to discredit Judaism, Spinoza advanced the thesis that the Bible has nothing to say to the intellect. It was in the spirit of Spinoza that the slogan was created: Judaism has no theology. As a result, modern Jewish education, with very few exceptions, neglected the field of inquiry into the world of Jewish thought. Jewish thought has been kept a well-guarded secret. The hundreds of books which reflect our people's wrestling with the difficulties of faith, with the profundities of biblical themes, are not even known by name.[2]

Intellectual evasion is the great sin of contemporary Jewish teaching. Urgent problems are shunned, the difficulties of faith are ignored. We have lost the sense for the relevance of Judaism, and we run for refuge to all sorts of substitutes.

Judaism today is an unknown religion. The vital issues it raises, the sublime views it discloses, the noble goals it points to are forgotten. We have failed to learn how much Judaism has to say to the mind, to the soul.

Judaism is not a mood, a feeling, a sentimental attachment to customs and ceremonies. Judaism is a source of cognitive insight, a way of thinking, not only an order of living.

We must learn to deal with the doubts, the confusions, and the distortions. Our task is not to satisfy complacency but to shatter it. Our duty is confrontation rather than evasion.

Our future depends upon the realization that to be a Jew means not only to do certain deeds but also to stand for certain thoughts. We must learn to discover the intellectual relevance of Judaism in terms of the moral and spiritual problems of human existence.

Judaism remains irrelevant unless we develop a degree of sensitivity to the ultimate questions which its ideas and acts are trying to answer. To cultivate such a sensitivity as well as a sense of horror to specious answers and to the attempts to vitiate the urgency of ultimate questions is the sacred task of a Jewish teacher.

Unless we overcome the externalization of Judaism, all our efforts will be futile. It is impossible to observe the Seventh Day, week after week, if one's inner life remains untouched and unenriched by it. Unless there is Sabbath in the soul, it is very difficult to remain loyal to the Sabbath laws.

Judaism today survives as a curious relic, of interest to antiquarians. It is becoming more and more parochial. Jewish poetry is dormant. Jewish thought is sterile. We appeal to Jewish loyalties, we have little to say to the imagination.

We are proud of our contributions to modern civilization. But many of these were contributions we made as men of the Western world. Where are the contributions of Judaism itself to modern civilization? How different the world would have been if Heine had been imbued with the spirit of the psalmist, Marx with the spirit of the prophets, and Freud with the spirit of the Ba'al Shem.

Our civilization is in need of redemption. The evil, the falsehood, the vulgarity of our way of living cry to high heaven. There is a war to be waged against the vulgar, against the glorification of power; a war that is incessant, universal. There is much purification that needs to be done, ought to be done, and could be done through bringing to bear the radical wisdom, the sacrificial devotion, the uncompromising loyalty of our forefathers upon the issues of our daily living.

I would be presumptuous were I to underestimate your difficulties. The numerous opportunities of my visits to congregations
gave me a degree of understanding of the loneliness and the manifold frustrations to which a rabbi is exposed. It is hard to preach
about God to people to whom material wealth is almost holy and
the right country club is heaven. It is hard to interpret the words of
the liturgy of the New Year's Day: "Blessed is the man who does
not forget Thee . . ." to people who at that very moment are in a
hurry to drive to the golf course. Yet, there are in every congregation those who are hungry for an inkling of the spirit, who would
appreciate the grandeur of the Torah. It is these people with whom
we must begin. The others may follow.

"The stone which the builders rejected has become the chief
cornerstone." American Jewish youth is one of the wonders of
Jewish history. There is a simplicity of spirit, a readiness for
reverence.

I repeat, it is hard to speak about the holy in an atmosphere
charged with complacency and presumption. Yet, that complacency
is frequently a veneer. Scratch the skin of a human being and you
come upon misery. But only a soul can reach a soul. Only out of a
certainty matured in inner experiences, out of the depth of one's
own silence come words which are audible to the souls of others.

The foremost sources of my own religious insights lie in reverence
for halacha, in my feeble effort to live by it. Elimination of
halacha would be spiritual suicide.

Halacha is the major form of personal and social sanctification
which is a prerequisite for the ultimate redemption of all men. The
fate of one generation may often be determined by the acts of one
man. The future of all peoples may be determined by the mode of
life of one people.

At most Rabbinical Assembly conventions, we spend our time
discussing the areas of public or congregational halacha involving
the function of the rabbi. I do not minimize their importance. But
pedagogically, it is a mistake to concentrate only on these. The
central and more difficult problem is the area of private observance

of both rabbis and laymen. *Halizah* happens once in many years, prayer we must lead every day. Every one of us lives in isolation. My observations told me that the rabbi himself is the *agunah*. He may have devotion to the highest goals, yet he becomes trapped in activities for which he does not care, and carried away by slogans in which he does not believe.

The congregations and national organizations push the rabbi into the role of public relations man, while the real task of the rabbi is to be a *private relations man*.

As a Jew committed to halacha, I say to you that halacha is not the central issue of this generation. This generation does not know how to study nor what to study. We have lost the way that leads to the Bible. We do not learn how to sense the presence of God in the words of the Bible. We all crave religious experiences. But we were not given the insights that would enable us to discover that the observance of the Law is the richest source of religious experience. The whole world is full of opportunities to acquire God. But *mitzvoth* are God's opportunities to take a hold of us.

Let us search for meanings in *mitzvoth*. Not only for meanings in terms of comfort and beauty, but for meanings that convey the certainty that man is more than a mere speck in the universe; he is a priest who carries out God's mission on earth.

Compassion without wisdom may breed cruelty. The sentimental generosity in proclaiming that everybody is a good Jew should be curbed occasionally. Such generosity is an antibiotic, not the food that will keep us alive.

We must not accept the present state of Judaism as final. We must not fail in the vital experiment of the making of the modern Jew. The love of Zion was only a dream, a prayer, and a vision. Yet the power of dedication turned the dream into a reality. Creative Judaism in America is only a dream. But wisdom, a prayer, and the power of dedication may turn it into a reality.

Our greatest mistake is to underestimate the spiritual power of the rabbi. Sermons may be forgotten, but the love, the reverence, the dedication of the rabbi affects the souls of his community and remains alive long after the rabbi has left this world.

Our greatest sin is to underestimate the layman. The best is not good enough. Dedication stirs dedication. We must raise our demands for education of the young and the commitment of the adults.

I do not for a moment underestimate the difficulties and the enormous obstacles we encounter in trying to bring back the spirit of the Sabbath into the Jewish home, or in trying to build day-schools, or in establishing the habit of studying Torah.

The five-day week is becoming a reality. The memories of Sabbath in parents' homes are still alive. It may be our greatest opportunity to face the challenge.

Soon America may have a four-day week. The chief problem will be: what to do with leisure time? The problem will be too much time rather than too little time. If we do not show a way how to sanctify time—by reviving intellectual pursuits—our laymen will have only one way, one solution: to kill time.

We must evolve positive forms. The women in particular can be the pioneers in the art of sanctifying the Seventh Day, provided concrete guidance is offered how to combine rest with spiritual delight.

The combined effort of all of us, the thinking, the imagination, and the dedication, concentrated on the task of disclosing the meaning and vital relevance of the Sabbath to the personal life of the Jew and its being the major source of strength in maintaining the integrity and beauty of the Jewish home and family, will undoubtedly result in a great achievement. It will be through the Sabbath that the Torah will come back to the Jewish home.

Let us go out to those who have gone astray and teach them to distinguish between the upper and the lower levels of life. Many people delight in their wealth and wit; let us delight in reciting Psalms as said by David and the afflicted and martyred Jews of all times. Let us adore the pioneers of prayer in an age of paganism and cruelty. Let us remember those who would never utter a lie, those who would always share their scanty meals with strangers. Let us follow those who kept the company of God in this world of misery, who welcomed angels to their homes on Friday evenings.

1. Compare the remarks on Israel, above, pp. 188 ff.
2. See Heschel, *God in Search of Man,* pp. 24 f., 321 ff.

15 / Jewish Education

I

Life can be seen from many perspectives, analyzed by various scientific methods. In modern times the sociological approach seems to dominate our thinking. One of the clearest examples of this dominance of sociology is the fact that the most frequently discussed topic on lecture platforms, as well as in essays, textbooks, magazines, and surveys, is the question: Are the Jews a race, a people, a religion, a cultural entity, a historic group, a linguistic unit? As if the only important question concerning Judaism and Jewish life were the sociological category to which it belongs! To protest against the autocracy of this way of thinking and to point out the importance of other problems and approaches is not to minimize the validity of the science of sociology. Our intention is to plead for equal rights for other sciences and perspectives, to call for a democracy of thinking. Surely ethics, philosophy, and religion as such are important perspectives. Yet how often do we ask ourselves, "What are we morally? What are we spiritually?" Is not the distinction between right and wrong of greater importance than the distinction between people and religious groups?

It is important that each of us concern himself about the group, but it is equally important that he concern himself about what he is as an individual, as a human being, that he ask himself: What am I, a mass of protoplasm, a complicated robot, a tool-making animal? What is the meaning of my individual existence? Am I anything more than just a physical being? The individual Jew in America today is, in fact, less concerned about whether we are a cultural entity or a historic group than about such problems as the meaning of life and death, the nature of good and evil, love and hatred, and the way to handle envy and jealousy.

The older anthropology used to teach us that there was no place in primitive society for the activities of the individual. The thoughts and actions of every human being were not spontaneous but were imposed on him by social pressures. This concept no longer holds a place in present-day anthropology. But in the last fifty or sixty years we Jews have fallen victim to this anthropological approach through its effects upon Christian theology. Christian theologians used to show the superiority of Christianity to Judaism and the Torah through asserting that Christianity is rooted in the soul of the individual, while supposedly inferior Judaism is nothing but a collective or social religion and hence a primitive one. Religious individualism, according to this theology, came on the scene only in comparatively recent times, as if there were no expression of the individual in the Bible, no command in the Torah, "Thou shalt love," in the second-person singular, no concern with the intimate needs of the individual soul. It was an individual, after all, who tried to save Sodom, an individual who led an impatient and weary-laden tribes for forty years through the wilderness. And it is as individuals, that we pray. We pray for the people, to be sure, but we do so as individuals.

Ethics when built on a sociological approach maintains that man's purpose is to serve society or mankind. The ultimate worth of a person would then be determined by his usefulness to others, by the efficiency of his social work. Yet, in spite of this instrumentalist attitude, man expects others to take him not for what he may mean to them but as a being valuable in himself. Even he who does not regard himself as an absolute end, rebels against being treated as a means to an end, as subservient to other men. The rich, the men of the world, want to be loved for their own sake, for their essence, whatever it may mean, not for their achievements or possessions. Nor do the old and sick expect help because of what they may give us in return. Who needs the old, the incurably sick, the maintenance of whom is a drain on the treasury of the state? It is, moreover, obvious that such service does not claim all of one's life and can therefore not be the ultimate answer of his quest of meaning for life as a whole. Man has more to give than what other men are able or willing to accept. To say that life could consist exclusively of care for others, of incessant service to the world, would be a vulgar boast. What we are able to bestow upon others is usually less and rarely more than a tithe.[1]

It is as individuals, not as members of a mass-mind that we are asked to observe *mitzvoth*. Mitzvoth are folkways in an extremely limited sense. Indeed, folkways cannot be regarded as our ideals or standards of behavior. There was once a folkway to worship a golden calf, to worship a Baal. What of the folkways which have been developed among the Jewish people of America? Does sending *mezuzoth* to the soldiers in Korea as a good luck charm express the spirit of Judaism?[2] We cannot accept social approval as a standard for good and evil or for Jewish authenticity, for the Jewish people may be wrong, just as any individual may be wrong. A group may often act as accumulated selfishness, as the seat of demonic forces. "Right," according to an official proclamation of the German government under Hitler, "is what is useful to the German people." But what is useful to the group may still be wrong and evil. Only false prophets flatter the pride of the people. The true prophets rebelled against folkways, against that which the group preferred. The sacrifice of flesh was known to other nations as well as to Israel; what the prophets called for was the sacrifice of a "broken spirit." "The sacrifice of the Lord is a broken spirit" was a new interpretation of sacrifice which centered it in the individual rather than in the group. When the Bible calls upon us to open the heart (see

Deuteronomy 10:16), it is appealing to the religion of the individual.

The significance of Judaism, therefore, does not lie in its being conducive to the survival of this particular people but in its being a source of spiritual wealth, a source of meaning relevant to all peoples. Sociology, as a result, is not competent to bring out the full significance of Jewish thought and life. It can at best explain the origin of certain phenomena—why they are the way they are—not their meaning and value—not why these phenomena should be maintained. Nor do we receive from sociology an answer to the metasociological question: What caused the causes by which sociology tries to explain those phenomena? The social aspect plays a very great role in Jewish life, but we cannot allow it to eclipse the individual. We teachers face the pupil as an individual: we have to take into consideration his rights and his tasks. To respect these rights and to think of these tasks is the great duty of educators, for to educate means to meet the inner needs, to respond to the inner goals of the child. We dare not commit human sacrifice by immolating the individual child upon the altar of the group.

A contemporary book about Jewish education contains the following passage:

> To the Jewish people as a whole the home and the synagogue customs have been indispensable as bonds of unity and as forces of survival. . . . In thousands of synagogues throughout the world, the same prayers are recited and identical portions of the Bible are read. People who observe the same customs naturally feel more closely united to one another.

Does this definition, which is quite acceptable to a great many of us, express the deeper significance and truth of Judaism? If we look for deeper unity, it must be found not on the level of customs, generalities, and external forms of conduct but on that of the inner life. Nor can the Jewish religion be justified as an instrument of Jewish survival, as this passage implies, any more than the meaning of music can be said to consist of its being an instrument for the survival of society.

II

Let us now discuss the role of psychology in contemporary thinking.

Just as in the Middle Ages sciences were regarded as *ancillæ theologiæ*, it is claimed today that the problems of metaphysics, religion, ethics, and the arts are essentially problems of psychology. There is a tendency which we should like to call *panpsychology*. It proclaims psychology as capable of explaining the origin and development of the laws, principles, and values of logic, religion, and ethics by reducing both form and content of thought and conduct to subjective psychical processes, to impulses and functions of psychical development.

The error of this view lies in its confounding values, laws, or principles with the psychical setting in which they come to our attention. It is fallacious to identify the content of knowledge with the emotional reactions which accompany its acquisition, or concepts with mental functions. Our affirming or denying a conclusion, our saying Yes or No to an idea, is an act in which we claim to assert the truth on the basis of either logical cogency or intuitive certainty. It is precisely the immunity to emotion that enables us to entertain a claim to knowing the truth.

Such a claim is entertained by the panpsychologist himself. Laws must be applied by him to the vague, manifold, and chaotic psychological processes if they are to be classified, interpreted, and made intelligible. But such laws, to be universally valid, must be capable of being logically and epistemologically defended; they must be categories, not psychical processes themselves. Otherwise they would be merely additional subject matter for psychological analysis without any cognitive value. Are we not, then, compelled to admit that there are cognitive acts the validity of which is independent of impulses?

From the point of view of panpsychology we would have to deny it. Yet we have no more right to say that logical categories are the offspring of impulses than to say that impulses are the offspring of categories. Categories are facts of human consciousness which are just as undeniably given as impulses. We seem, in fact, to be more dependent on categories in trying to understand impulses than we are in need of impulses in developing our categories.

Good and evil are not psychological concepts, although the ways in which they are understood are affected by the psychological conditions of the human personality, just as the particular forms in which they are realized are often determined by historical, political, and social conditions. However, good and evil as such do not denote functions of the soul or society but goals and ends, and are, in their essence, independent of the psychical chain of causation.

In his consciousness of good and evil or in complying with religious precepts even at the price of frustrating personal interests, man does not regard his attitude as a mere expression of a feeling: he is sure of reflecting objective requiredness, of striving for a goal which is valid regardless of his own liking. Should we, against the empirical fact of such consciousness, condemn it as wishful thinking or, rather, say that our theories about the relativity of all moral goals result from a time-conditioned decline of attentiveness to ultimate goals?

Man's consciousness of requiredness is, of course, no proof that the particular forms in which he tries to attain his moral or religious ends are absolutely valid. However, the fact of such consciousness may serve as an index of his being committed to striving for valid ends. Man's conception of these ends is subject to change; his being committed endures forever.

In the light of such a realization, it is improper to maintain that our supreme goal is to express the self. What is the self that we should idolize it? What is there in the self that is worthy of being expressed and conveyed to others? The self gains when it loses itself in the contemplation of the nonself, in the contemplation of the world, for example. Our supreme goal is *self-attachment* to what is greater than the self rather than *self-expression*.

Analyze the process of our enjoyment of art. You might mistake it at first as being motivated by the need to find expression for feelings latent in our soul. Yet this would imply that a work of art could not produce an emotion in us if we had not already experienced it in real life; that we would not be capable of responding to a motif if we had not already registered it, though vaguely, in our own heart.

The fact is that we do not turn to art in order to gratify, but in order to create interests and feelings. A work of art introduces us to emotions which we have never cherished before. It is boring unless we are surprised by it. Great works produce rather than satisfy needs by giving the world fresh craving. By expressing things we were not even aware of, works of art inspire new ends, unanticipated visions.

Or does the creative act of the artist originate in a need for self-expression? It is obvious that an artist who is engaged in satisfying his personal need is of little concern to society. His work becomes relevant to the world when in the process of expression he succeeds in attaining ends which are relevant to others. If Honoré de Balzac were solely interested in satisfying his desire for money and prestige, his achievements would have been pertinent to no one else but him. His significance became universal when he succeeded in creating types and situations, the relevance of which had little to do with his own private needs.

It is not the blind need for self-expression that is the secret of a creative personality. Only he who has nothing to say boasts of his urge for self-expression. There must be something to be expressed, an emotion, a vision, an end, which produces the need for expressing it. The end is the basic number, the need is but the coefficient.

I do not want to minimize the great importance of self-expression in the realm of education. I only claim that in order to help a pupil to attain self-expression we must first help him to attain self-attachment, attachment to sources of value experience.

III

As serious as is the problem of autocracy in our thinking, the problem of *apologetics* is equally serious. In the face of the fabulous progress made in secular civilization, the religious man became obsessed with an excessive inferiority complex. In all religions men began to suffer from *a thirst for approbation,* from an eagerness to receive the approval of scientists or men of affairs for the principles of their faith. In some cases faith became contingent on the sanction of the scientists. The religion by approval degenerated into a religion of approval.

But is approbation the test of religious truth? Was it the approval that Abraham received from the sages of Mesopotamia that encouraged him in his lonely faith?

The man who lives by his faith is he who—even if scholars the world over should proclaim, if all mankind by an overwhelming majority of votes should endorse and if experiments, which at times adapt themselves to man's favorite theories, should corroborate that there is no God—would rather suffer at the hands of reason than accept his own reason as an idol; who would grieve, but neither totter nor betray the dignity of his sense of inadequacy in the presence of the ineffable. For faith is an earnest we hold till the hour of passing away, not to be redeemed by a doctrine or even exchanged for insights.

One of the greatest modern scholars the Jewish people has produced, a man to whom we owe a great deal, a man of simply inexhaustible information, is Moritz Steinschneider. One of Steinschneider's books is *Die Arabische Literatur der Juden,* "The Arabic Literature of the Jews." The Arabic writings of Jews include treatises on medicine and philosophy, commentaries on the Mishnah and the Talmud, Responsa, homiletics, works such as Bahya's *Duties of the Heart.* Yet Steinschneider characterizes the significance of his book in his subtitle as *Ein Beitrag zur Literaturge-schichte der Araber*, "A Contribution to the Literary History of the Arabs."

Judaism is not merely a matter of external forms—it is also a matter of inner living. The Sabbath is not essentially a matter of external performance, of prohibitions, restrictions, customs, and ceremonies. It is an answer to one of the deepest problems of human existence, to the problem of civilization. What is happening today? Is Judaism still aware of inner living? We have synagogues, certainly, but we have very little prayer. We have important institutions, but how much spirit do we have? We have observances, but what about principles? We have a great deal of information, but how much appreciation? We have plenty of organization, but how much fellowship? Perhaps our greatest curse is the trend toward *vulgarization* which is taking hold of our lives and of our activities. This trend is in part, at least, a product of *religious behaviorism*— the belief that Judaism glorifies the deed, that it consists exclusively of external conformity, that to be religious is a matter of outward action.

Is it true that Judaism glorifies the deed, regardless of intention and motive? Is it action that is called for and not inner devotion? Is a Jew judged only by what he *does* and not by what he *is*? Religious deeds can be performed in a spiritual wasteland, in the absence of the soul and with a heart hermetically sealed. There are people who believe that external action is the essential mode of worship, that pedantry is the same as piety, that what matters to God is not the inner life but how men behave in physical terms. But *Shema Yisrael* is something more than an external action. *Shema* means "to hear": we have to hear as well as say; we have to understand, to respond. "God asks for the heart." External performance is important, but it must be accompanied by the soul. The mind, the heart are never exempted from being engaged in the service of God. The *mitzvoth* demanding the heart are more numerous even than the *mitzvoth* merely demanding external performance. They are limitless, those *mitzvoth* that require an action of the soul. Every act of man and

especially every *mitzvah* rests on both performance and inner intention, on the deed as well as on the *kavanah*. The duties of the heart
take precedence, in fact, over the duties to fulfill practical precepts.
"They are binding upon us at all seasons, in all places, at every hour,
at every moment, under all circumstances as long as we have life
and reason" (Bahya).

In Jewish tradition we exalt the deed, but we do not idolize
external performance. Nor was this so in the past, not even in the
ritual in the Temple in Jerusalem, whose celebration was surrounded
by great formality. The minutiae of the ritual were very highly
developed, and strange things are still to be found in the laws
concerning the sacrifices in the Temple. The first two tractates of
the Fifth Section of the Mishnah, called Zevachim and Menachot,
are practically like one tractate dealing with these sacrifices. They
begin (Zevachim) with the problems of the inner attitude of the
priest. If the inner attitude of the priest is improper, the sacrifice is
improper. The validity of the ceremony of sacrifice thus depends on
what goes on in the mind of the priest. And at the end of the
tractate of Menachot, the climax of all the laws of sacrifice in which
the minutiae are of so great importance, we read: "It is all the same
whether one offers much or little, provided one directs his heart to
heaven."

It is not only important what a person *does;* it is equally and even
more important what a person *is.* Spiritually speaking, what he does
is a minimum of what he is. Deeds are outpourings, they are not the
essence of the self. Deeds reflect or refine but they remain functions.
They are not the substance of the inner life. Hence it is the inner life
that is the problem for us, Jewish educators, and particularly the
inner life of the Jewish child. On the other hand, we must never
forget that in Judaism we answer God's will in deeds. God asks for
the heart, but the heart is often a lonely voice in the market place of
living, oppressed with uncertainty in its own twilight. God asks for
faith, and the heart is not sure of its faith. It is good, therefore, that
there is a dawn of decision for the night of the heart, deeds to
objectify faith, definite forms to verify belief. A man may entertain

lofty ideals, we know, and behave like an ass. The problem of the soul is how to live nobly in an animal environment, how to persuade and train the tongue and senses to behave in agreement with the insights of the ages. It is to this problem that Jewish observance is meant to be an answer. But do we still teach Judaism as an answer to the questions of the inner life?

To say that the Jewish religion is but a set of rituals is to reduce Judaism to a parochial affair. It is to transform it, as said above, into a system of "sacred physics," rather than a spiritual outlook toward the world and life. A book on education published several years ago says: "Judaism is not a creed, authority within the religion inheres in the code of laws developed through the ages." But this is not true. In Judaism it is necessary to believe in God, to believe that God's revelation is in Torah. It is true that Judaism is much more than a dogma. But this is not because it has no dogmas. It is rather because there are no dogmas which can sufficiently express the depth and grandeur of its insights. Judaism is *not* legalism; this is precisely what the opponents of Judaism claim. It is an answer to the ultimate problems of the individual and of society.

We Jews must not claim that we are better than others. We only claim that we have experienced more than others. Experience passes, but having experienced never passes. Let us remain true to our destiny, to the accumulated experience of ages. A Jew once said a hundred years ago that it is better to have Jews without science than to have science without Jews. How reactionary we thought he was! But today we have a great deal of science and very few Jews. Let us try to save the Jews. Civilization is not our religion, nor is it the religion of any other group in the world. It cannot be. *Civilization is our problem. Judaism is the art of surpassing civilization.* It teaches us how to help cure civilization's ills. Our historic experience has taught us that in order to be human, man must be more than human; that in order to be a people, the Jews must be more than a people. What we must learn all the time is how to rise a little bit above ourselves, how to be a little holy for the sake of our own souls.

Recognizing the vital importance of Jewish education, we should worry less about technique and more about content. We should concern ourselves not only with sociological surveys of education but also with the religious and spiritual aspects of Jewish education. Are we not in need of a survey of its spiritual aspects? I would like to suggest as a goal of Jewish education that every Jew become a representative of the Jewish spirit, that every Jew become aware that Judaism is an answer to the ultimate problems of human existence and not merely a way of handling observances. The philosophy of Jewish education ought to formulate what insights to set forth from and about our tradition. It should also help us technically by showing us how to adjust and express these insights so that they may become a part of the personality of every pupil.

At all religious schools, pupils are taught the benediction to be said before drinking a beverage. It is taught as a custom, as a practice. But how many teachers attempt to convey the grand mystery and spiritual profundity contained in these three Hebrew words—"Everything came into being by His word"? It is unfair and unfortunate that we ignore, withhold, or fail to communicate the spiritual substance of our tradition.

A reorientation in our educational work both in the schools and on the adult level will have to take place. Our goal must be to teach Judaism as a subject of ultimate personal significance. But do we teach it in this way? I taught a class once whose students, young men of about twenty, had studied for many years at Hebrew schools. In this class the problem came up, whether from the point of view of Judaism it is allowed to take revenge. "Of course, it is allowed," they said. In spite of their having gone to Hebrew schools for almost fifteen years, my students had simply never heard of the injunction, "Thou shalt not take vengeance or bear any grudge," words which are a part of the same verse as the words "love your neighbor as yourself." I once examined a student who was interested in becoming a rabbi and asked him the following question: "Will you give me the source of the statement 'Love thy neighbor as thyself'?" The answer was prompt: "The New Testament." Yet this was a student who went to Talmud Torahs and Yeshivahs! Is it not more meaningful for the life of a man that he know the rabbinic interpretation of "Thou shalt not take vengeance or bear any grudge," quoted in Rashi's commentary to that passage, than so many stories which are contained in contemporary Hebrew textbooks? The attitudes recorded in some of the Psalms are no less important, we might assume, than the events recorded in the Book of Judges. Yet how few Psalms are taught in our schools while the Books of Judges and Samuel are always taught. "Christianity is a wonderful religion," a Jewish woman active in a Temple, remarked. "Why does not Judaism have a Book of Psalms?" We say that we have given the Bible to the world. Have we not given it away?

I have asked mature students what the thirteen *middoth* are. Some of them have heard of the thirteen *middoth* of Rabbi Ishmael, the thirteen principles of interpretation. They had never heard, never been moved by one of the central insights of Moses which became the heart of the liturgy on the Day of Atonement: "The Lord, the Lord, a God merciful and gracious. . . ." The most popular Hebrew text taught in America is the berachoth that a Jew is supposed to say when he has an Aliyah. It is something which every Bar Mitzvah boy must know. I have often asked those who teach these berachoth to the boys who are to become Bar Mitzvah whether they pay attention to the meaning of the term *hayye 'olam* and the profound message contained in the phrase "He has implanted in us eternal life." What do we teach the Bar Mitzvah boys? Generalities and externalities. Why not try to teach them the lofty claim of the Jewish spirit? Judaism is a way of action, but it is also a way of inner living. Is it not important to teach our students a verse such as this: "For thus says the high and lofty one who inhabits eternity whose name is holy, 'I dwell in the high and holy place and also with him who is of a contrite and humble spirit'?" (Isaiah 57:15.)

Teaching a child is in a sense preparing him for adolescence. We have to teach him ideas which he can carry over to his maturity. Some of our schools teach subjects which are very entertaining and have their place in the curriculum, but I wonder whether in the later crises of life they will prove to be very helpful. Will they remain alive in his years of maturity, in his bitter trials, disappointments, and frustrations? All our lives we draw upon the inspiration we received in childhood. We have to remember *that* when we face our pupils, when we ask ourselves what we should teach them. I am committing a heresy, I know, if I suggest that we ought to teach them a phrase such as, "Ye shall be holy," the vision of a *neshamah yetherah,* the meaning of *Schechinah,* rather than words such as *kaddur basis,* but heretical I must be. For difficult as it is to teach these matters, it is not impossible. If it is so easy for the scoffers and cynics to teach successfully in an attitude of contempt, the art of being supercilious, why should we completely fail in teaching how to revere? Indeed, if teaching spiritual attitudes is an impossibility, then all of Judaism is a mistake.

The Hebrew term for education means not only to train but also to dedicate, to consecrate. And to consecrate the child must be our goal, difficult as it may be. The survival of the Jewish people is our basic concern. But what kind of survival, we must continually ask, and for what purpose? Many questions come to mind when one analyzes the ideology underlying the content and composition of contemporary textbooks. Is not the Ba'al Shem as relevant as Bar Kochba? Why are there so few studies in the teaching of the Prayer Book? We are divided among ourselves as to ritual observance, it is true. But we must not be divided when it comes to teaching the spiritual attitudes of Judaism. Let us remember that it is not enough to impart *information*. We must strive to awaken *appreciation* as well.

Our goal must be to enable the pupil to participate and share in the spiritual experience of Jewish living; to explain to him what it means to live as a likeness of God. For what is involved in being a Jew? Duties of the heart, not only external performance; the ability to experience the suffering of others, compassion and acts of kindness; sanctification of time, not the mere observance of customs and ceremonies; the joy of discipline, not the pleasures of conceit;

sacrifice not casual celebrations; contrition rather than national pride.

The key word is not "the book." The key word is *talmud torah*, study. What we glorify is not knowledge, erudition, but study and the dedication to learning. According to Rabba "when man is led in for judgment, he is asked . . . did you fix time for learning?" (*Shabbat* 31a).

Man is not asked how much he knows but how much he learns. The unique attitude of the Jew is not the love of knowledge but the love of studying. A learned rabbi in Poland, the story goes, was dismissed by his community because no light was seen in his house after midnight—a sign that he was not studying enough. It is not the book, it is the dedication that counts. Study is an act which is analogous to worship.

Here, of course, everything depends on the person who stands in the front of the classroom. The teacher is not an automatic fountain from which intellectual beverages may be obtained. He is either a witness or a stranger. To guide a pupil into the promised land, he must have been there himself. When asking himself: Do I stand for what I teach? Do I believe what I say? he must be able to answer in the affirmative.

What we need more than anything else is not *textbooks* but *textpeople*. It is the personality of the teacher which is the text that the pupils read; the text that they will never forget. The modern teacher, while not wearing a snowy beard, is a link in the chain of a tradition. He is the intermediary between the past and the present as well. Yet he is also the creator of the future of our people. He must teach the pupils to evaluate the past in order to clarify their future.

Nations are represented by the heads of state. The Jewish people is represented by every individual Jew. This is our message to the world: Man has to learn that the meaning of living is to be an example. A man should always regard himself as though the world were half guilty and half meritorious. One (good) deed may turn the scale of the whole world on the side of guilt or on the side of merit (see *Kiddushin* 40b). Every person participates at all times in the act of either destroying or redeeming the world. The Messiah is in us. This is why every child is of such immense importance.

Implant in each pupil the consciousness that it was for his sake that generations have in spite of suffering insisted upon preserving our tradition. That it is his personal responsibility and high privilege to continue what Abraham inaugurated.

We live in an age in which man's ultimate problems are his most pressing, his most urgent ones. The world is in turmoil and its crisis is not primarily political but spiritual. In this crisis people would in vain turn to psychology or sociology for solutions because these sciences, important as they are, do not have the answer to ultimate problems. There is, in fact, no such thing as "psychology" or "sociology," but only particular theories of psychology or sociology. It is not within their power to answer certain problems with which we are all faced: How can one preserve one's integrity in a world filled with intrigue, flattery, and falsehood? How can a man be constantly exposed to meanness, malice, and jealousy and not be corrupted himself? What is the value of being moral in spite of the defeats of the moral man in the atmosphere of cynicism in which we live? What is the meaning of being alive and of living at this particular time? There is a great deal that philosophy can learn from the Bible, for it is here rather than in formal systems that the answers to these questions are found.

IV

The stream of Sephardic Jewish culture was not confined within the so-called Spanish-Portuguese communities. In the modern period, its influence permeated other Jewish groups, especially in Germany. It was the admiration of nineteenth-century German Jewish scholars for the Sephardic Middle Ages that determined the mood of the modern "science of Judaism" (*Wissenschaft des Judentums*).[3]

The scholars of emancipated German Jewry saw in the Spanish period the "Golden Age" of Jewish history, and celebrated it as a

happy blend of progress and traditionalism upon which they desired
to model their own course. In their research they went to the point
of applying the cultural standards of the "Golden Age" to the literature of later centuries. For some Jewish scholars, any Jewish literature dating after 1492, the year in which Jewish life in Spain ceased,
was not considered worthy of scholarly investigation. Their example
was followed in forming the curricula of the higher schools of
Jewish learning, which gave no place to works written after 1492
and before the beginning of modern Hebrew literature.

This desire for inner identification with the Spanish-Jewish period
reflected itself in the synagogue architecture of the nineteenth
century. Liberal Jewish synagogues in Central Europe were built in
the Moorish style as if the stucco arabesque, horseshoe arches, and
dados of glazed and painted tiles were the aptest possible expressions
of the liberal Jew's religious mood.

Hand in hand with the romantic admiration of the Sephardim
that became one of the motifs of Reform Judaism in Germany went
social aspirations, too. The social standing of the few Sephardim in
Germany was superior to that of the Ashkenazim, and the leaders of
the new Reform movement, anxious to develop a new and more
advanced way of Jewish life that would abandon the traditional
forms still adhered to by the Jewish masses, often blatantly imitated
the manners of the Sephardim. In the Portuguese synagogues they
found that solemnity and decorum which they missed in the old
shul. It was hardly for scientific reasons that the Sephardic pro-
nunciation of Hebrew was introduced in the early "temples."

In consequence, the modern Ashkenazic Jew, particularly in
Central Europe, often came to lose his appreciation of the value of
his own original way of life. He developed an embarrassed aversion
for the dramatic, for the moving and vivid style, whether in the
synagogue or in human relations. For him dignity grew to mean
something to be achieved by strict adherence to an established, well-
balanced, mannerly form undisturbed by any eruption of the sudden
and spontaneous. Thus Hermann Cohen wrote in 1916 that the
elimination of the dramatic manner from the worship of East

European Jews would turn the synagogues into "seats of true culture."

This lack of understanding for and alienation from the values of the Ashkenazic traditions became complete. Describing the way in which the Hasidim prayed, a prominent Jewish historian, in a work first published in 1913 and reprinted in 1931, could write:

> The [Hasidic] movement did not signify a gain for religious life; the asset that lay in its striving for inwardness was more than cancelled out by the preposterousness of its superstitious notions and of its unruly behavior. . . . According to its principles, Hasidism meant a total revolt against the divine service [sic]; nothing could have made the untenability of the latter more striking than the fact that great numbers of people should turn away from it, not out of scepticism or doubt, but out of a most intense yearning for piety. . . . Hasidism contributed to the deterioration rather than to the improvement of the divine service. . . . its noise and wild, restless movements brought new factors of disturbance. . . . It is no wonder that at such a time complaints were made about the lack of devoutness and attention, about the disorder and interruptions. The divine service stood in need of a thorough renovation and restoration if it was to survive. The modern age [the Reform movement] supplied both.

In looking for an orientation for American Jewry, it seems clear that neo-Sephardic modes do not represent the spirit of our own generation. Often they only conceal, or even eradicate, precious elements deeply rooted in the inner life of our people. We cannot afford to dispense with the *niggun,* the spontaneous note that rises from within, simply for the sake of acquiring solemnity an artificial decorum, qualities that hardly express the essential mood of the modern Jew.

Our generation can hardly think of Jewish religious life as an objectivized, ceremonious cult, repeating what is derived from whatever philosophy happens to be in vogue at the moment, and

strictly congruous with contemporary tendencies. Though the ana-
lytical study of Jewish literature and history carried out by the neo-
Sephardic movement has greatly enriched and widened our knowledge, its pedantic and abstract knowledge must be supplemented by
inwardness and spontaneity, by the common experiences and expressions of the people, by the powers won in struggle with immediate
problems, by grief and joy.

We still carry deeply rooted prejudices against the Ashkenazic
heritage, particularly as it was developed in Eastern Europe. That
prejudice has divided us and distorted our sense of values—it has
also had tragic results. In our zeal to expand the scope of our
intellectual endeavors we should beware lest we lose the sense of
that which is our very essence. Hardly a better mirror exists in
which to recognize the unique features of our own origins than the
cultural life of East European Jewry. This must not be measured by
Sephardic standards—to do so would be equivalent to weighing the
beauties of Gothic architecture on the scales of classical Greek. On
the other hand, if the right categories are applied, unique values
will be revealed.

Magnificent synagogues are not enough if they mean a petrified
Judaism. Nor will the stirrings of creative life in the land of Israel
find any echo if brilliance is held more important than warmth.

NOTES

1. See Heschel, *Man Is Not Alone* (New York: Farrar, Straus, 1951);
Who Is Man (Stanford: Stanford University Press, 1965); see also above,
"To Grow in Wisdom," pp. 75 f.

2. The people who sell *mezuzoth* to be worn as amulets, adding, e.g.,
names of angels to the texts, are "among those who have no share in the
world to come. These fools not only fail to fulfill the commandment but
treat an important *mitzvah* that expresses the unity of God, the love of
Him and His worship, as if it were an amulet to promote their own
personal interests; for according to their foolish minds the *mezuzah* is
something that will secure for them advantages in the vanities of this
world," Maimondes, *Mishneh Torah*, Hilchoth Tefillin, 5, 4.

3. See Heschel, *The Earth is the Lord's* (New York: Abelard-
Schuman), pp. 23 ff.

16 / *The Vocation of the Cantor*

What does a person expect to attain when entering a synagogue? In the pursuit of learning one goes to a library; for aesthetic enrichment one goes to the art museum; for pure music to the concert hall. What then is the purpose of going to the synagogue? Many are the facilities which help us to acquire the important worldly virtues, skills, and techniques. But where should one learn about the insights of the spirit? Many are the opportunities for public speech; where are the occasions for inner silence? It is easy to find people who will teach us how to be eloquent; but who will teach us how to be still? It is surely important to develop a sense of humor; but is it not also important to have a sense of reverence? Where should one learn the eternal wisdom of compassion? the fear of being cruel? the danger of being callous? Where should one learn that the greatest truth is found in contrition? Important and precious as the development of our intellectual faculties is, the cultivation of a sensitive conscience is indispensable. We are all in danger of sinking into the darkness of vanity; we are all involved in worshiping our own egos. Where should we become sensitive to the pitfalls of cleverness, or to the realization that expediency is not the acme of wisdom?

We are constantly in need of self-purification. We are in need of experiencing moments in which the spiritual is as relevant and as concrete, for example, as the aesthetic. Everyone has a sense of beauty; everyone is capable of distinguishing between the beautiful and the ugly. But we also must learn to be sensitive to the spirit. It is in the synagogue where we must try to acquire such inwardness, such sensitivity.

To attain a degree of spiritual security one cannot rely upon one's own resources. One needs an atmosphere, where the concern for the spirit is shared by a community. We are in need of students and scholars, masters and specialists. But we need also the company of witnesses, of human beings who are engaged in worship, who for a moment sense the truth that life is meaningless without attachment to God. It is the task of the Cantor to create the liturgical community, to convert a plurality of praying individuals into a unity of worship.

Pondering his religious existence a Jew will realize that some of the greatest spiritual events happen in moments of prayer. Worship is the source of religious experience, of religious insight, and religiously some of us live by what happens to us in the hours we spend in the synagogue. These hours have been in the past the wellsprings of insight, the wellsprings of faith. Are these wellsprings still open in our time?

Following a service, I overheard an elderly lady's comment to her friend, "This was a charming service!" I felt like crying. Is this what prayer means to us? God is grave; He is never charming. But we think that it is possible to be sleek and to pray, "Serve the Lord with fear and rejoice with trembling" (Psalm 2:11). Prayer is joy and fear, trust and trembling together.

I grew up in a house of worship where the spiritual was real. There was no elegance, but there was contrition; there was no great wealth, but there was great longing. It was a place where when seeing a Jew I sensed Judaism. Something happened to the people when they entered the house of worship. To this day every time I go to the synagogue my hope is to experience a taste of such an atmosphere. But what do I find within the contemporary synagogue? We are all in agreement about the importance of prayer. Cantors dedicate their lives to the art of leading our people in prayer. Indeed, of all religious acts, prayer is the most widely observed. Every Seventh Day hundreds of thousands of Jews enter the synagogue. But what comes to pass in most of our services?

One must realize the difficulties of the Cantor. The call to prayer often falls against an iron wall. The congregation is not always open and ready to worship. The Cantor has to pierce the armor of indifference. He has to fight for a response. He has to conquer them in order to speak for them. Often he must first be one who awakens those who slumber, before he can claim to be a *sheliaḥ ṣibbur*. And yet we must not forget that there is a heritage of spiritual responsiveness in the souls of our people. It is true, however, that this responsiveness may waste away for lack of new inspiration, just as fire burns itself out for lack of fuel.

The tragedy of the synagogue is in the depersonalization of prayer. *Ḥazzanuth* has become a skill, a technical performance, an impersonal affair. As a result the sounds that come out of the *ḥazzan* evoke no participation. They enter the ears; they do not touch the hearts. The right Hebrew word for Cantor is *ba'al tefillah*, master of prayer. The mission of a Cantor is to lead in prayer. He does not stand before the Ark as an artist in isolation, trying to demonstrate his skill or to display vocal feats. He stands before the Ark not as an individual but with a Congregation. He must identify himself with the Congregation. His task is to represent as well as to inspire a community. Within the synagogue music is not an end in itself but a means of religious experience. Its function is to help us to live through a moment of confrontation with the presence of God; to expose ourselves to Him in praise, in self-scrutiny and in hope.

We have adopted the habit of believing that the world is a spiritual vacuum; whereas the seraphim proclaim that "the whole earth is full of His glory." Are only the seraphim endowed with a sense for the glory? "The heavens declare the glory of God." How do they declare it? How do they reveal it? "There is no speech, there are no words, neither is their voice heard." The heavens have no voice; the glory is inaudible. And it is the task of man to reveal what is concealed; to be the voice of the glory, to sing its silence, to utter, so to speak, what is in the heart of all things. The glory is here—invisible and silent. Man is the voice; his task is to be the song. The cosmos is a congregation in need of a Cantor. Every Seventh Day we proclaim as a fact.

> They all thank Thee,
> They all praise Thee,
> They all say,
> There is none holy like the Lord.

Whose ear has ever heard how all trees sing to God? Has our reason ever thought of calling upon the sun to praise the Lord? And yet, what the ear fails to perceive, what reason fails to conceive, our prayer makes clear to our souls. It is a higher truth, to be grasped by the spirit: "All Thy works shall give Thee thanks, O Lord" (Psalm 145:10).

We are not alone in our acts of praise. Wherever there is life, there is silent worship. The world is always on the verge of becoming one in adoration. It is man who is the Cantor of the universe, and in whose life the secret of cosmic prayer is disclosed. To sing means to sense and to affirm that the spirit is real and that its glory is present. In singing we perceive what is otherwise beyond perceiving. Song, and particularly liturgical song, is not only an act of expression but also a way of bringing down the spirit from heaven to earth. The numerical value of the letters which constitute the word *shirah*, or song, is equal to the numerical value of the word *tefillah*, or prayer.[1] Prayer is song. Sing to Him, chant to Him, meditate about all the wonders (I Chronicles 16:9), about the mystery that surrounds us. The wonder defies all descriptions; the mystery surpasses the limits of expression. The only language that seems to be compatible with the wonder and mystery of being is the language of music. Music is more than just expressiveness. It is rather a reaching out toward a realm that lies beyond the reach of verbal propositions. Verbal expression is in danger of being taken literally and of serving as a substitute for insight. Words become slogans, slogans become idols. But music is a refutation of human finality. Music is an antidote to higher idolatry.

While other forces in society combine to dull our mind, music endows us with moments in which the sense of the ineffable becomes alive.

Listening to great music is a shattering experience, throwing the soul into an encounter with an aspect of reality to which the mind can never relate itself adequately. Such experiences undermine conceit and complacency and may even induce a sense of contrition and a readiness for repentance. I am neither a musician nor an expert on music. But the shattering experience of music has been a challenge to my thinking on ultimate issues. I spend my life working with thoughts. And one problem that gives me no rest is: do these thoughts ever rise to the heights reached by authentic music?

It has been said that at the time when one who had transgressed the Law brought his sacrifice to the holy temple in Jerusalem, the priest would look at him and perceive all his thoughts. If he found that the man had not yet repented completely, the priest would direct the Levites to begin to chant a melody, in order to bring the sinner to *teshubah.*

Music leads us to the threshold of repentance, of unbearable realization of our own vanity and frailty and of the terrible relevance of God. I would define myself as a person who has been smitten by music, as a person who has never recovered from the blows of music. And yet, music is a vessel that may hold anything. It may express vulgarity; it may impart sublimity. It may utter vanity; it may inspire humility. It may engender fury, it may kindle compassion. It may convey stupidity and it can be the voice of grandeur. If often voices man's highest reverence, but often brings to expression frightful arrogance.

Cantorial music is first of all music in the service of the liturgical word. Its core is *nussaḥ,* and its integrity depends upon the cultivation of *nussaḥ.* Elsewhere I have suggested[2] that one of the main causes of the decay of prayer in the synagogue is the loss of *nussaḥ,* the loss of chant; and surely the disengagement of cantorial music from the *nussaḥ* has been most harmful. To pray without *nussaḥ* is to forfeit the active participation of the community. People may not be able to pray; they are all able to chant. And chant leads to prayer. What I mean by the disengagement of cantorial music from the liturgical word is not singing without words, but singing in a way which contradicts the words. It is both a spiritual and a technical matter. The Cantor's voice must neither replace the words nor misinterpret the spirit of the words. The Cantor who prefers to display his voice rather than to convey the words and to set forth the spirit of the words, will not bring the congregation closer to prayer. "Be humble before the words," should be the cantorial imperative.

Music is a serious pretender to the place of religion in the heart of man, and the concert hall is to many people a substitute for the synagogue. The separation of music from the word may, indeed, foster a spirituality without a commitment and render a greater service to the advancement of concert music than to the enrichment of synagogue worship.

A Cantor who faces the holiness in the Ark rather than the curiosity of man will realize that his audience is God. He will learn to realize that his task is not to entertain but to represent the people Israel. He will be carried away into moments in which he will forget the world, ignore the congregation, and be overcome by the awareness of Him in whose presence he stands. The congregation then will hear and sense that the Cantor is not giving a recital but worshiping God, that to pray does not mean to listen to a singer but to identify oneself with what is being proclaimed in their name.

Entering the synagogue, I first relinquish all I know and try to begin all over again. The words are sometimes open, and at other times locked. Even in such embarrassment song is a sphere that will admit even the poor in faith. It is so far off, and yet we are all there. Pride begins to fade bit by bit, and praise begins to happen. The cantorial voice is a door, but often the banging of the door jars and tears our sensitivity to shreds.

Mankind is always on trial, and the cross-examination of the soul is audible in music. One of the things reflected in modern cantorial music is the lack of the sense of mystery which is at the very root of religious consciousness. Music gains its religious dimension when ceasing to be satisfied with conveying that which is within the grasp of emotion and imagination. Religious music is an attempt to convey that which is within our reach but beyond our grasp. The loss of that tension throws all cantorial music into the danger of becoming a distortion of the spirit.

Music is the soul of language. A good sentence is more than a series of words grouped together. A sentence without a tone, without a musical quality, is like a body without a soul. The secret of a good sentence lies in the creation of a tonal quality to correspond to the meaning of the words. There has to be a harmony of the right tone and the right words. Such harmony is often painfully missing in cantorial expression. One is shocked to hear how magnificent thoughts are uttered in a false tone: sublime words and crude melodies. So much of what we hear in the synagogue is alien to our liturgy. So much of the music we hear distorts and even contradicts the words, instead of enhancing and glorifying them. Such music has a crushing effect upon our quest for prayer. One feels frequently hurt when listening to some of the melodies in modern synagogues.

It is a fact that just as there are speakers who are better than their words, there are Cantors who are better than their melodies. But this is not only a matter of personal importance. The future of Jewish prayer is to a considerable degree in the power of the Cantor

The *siddur* is a book which everyone talks about, but few people have really read; a book which has the distinction of being one of the least known books in our literature. Do we ever ponder the meaning of its words? Do we seek to identify our inner life with what is proclaimed in the *nishmath:* "The soul of every living being blesses Thy name, Lord our God . . ."? And yet, there are those who claim that the *siddur* does not express the needs, wants, aspirations of contemporary man.

We must learn how to study the inner life of the words that fill the world of our Prayer Book. Without intense study of their meaning, we indeed feel bewildered when we encounter the multi-

THE VOCATION OF THE CANTOR

tude of those strange, lofty beings that populate the inner cosmos of the Jewish spirit. The trouble with the Prayer Book is that it is too great for us, too lofty. Our small souls must first rise to its grandeur. We have failed to introduce our minds to its greatness, and our souls are lost in its sublime wilderness. It is not enough to know how to translate Hebrew into English; it is not enough to have met a word in the dictionary and to have experienced unpleasant adventures with it in the study of grammar. A word has a soul, and we must learn how to attain insight into its life. Words are commitments, not only the subject matter for aesthetic reflection.

This is our affliction. We say words but make no decisions. We do not even know how to look across a word to its meaning. We forget how to find the way to the word, how to be on intimate terms with a few passages in the Prayer Book. We are familiar with all words, but at home with none. The *siddur* has become a foreign language which the soul does not know how to pronounce.

In order for cantorial music to regain its dignity, it will not be enough to study the authentic pattern of our musical tradition. What is necessary is a *liturgical revival*. This will involve not only a new sense of reverence and faith, but also a new insight into the meaning of the liturgical words as well as an intimate way of uttering and appropriating the words. The decline of *hazzanuth* will continue as long as we fail to realize that reverence and faith are as important as talent and technique, and that the music must not lose its relationship to the spirit of the words.

It is important for the Cantor to study the score, but it is also important to study the words of the Prayer Book. The education of the Cantor calls for intellectual and not only aesthetic achievements. In Judaism study is a form of worship, but it may also be said that worship is in a sense a form of study; it includes meditation. It is not enough to rely on one's voice. It takes a constant effort to find a way to the grandeur of the words in the Prayer Book.

What are we exposed to in the atmosphere of the synagogue? We are exposed neither to sacred words alone, nor to spiritual tunes alone. This, indeed, is the essence of our liturgy. It is a combination of word *and* music. Great as music is, it is neither the ultimate nor the supreme. The ultimate is God, and the medium in which His guidance has been conveyed to us is *the word*. We have no holy music; we revere sacred Scripture, sacred words. Music is the language of mystery. But there is something which is greater than mystery. God is the meaning beyond all mystery. That meaning is concealed in the biblical words, and our prayers are an attempt to disclose to ourselves what is concealed in those words.

For all its grandeur, there is something greater than music. At Sinai we heard thunder and lightning, but it was not the music of the elements but the word, for the sake of which the great event happened. The Voice goes on forever, and we are being pursued by it. We have neither icons nor statues in our synagogue. We are not even in need of visible symbols to create in us a mood of worship. All we have are words in the liturgy and reverence in our hearts. But even these two are often apart from each other. It is the task of music to bring them together.

"Who shall ascend the hill of the Lord, and who shall stand in His holy place? He who has clean hands and a pure heart, and who does not lift up his soul to what is false and does not swear deceitfully" (Psalm 24:3-4). Not by might of voice, not by strength of talent alone, but by the sense of awe and fear, by contrition and the sense of inadequacy, will a Cantor succeed in leading others to prayer. The Cantor must constantly learn how to be involved in what he says, realizing that he must also teach others how to attach themselves to the words of the liturgy. He has a secret mission to convert, to lead people to a point where they can sense that arrogance is an abyss and sacrifice is eternity.

There are hardly proofs for the existence of God, but there are witnesses. Foremost among them are the Bible and music. Our liturgy is a moment in which these two witnesses come to expression. "On the evidence of two witnesses a claim is sustained." Our liturgy consists of the testimony of both music and the word. Perhaps this is the way to define a *ba'al tefillah*. He is a person in whom the two witnesses meet. He is a person in whom a spiritual equation takes place—the equation of song and soul, of word and mind. The self and prayer are one.

I should like to conceive *hazzanuth* as the art of *siddur* exegesis, as the art of interpreting the words of the liturgy. Words die of routine. The Cantor's task is to bring them to life. A Cantor is a person who knows the secret of the resurrection of the words. The art of giving life to the words of our liturgy requires not only the personal involvement of the Cantor but also the power contained in the piety of the ages. Our liturgy contains incomparably more than what our hearts are ready to feel. Jewish liturgy in text and in song is a spiritual summary of our history. There is a written and an unwritten Torah, Scripture and tradition. We Jews claim that one without the other is unintelligible. In the same sense we may say that there is a *written and an unwritten liturgy*. There is the liturgy but there is also an inner approach and response to it, a way of giving life to the words, a style in which the words become a personal and unique utterance.

The Lord commanded Noah: "Go into the *tevah,* you and all your household" (Genesis 7:1). *Tevah* means ark; it also means word. In prayer a person must enter the word with all he has, with heart and soul, with thought and voice. "Make a light for the *tevah.*" The word is dark. This is the task of him who prays: to kindle a light in the word.[3] Humbly we must approach both the word and the chant. We must never forget that the word is deeper than our thought, that the song is more sublime than our voice. The words enhance us. The rabbis maintain that "those who carried the Ark were actually carried by the Ark."[4] And indeed he who knows how to carry a word in all its splendor is carried away by the word. He who has succeeded in kindling a light within the word will discover that the word has kindled a light within his soul. Where is the *Shekhinah?* Where is the presence of God to be sensed? According to *Tikkune Zohar* the *Shekhinah* is in words, God is present in sacred words. In praying we discover the holiness in words.

Song is the most intimate expression of man. In no other way does man reveal himself so completely as in the way he sings. For the voice of a person, particularly when in song, is the soul in its full nakedness. When we sing, we utter and confess all our thoughts. In every sense *hazzanuth is hishtapkhuth hanefesh* (outpouring of the heart). There is a story about the Ba'al Shem who was once listening most intently to a musician. When his disciples asked him why he was so absorbed in what he heard, the Ba'al Shem replied: When a musician plays he pours out all he has done.

Indeed, a Cantor standing before the Ark reveals all his soul, utters all his secrets. The art of being a Cantor involves the depth, richness and integrity of personal existence. There is a story about a hasidic rabbi in Galicia, among whose adherents were many *hazzanim*. Their custom was to gather at the rabbi's court for the Sabbath which precedes Rosh Hashanah. At the end of their stay they would enter the rabbi's chamber and ask for his blessing that their prayers on Rosh Hashanah be accepted in heaven. Once, the story goes, one of the *hazzanim* entered the rabbi's chamber immediately after the Sabbath to take leave of the rabbi. When the rabbi asked him, why he was in a hurry to leave, the *hazzan* replied, "I must return home in order to go through the *Mahzor* (The Liturgy for the Days of Awe) and to take a look at the notes." Thereupon the rabbi replied, "Why should you go through the *Mahzor* or the notes; they are the same as last year. It is more important to go through your own life, and take a look at your own deeds. For you are not the same as you were a year ago." The *hazzan* was no longer in a hurry to leave.

Awe is the prerequisite of faith and an essential ingredient of being a Cantor. The loss of awe one must feel in the presence of a congregation, unawareness of how poor we are in spirit and in deeds, is a dangerous deprivation.

A learned man lost all his sources of income and was looking for a way to earn a living. The members of his community, who admired him for his learning and piety, suggested to him to serve as their Cantor on the Days of Awe. But he considered himself unworthy of serving as the messenger of the community, as the one who should bring the prayers of his fellow men to the Almighty. He went to his master, the rabbi of Husiatin, and told him of his sad plight, of the invitation to serve as a Cantor in the Days of Awe, and of his being afraid to accept it and to pray for his congregation. *"Be* afraid—and pray," was the answer of the rabbi.

NOTES

1. Rabbi Bahya ben Asher, *Commentary,* Numbers 21:19.
2. See Heschel, *Man's Quest for God,* "Studies in Prayer and Symbolism" (New York: Charles Scribner's Sons, 1954), pp. 51, 89.
3. According to the Ba'al Shem.
4. When the priests that bore the ark of the covenant of the Lord crossed the waters of Jordan (Joshua 4:11 ff.), "the ark carried its bearers" (Babylonian Talmud, Sotah 35a).

17 / Prayer as Discipline

The universe would be an inferno without a God who cares. There is no echo within the world for the agony and cry of humanity. There is only God who hears.

Consider the disproportion of misery and compassion. The depth of anguish is an abyss, its intricacies are a veritable labyrinth, and our grasp of it may be compared to the grasp of a butterfly flying over the Grand Canyon. Callousness, the dreadful incompatibility of existence and response, is man's outstanding failure. For the sin we have sinned in not knowing how much we sin, we cry for forgiveness. Dark is the world for me for all its cities and stars. If not for the certainty that God listens to our cry, who could stand so much misery, so much callousness?

The mystery and the grandeur of the concern of the infinite God for the finite man is the basic insight of biblical tradition. This mystery is enhanced by the aspect of immediacy. God is *immediately* concerned. He is not concerned through intermediate agents. He is personally concerned.

I

Prayer is more than a cry for the mercy of God. It is more than a spiritual improvisation. Prayer is a condensation of the soul. It is the whole soul in one moment, the quintessence of all our acts, the climax of all our thoughts. For prayer to live in man, man has to live in prayer. In a sense, prayer is a part of a greater issue. It depends upon the total moral and spiritual situation of man, it depends upon a mind within which God is at home. Of course, there are lives which are at the bottom too barren to bring forth a thought in the presence of God. If all the thoughts and anxieties of such people do not contain enough spiritual substance to be distilled into prayer, an inner transformation is a matter of emergency.

The only way we can discuss prayer is on the basis of self-reflection, trying to describe what has happened to us in a rare and precious moment of prayer. The difficulty of self-reflection consists in the fact that what is given to us is only a recollection. You cannot, of course, analyze the act of prayer while praying. To worship God means to forget the self; an extremely difficult, though possible, act. What takes place in a moment of prayer may be described as a shift of the center of living—from self-consciousness to self-surrender. This implies, I believe, an important indication of the nature of man. Prayer begins as an "it-He" relationship. I am not ready to accept the ancient concept of prayer as a dialogue. Who are we to enter a dialogue with God? The better metaphor would be to describe prayer as an act of immersion, comparable to the ancient Hebrew custom of immersing oneself completely in the waters as a way of self-purification to be done over and over again. Immersion in the waters! One feels surrounded, touched by the waters, drowned in the waters of mercy. In prayer the "I" becomes an "it." This is the discovery: what is an "I" to me is, first of all and essentially, an "it" to God. If it is God's mercy that lends eternity to a speck of being which is usually described as a self, then prayer begins as a moment of living as an "it" in the presence of God. The closer to the presence of Him, the more obvious becomes the absurdity of the "I." The "I" is dust and ashes. "I am dust and ashes," says Abraham; then he goes on in dialogue to argue with the Lord, about saving the cities of Sodom and Gomorrah. How does Moses at the burning bush respond to the call to go to the people of Israel and to bring to them the message of redemption? "Who am I that I should go to Pharaoh and bring the children out of Egypt?" Only God says "I." This is how the Ten Commandments begin: "I am the Lord."

Prayer is a moment when humility is a reality. Humility is not a virtue. Humility is truth. Everything else is illusion. In other words it is not as an "I" that we approach God, but rather through the realization that there is only one "I." Now it is our being precious to Him that sets us apart from being merely an accidental by-product of the cosmic process. This is why in Jewish liturgy primacy is given to prayer of praise. One must never begin with supplication. One begins with praise because praise is the prerequisite and essence of prayer. To praise means to make Him present, to make present not only His power and splendor but also His mercy. His mercy and His power are one.

II

How does man become a person, an "I"? By becoming a thought of God. Man lives on earth as a self but also as an object of divine concern. Such discovery is the reward of prayer. Such realization is the major motivation in piety. This is the goal of the pious man: to become worthy to be remembered by God.

Thus the purpose of prayer is to be brought to God's attention: to be listened to, to be understood by Him. In other words, the true task of man is not to know God but to be known to God. Here lies the meaning of living according to religious discipline: to make our existence worthy of being known to God. This may not be the essence of grace but it is the gate to grace.

Are we worthy of entering into His mercy, of being a matter of concern to Him? The answer is given in prayer. Prayer is the affirmation of the preciousness of man. Prayer may not save us, but it makes us worthy of being saved.

There is no human misery more strongly felt than the state of being forsaken by God. Nothing is more dreadful than rejection by Him. Rejection, being forsaken, living a life deserted by God, is possible. But it is the fear of being forgotten that is a powerful spur to a person to enter prayer, to bring himself to the attention of God. In prayer we learn that it is better to be smitten by His punishment than to be left alone. Perhaps all prayer may be summarized in one utterance: "Do not forsake us, O Lord."

Prayer is not speculation. In speculation, God is an object; to the man who prays, God is the subject. When awakening to the presence of God, we do not strive to acquire objective knowledge but to deepen a mutual allegiance. What we long for in such moments is not to know Him but to be known to Him; not to form judgments about Him but to be judged by Him; not to make the world an object of our mind but to augment His, rather than our, knowledge. We endeavor to disclose ourselves to the Sustainer of all rather than to enclose the world in ourselves.

To disclose the self we must learn how to cast off the shells of ambition, of vanity, of infatuation with success. We are all very poor, very naked, and rather absurd in our misery and in our success. We are constantly dying alive. From the view of temporality we are all dead except for a moment. There is only one bridge over the abyss of despair: prayer.

The presence of God is the absence of despair. In the stillness of sensing His presence misery turns to joy, despair turns to prayer. I repeat, prayer is more than a cry out of anguish. It is rather a moment of sensing His mercy. Let me make clear what I mean. A moment of supplication is an expression of what we need at the moment. A person may go on pondering deeply in intense emotion about his needs, about the need of the moment. That is not yet prayer. Adding "in the name of God" to it will not make it prayer. It is the cry of anguish which becomes a realization of God's mercy that constitutes prayer. It is the moment of a person in anguish forgetting his anguish and thinking of God and His mercy. That is prayer. Not self-reflection, but the direction of the entire person upon God. It is a difficult but not impossible situation. It may last a moment but it is the essence of a lifetime.

III

The true motivation for prayer is not, as it has been said, the sense of being at home in the universe, but rather the sense of not being at home in the universe. Is there a sensitive heart that could stand indifferent and feel at home in the sight of so much evil and suffering, in the face of countless failures to live up to the will of God? On the contrary, the experience of not being at home in the world is a motivation for prayer. That experience gains intensity in the amazing awareness that God himself is not at home in the universe. He is not at home in a universe where His will is defied and where His kingship is denied. God is in exile; the world is corrupt. The universe itself is not at home. To pray means to bring God back into the world, to establish His kingship for a second at least. To pray means to expand His presence. In the most important moment of the Jewish liturgy, we cry out of the depth of our disconcerted souls a prayer for redemption. "Lord our God, put Thy awe upon all whom Thou hast made, Thy dread upon whom Thou hast created, so that all Thy works may revere Thee, and all that Thou hast created may prostrate themselves before Thee, and all form one union to do Thy will wholeheartedly." To worship, therefore, means to make God immanent, to make Him present. His being immanent in the world depends upon us. When we say "Blessed be He," we extend His glory, we bestow His spirit upon the world. In other words, what underlies all this is not a mystic experience of our being close to Him but the certainty of His being close to us and of the necessity of His becoming closer to us.

Let me warn against the equating of prayer with emotion. Emotion is an important component of prayer, but the primary presupposition is conviction. If such conviction is lacking, if the presence of God is a myth, then prayer to God is a delusion. If God is unable to listen to us, then we are insane in talking to Him. All this presupposes conviction. The source of prayer then is an insight rather than an emotion. It is the insight into the mystery of reality;

it is, first of all, the sense of the ineffable that enables us to pray. As long as we refuse to take notice of what is beyond our sight, beyond our reason, as long as we are blind to the mystery of being, the way to prayer is closed to us. If the rising of the sun is but a daily routine of nature there is no reason for us to praise the Lord for the sun and for the life we live. The way to prayer leads to acts of wonder and radical amazement. The illusion of total intelligibility, the indifference to the mystery that is everywhere, the foolishness of ultimate self-reliance, are serious obstacles on the way. It is in the moment of our being faced with the mystery of living and dying, of knowing and not knowing, of loving and the inability to love that we pray, that we address ourselves to Him who is beyond the mystery.

IV

Finally, I should like to mention an important problem to which, I believe, proper attention has not been given. It is the problem of the relation between words and prayer. One of the major symptoms of the general crisis existent in our world today is our lack of sensitivity to words (see "Religion in a Free Society," p. 17). We use words as tools. We forget that words are a repository of the spirit. The tragedy of our times is that the vessels of the spirit are broken. We cannot approach the spirit unless we repair the vessels.

Reverence for words—an awareness of the wonder of words, of the mystery of words—is an essential prerequisite for prayer. By the word of God the world was created. Without sensitivity to words there can be no relationship to the Bible and no prayer in the tradition of the Bible. We have forfeited reverence for words. We have trifled with the name of God. We have taken his commandments in vain. Purification of language, therefore, remains a major task in theological discipline. Beginning by stressing strongly sensitivity to words, its goal must be the sanctification of human speech.

It takes two things for prayer to come to pass—a person and a word. Prayer involves a right relationship between those two things. But we have lost that relationship. Involved as we are in many relationships, our relationship to words has become totally obscured. We do not think about words, although few things are as important for the life of the spirit as the right relationship to words. Words have become clichés, objects of absolute abuse. They have ceased to be commitments. We forget that many of our moral relationships are based upon a sense of the sacredness of certain words. It is true that prayer is not only an act that takes place by means of words. There is also a form of prayer that is beyond expression. But this is a rare form. For the most part prayer lives in words, and it is in the relationship to the word of prayer, it is in a wrestling with the soul of words that an act of worship comes about. We must learn to face the grandeur of words, and the fact that it is very hard to live up to the height of a great word. We must learn to establish the right relationship between the heart and the word we are about to utter.

· The words of prayer are an island in this world. Each time when arriving at the shore, we face the same hazards, the same strain, tension and risk. Each time the island must be conquered as if we had never been there before, as if we were strangers to the spirit. Rugged is the shore. In the sight of majestic utterances we stand, seeking a kindred word on which to gain a foothold for our souls. The words we face are lofty, and the humble ones are concealed beyond our reach. We must not be shaken, we must learn to crawl if we do not know how to leap. Prayer does not complete itself in an instant, nor does it move on a level plain. It thrusts itself forward through depths and heights, through detours and by-ways. It advances gradually from word to word, from thought to thought, from feeling to feeling. Arriving, we find, on a level where words are treasures, where meanings lie hidden, still to be discovered. Restrained insight, slumbering emotions, the subdued voice of deeper knowledge bursts upon the mind.

To speak about prayer is indeed presumptuous. There are no devices, no techniques; there is no specialized art of prayer. All of life must be a training to pray. We pray the way we live. Prayer depends not only upon us but also upon the will and grace of God. Sometimes we stand before a wall. It is very high. We cannot scale it. It is hard to break through it, but even knocking our heads against the wall is full of meaning. Ultimately, there is only one way of gaining certainty of the realness of any reality, and that is by knocking our heads against the wall. Then we discover there is something real outside the mind.

18 / Jews in the Soviet Union

I

We are all involved in the great battle for equal rights being waged in America and rejoice in the fact that millions of Americans are wholeheartedly taking part in the effort to eliminate the inequities that result from prejudice and discrimination.

While this victorious drama has electrified all Americans, another drama is being enacted which, though agonizing and heartrending, and perhaps more tragic than the story of the Negro people, is being ignored. I mean the plight of the Jews in Soviet Russia.

There is no other people in the world which by destiny and necessity is so committed to the sanctity of human rights and the equality of all men. History is the most emphatic testimony that injustice to some men spells the doom of all men. Prejudice is like a Hydra, a monster which has many heads, an evil the overcoming of which requires many efforts. One head sends forth poison against people of a different race, another head sends forth poison of a different religion or culture. Thus the evil of prejudice is indivisible. Discrimination against the political rights of the Negro in America and discrimination against the religious and cultural rights of the Jews in the Soviet Union are indivisible.

To be sensitive to the interdependence of all deeds and all men is an essential part of the great calling of the rabbi. It is the destiny of a rabbi to be implicated, to be involved in the plight of our people. A hasidic rabbi was asked: "Why are your prayers accepted by the Lord?" And he answered: "All of Israel is one body. If one limb is sick, the whole body feels it. Now I am one with Israel. Wherever a person suffers, I feel his pain and his anguish."

A rabbi is intensely implicated in the situation of our people. He is involved with heart and soul in the lives of other human beings. He suffers by association. His chief quality is compassion.

Rabbis are called the "elders of the community," and are charged with a supreme responsibility.

The moral implications of the rabbinate are set forth in "the rite of the 'eglah 'erufah" of "the heifer whose neck is to be broken," as described in Deuteronomy:

> If, in the land that the Lord your God is giving you to possess, someone slain is found lying in the open, the identity of the slayer not being known, your elders and officials shall go out and measure the distances from the corpse to the nearby towns. The elders of the town nearest to the corpse shall then take a heifer which has never been worked, which has never pulled in a yoke; and the elders of that town shall bring the heifer down to a watered wadi, which is not tilled or sown. There, in the wadi, they shall break the heifer's neck. The priests, sons of Levi, shall come forward; for the Lord your God has chosen them to minister to Him and to pronounce blessing in the name of the Lord, and every disputed case of assault is subject to their ruling. Then all the elders of the town nearest to the corpse shall wash their hands over the heifer whose neck was broken in the wadi. And they shall pronounce this declaration: "Our hands did not shed this blood, nor did our eyes see it done. Absolve, O Lord, Your people Israel whom You redeemed, and do not let guilt for the blood of the innocent remain among Your people Israel." And they will be absolved of bloodguilt. Thus you will remove from your midst guilt for the blood of the innocent, for you will be doing what is right in the sight of the Lord.

> Deuteronomy 21:1–9

Jewish tradition ponders the meaning of this strange rite. "The elders of that city then wash their hands and declare, Our hands have not shed this blood, neither have our eyes seen it." But can it enter our minds that the elders of a court of justice are shedders of blood? The meaning of their statement, however, is that the man found dead did not come to us for help—and we dismissed him without supplying him with food, we did not see him and let him go without escort.[1]

The importance of offering escort, of not leaving a person alone, unattended, an act both vital and discreet, has often been stressed in our tradition.

"Rab Judah said in the name of Rab: Whoever accompanies his neighbour four cubits in a city will come to no harm."

The thoughtfulness experienced in being escorted, even when not in need of protection, namely within the city, gives a person a feeling of security even after he left the city and is on the road.[2] How much more important is companionship when a person is in distress.

The promise of the Lord is phrased: "I will be with him in distress" (Psalm 91:15). It is absurd to be alone in delight, it is dreadful to be alone in distress. Rabbi Johanan said in the name of Rabbi Meir: "Whoever does not escort others or allow himself to be escorted is as though he shed blood."

The Russian Jews do not feel escorted. They feel abandoned. Zion said: "The Lord has forsaken me; and the Lord has forgotten me" (Isaiah 49:14). Russian Jewry says: The Jewish people has forsaken me, the Jewish people has forgotten me.

II

How should one describe the way we have behaved toward our brethren in Soviet Russia during the last forty-five years? Except for a brief period of extending financial aid the total picture reveals a vast amount of self-delusion, no imagination, increasing inattentiveness of the most, and intermittent concern of the few.

In the nineteen-twenties American Jewish welfare organizations spent considerable funds in support of Jewish agricultural settlements in the Crimea and the Ukraine. In those years many of us, especially molders of public opinion, had a rendezvous with fantasy —at a castle in the air. The Yiddish language was given official status, cultural activities, such as publication of books, Yiddish theater and concerts, were encouraged, though Hebrew was suppressed, Zionism and the teaching of religion considered a crime.

In the nineteen-thirties the Jews of the world were too overwhelmed with anxiety over the threat of the Nazi movement to pay attention to the plight of their brethren in Russia. In the forties we were all stunned by the experience of the Nazi war and the holocaust.

It was in 1948 that the rude awakening began. The Soviet government, it became clear, was bent upon the blotting out of all signs, memories and expressions of Jewish tradition, forcibly destroying dignity, loyalty, legacy. What started in Ur at the time of Abraham and survived Egypt and Assyria, Babylonia and ancient Rome, the Crusades and the Inquisition—remnants of Hitler's holocaust—was now condemned to silent extinction.

Many years have passed. What have we done in the face of this emergency? The situation calls for action, for pleading, for protest, for crying out, yet all that comes about is a spurt that comes and goes. There is no sustained action, no program of informing or impressing upon our own people and the people all over the world of being witness to spiritual genocide.

We have dealt with this issue in the way we act when facing a moral emergency: unprepared, disunited, irresolute, reluctant, harassed by inhibition, bereft of imagination. We may think clearly, feel deeply, yet our initiative is easily stunned by realizing the ramifications and complexity of the problem we face and the enormous obstacles we encounter, though all we ask of the Soviet Union is to implement the guarantees offered by her own constitution for equal cultural and religious rights for all citizens. Of what avail is sadness without imagination, compassion without action?

When leaders of Jewish organizations are asked the question: How do you account for your equanimity in relation to the Jews of Soviet Russia? their answer is always the same: There is little we can do, there is so much else we are committed to.

Those who are busy with private careers are hardly aware of the drama of extinction that goes on behind the Iron Curtain. When occasionally confronted with it they are sad about it for a reasonable amount of time.

Comfort is easily derived from the fact that while Russian Jewry as a whole is exposed to deprivation, individual Jews have been given the opportunity to make notable contributions. So many men of genius have been permitted to add to the advancement of Russia's supremacy in the field of space-research or to Russia's glory on the concert stage, in spite of their being of Jewish descent.

Perhaps our apathy is due to the fact that we do not really care whether the covenant between God and His people is kept alive in the hearts of all the children of Israel.

Cain's famous recipe, "Am I my brother's keeper?" is the universally acclaimed antibiotic to a sensitive conscience. Indeed, perfect immunity to the discomfort caused by pangs of conscience is about to be achieved.

A prudent man is he who minds his own business, who is busy making money, buying a new car, and being proud of his success in society. And who among us is not practical and prudent?

Our conscience dwells secure, we cast the blame on inevitable Fate. The rhetoric of indifference is highly effective. It is extremely easy to adjust to other people's suffering graciously.

Discomfort and disturbance which come with compassion are feelings which a normal person, it seems, instinctively abhors. Not to think of the Russian Jews is a habit smoothly acquired and effectively preserved.

The quality of concern for those in distress has always been the heart of Jewish existence. Today we are too busy to be concerned. The heart is made of clay, indifference gives it form. There is no guilt which the mind cannot excuse, particularly when our only transgression is in being passive. A bad conscience does not resist the cure of a claim: There is nothing we can do. We are strangely unaware that indifference is a silent Amen, a form of participation.

We rabbis and scholars are occupied with more sublime issues, like doing research, composing books, arguing whether to cooperate with rabbis whose outlook or affiliation does not conform to certain standards. We are busy raising funds for new synagogues, celebrating Bar Mitzvahs and testimonial dinners. We are busy in the nineteen-sixties just as we were busy in the nineteen-forties.

IV

According to our tradition, whoever forgets even one fragment of the Torah commits a grave sin.[3] How much more is a person guilty if he remains callous to the agony of one human being.

When I was a young boy I asked myself again and again: Was there no moral indignation in Europe, when a whole people was driven out of Spain? Was there no outcry, no outburst of anger when human beings were burned alive at the auto-da-fé?

There was no outcry, there was no public protest.

"Do not stand idly by the blood of your neighbor: I am the Lord" (Leviticus 19:16).

"Whence do we know that if a man sees his neighbor drowning, mauled by beasts, or attacked by robbers, he is bound to save him? From the verse you shall not stand idly by the blood of your neighbor." This, we are told, is not only a personal obligation, to do personally whatever one can do in saving a person. One is also obligated to hire another man, if he himself cannot deliver the person who is in peril.[4]

To be sure, there is a risk to be taken whenever we undertake to challenge the policy or the acts of a mighty power. At this juncture of history when the Test Ban Treaty between U.S.A. and U.S.S.R. has been signed and may, as we wholeheartedly hope and pray, initiate an era of peace and reconciliation between the world's great powers, our plea on behalf of the Jews of Russia may be attacked as inopportune. Political experts may rebuke us for calling attention to a minor issue when major issues are at stake. Yet the process of liquidating a great Jewish community is not a minor issue.

Risk is involved in every decision, in every action. Weighing the risk that the Jewish community may assume in fighting with moral and spiritual means for the rights of the Jews in Russia, we must be ready to suffer ourselves in order to assure their survival!

If a hostile official says to a Jew: "Let me cut off a limb from your body or I will murder another Jew," you must let him cut off a limb. Because, if in order to save human life you are commanded to desecrate the Sabbath, then you must certainly let him cut off a limb in order to save human life.

The precept "You shall not stand idly by the blood of your neighbor" implies that one is obliged to render help even at the cost of personal danger. You will say: Impossible! Nothing can be achieved, all efforts will remain futile. But to do the impossible is the beginning of faith, the beginning of greatness. Is not Judaism the art of the impossible?

Every man, Maimonides maintains, has the capacity for doing great deeds, for being as great as Moses. And Moses was the instrument of redemption, for redeeming a people deprived of equal rights.

We must not underestimate the power of justice, the power of compassion.

In the words of the prophet Amos (5:24):

> Let justice roll down like waters,
>   and righteousness like a mighty stream.

Mankind lies groaning, afflicted by fear, frustration, and despair. But in spite of our own dismay, in spite of Auschwitz and man's indifference to Auschwitz, we remain committed to the certainty of ultimate redemption as well as to the belief in the possibility of bringing about redemption every day. Just as bread and water may be obtained every day, redemption comes about every day.

Jewish history is rich in important, even momentous events.

However, they are hardly mentioned in our liturgy. Even the great moment at Sinai while recalled in our spirit is only rarely spelled out in our prayers. The one event mentioned continually, almost incessantly, is the exodus from Egypt.

The exodus from Egypt is one of the central ideas in Judaism. God redeems the slaves. God saves the oppressed. What is meant is redemption of spirit as well as a social and concrete event in history, for all men to see.

If we are ready to go to jail in order to destroy the blight of racial bigotry, if we are ready to march to Washington in order to demonstrate our identification with those who are deprived of equal rights, should we not be ready to go to jail in order to end the martyrdom of our Russian brethren? To arrange sit-ins, protests, days of fasting and prayer, public demonstrations to which even Russian leaders will not remain indifferent? The voice of our brother's agony is crying to us! How can we be silent? How can we remain passive? How can we have peace of mind or live with our conscience?

The Jewish scientists who meet Russian scientists at international conventions never make reference in their private conversations to the plight of their brethren in Russia. They fail to do so because we have failed to impress upon our own Jews a sense of compassion and concern for what is going on at this moment in the Soviet Union.

What is called for is not a silent sigh but a voice of moral compassion and indignation, the sublime and inspired screaming of a prophet uttered by a whole community.

What is happening in our days in America proves beyond doubt that a strong voice ringing with force and dignity has the power to pierce the iron shield of a dormant conscience. Involved as we Jews are in the struggle for equal rights for the Negroes, we are sure that the Negroes will be ready to join us in efforts on behalf of equal rights for Jews in Russia. We should try to gain public support from Protestant and Catholic leadership, from statesmen, artists and scientists.

The trouble with our morality is its moderation. We try to strike a balance, while the world is out of joint. We try to keep a happy medium while the agony is extreme.

> Cry aloud, spare not,
> Lift up your voice like a trumpet. . . .
> Let us not keep silent
> Let us not rest,
> Let us do our utmost
> To loose the bonds of wickedness
> To undo the thongs of yoke,
> To let the oppressed go free,
> And to break every yoke.
>
>   Isaiah 58:1, 5.

I mentioned before the rite of breaking the heifer's neck. An ancient homily says: "Saul came to the city of Amalek, and lay in wait in the valley" (I Samuel 15:5). Saul began to complain about the law of breaking a heifer's neck: Lord of the universe, a human being has committed murder, and a heifer's neck should be broken in order to atone for his crime!

How to break the heifer's neck? When acts of murder became numerous, the rite of breaking a heifer's neck was abolished.

What we must do is to break the stiff neck of callousness. We have become accustomed to accept other peoples' suffering, painlessly. Insensitivity to the plight of the Russian Jews has become our second nature. Let us break our habit!

In the third century of our common era Rabbi Assi said: "If at the present time a Gentile betroths a daughter in Israel, note must be taken of the legal-religious validity of such betrothal, since it may be that he is of the Ten Tribes."[5]

A serious awareness of the real existence of the lost tribes was still alive in the Middle Ages. Subsequently, their existence became a matter of half-knowledge and half-legend. The Ten Tribes, or at least some of the tribes, dwell beyond the legendary river Sambation. That river is full of sand and stones which during the six working days tumble over each other with such vehemence that makes it impossible to cross it. On the Sabbath the tumultuous river subsides into quiet, yet a column of cloud stretches along the whole length of the river, and none can approach the Sambation within three miles.

Shall we permit a Sambation river to separate us forever from a major part of our fellow Jews? Shall Russian Jewry be reduced to the plight of the lost tribes? Our guilt in having been indifferent for so long is rapidly reaching a climax. A brother is never an innocent bystander. No heifer will atone, no pretext will excuse. We stand guilty of obtuseness! Forgive us, O Lord, the sin which we have committed before Thee because of hardness of heart. Let us cease to be obtuse. We must break the heifer's neck. "Because I know that thou art obstinate, and thy neck is an iron sinew, and thy brow brass" (Isaiah 48:4).

One of the tragic failures of ancient Judaism was the indifference of our people to the Ten Tribes of Israel which were carried away into exile by Assyria after the Northern Kingdom of Samaria was destroyed. Uncared for, unattended to, overlooked and abandoned, the Ten Tribes were consigned to oblivion, lost sight of. At the end, they vanished.

Irretrievably? When Rabbi Akiba proclaimed: "The Ten Tribes will never return," Rabbi Johanan said: "Here Rabbi Akiba abandoned his love." And Rabbi Eliezer said: "Just as the day darkens and then becomes light again, so the Ten Tribes—even as it went dark for them, so will it become light for them."[6]

Brother may forget brother; a mother does not forsake her children. What the prophet Jeremiah is reminded of in relation to the Ten Tribes applies, we pray, to the Jews in Soviet Russia,

> Thus saith the Lord:
> A voice is heard in Ramah,
> Lamentation, and bitter weeping;
> Rachel weeping for her children;
> She refuseth to be comforted for her children,
> Because they are not.

Thus saith the Lord:
Refrain thy voice from weeping,
And thine eyes from tears;
For thy work shall be rewarded, saith the Lord;
And they shall come back from the land of the enemy.
And there is hope for thy future, saith the Lord;
And thy children shall return to their own border. . . .

Is Ephraim a darling son unto Me?
Is he a child that is dandled?
For as often as I speak of him,
I do earnestly remember him still;
Therefore My heart yearneth for him,
I will surely have compassion upon him, saith the Lord.

Jeremiah 31:15–17, 20

The six million are no more. Now three million face spiritual extinction.

We have been guilty more than once of failure to be concerned, of failure to cry out, and failure may have become our habit.

Once a person has committed a sin once and repeated it, it appears to him to be no sin anymore.[7]

The old tragedies make us forget the new ones.

The test of the humanity of a human being is the degree to which he is sensitive to other people's suffering.

This is the deeper meaning of our history: The destiny of all Jews is at stake in the destiny of every Jew; the destiny of all men is at stake in the destiny of every man.

The problem, therefore, which we are discussing here tonight, while affecting three million human beings directly is really affecting the lives of all human beings wherever they are.

It is the duty of the American rabbinate, with its tradition of leadership in many social issues, to assume moral and spiritual leadership in this great emergency; to proclaim, to teach, to preach that the plight of the Jews in Russia is a matter of utmost priority.

Inform your congregants, preach, write, urge, stir.

The Negro problem is on the way to a solution, because of the decision of the Supreme Court. Yet if not for personal involvement, if not for action on the part of the Negroes, the decision of the Supreme Court would have remained a still small voice. The hour calls for the voice of justice as well as for concerted and incessant action.

There is a dreadful moral trauma that haunts many of us: The failure of those of us who lived in free countries to do our utmost in order to save the Jews under Hitler.

There is a nightmare that terrifies me today: the unawareness of our being involved in a new failure, in a tragic dereliction of duty.

East European Jewry vanished. Russian Jewry is the last remnant of a people destroyed in extermination camps, the last remnant of a spiritual glory that is no more. We ask for no privilege, all we demand is an end to the massive and systematic liquidation of a religious and cultural heritage of an entire community and equality with all other cultural and religious minorities. Let the twentieth century not enter the annals of Jewish history as the century of physical and spiritual destruction!

If I forget thee, O Russian Jewry . . .

NOTES

1. *Sotah* 38a.
2. See *Sotah* 46b, and Maharsha.
3. *Aboth* III, 8.
4. *Sanhedrin* 73a.
5. *Yebamoth* 17a.
6. *Sanhedrin* 110b.
7. *Yoma* 86b.

19 / A Declaration
of Conscience

We have just gone through days that shook the world: the change of leadership in Soviet Russia. It is a sign of genuine good will and affection that we all hope and pray that the effect of that change may be the enhancement of liberty and prosperity and the elimination of injustice in that great country. Khrushchev who had the courage of exposing the evils of Stalinism and modern-day inquisition failed to be consistent in uprooting those evils. Regretfully his achievements fell short of the world's expectations. This, then, is a great hour for the new leaders to proclaim that respect for genuine humanity is the supreme law of the land. Proclaim spiritual liberty throughout the land and the right of all cultural communities to survive.

Our meeting tonight is much more than a public demonstration. The sorrow, the shame, and the pain burning in our hearts cannot be on public display. The issue is so piercing, so bitter, so grave, that all words are preposterous understatements. The scandal of discrimination against three million people is an evil so absurd, so unnecessary, so stunning that our basic reaction is one of dismay.

Our meeting tonight is not only a demonstration of protest; it is a convocation of prayer as well as an appeal to the soul and the conscience of the great Russian people; it is an assembly of compassion, of people pleading for justice.

Our assembly tonight is completely devoid of any desire to debate or to attack other peoples' system of political philosophy. Our only motivation is care and compassion for man as well as a sense of righteous indignation at the fact that in one of the great countries in the world cultural and spiritual atrocities are being committed resulting in anguish, depravity and irreparable loss to all humanity. All these atrocities, which bring discredit to the name of Russia in the eyes of the world, can only be described as acts of sadism or political senility, as sordid after-effects of that dreadful pestilence known in Russia under the name of Stalinism, a blight that for many years ravaged and defiled the soul of Russia, the fruits of which the new leadership is seeking to eliminate. Regretfully the achievements of the new leaders, impressive as they are on many levels, fall short of the world's expectations as far as they relate to one people.

Stalin is dead, but in relation to the Jews Stalinism is very much alive, ugly, active, stubborn, and zealous.

Malice, madness and blind hatred had combined in Stalin's mind to produce a foul monster whose work goes on to this very day. It is a sinister fiend whose work is a kind of blood-sucking cruelty in depriving Jewish citizens of their pride, of their human dignity, of their spiritual authenticity. I refer to a continuous policy of depriving the Jews of their right to preserve their heritage, a heritage more ancient than the heritage of any people anywhere in the world, a heritage that brought so many precious qualities to the human race. I refer to the insults heaped on the Jewish community and to the consistent effort in forcing the Jews to betray what they revere, to despise their own identity.

We are most eager, most anxious to trust in Russia's striving for world peace. But peace, like charity, begins at home. Its premise is respect for other peoples' right to live and to survive.

The Jews of Russia are being conditioned to believe that they are the last of their people to live as Jews, that they just smolder and will soon be blown out. Russia is a vast spiritual cemetery where souls of our people are buried alive. Is this the dream of today's leaders: to be remembered as Pharaohs in the annals of history?

The right of every cultural or religious community to survive is acknowledged and respected in civilized society; the Jewish minority in Soviet Russia, with over three million human beings, is the only community in the world which is denied the right of survival.

National minorities in different parts of Czarist Russia that were unable to read or write—that lacked the most elementary instruments for the perpetuation of their national cultures—have been enabled to establish their cultures in the U.S.S.R. and provided with the means that enable them to flourish. These minorities have been given all the facilities to develop their national language, their literatures and their arts—to establish foundations for their schools, to perpetuate folklore and songs and their national arts. There is one exception: the Jews. What a tragic distinction: the only community considered unworthy of survival.

.We are gathered here to appeal to the conscience of the leaders of Russia to acknowledge the sacrifices made by her Jewish citizens in times of war as well as their contributions in times of peace, not to regard the Jews as a group to be wiped out but as a minority having equal rights with other minorities, to be given the opportunity to preserve its own heritage.

I have a dream that attends all my thoughts. A dream that the present-day leaders will proclaim: The humanity of man transcends all ideologies. The name "Jew" is not a word of disgrace. Every Jewish child has a right to acquire knowledge of his heritage. The Jews of the Soviet Union have a right to meet together and to decide what steps to take in order to attain their spiritual and cultural goals. They are allowed to enter a dialogue with their brethren in the rest of the world. They are allowed to publish books which they need and cherish, magazines for self-expression, to create works of thought and works of art reflecting authenticity; to build Jewish schools, libraries, synagogues. I am holding steadfastly to my dream. I refuse to despair. For the alternative of my dream is a veritable nightmare. Hundreds of thousands of Russian Jews have shed their blood in the fight against the forces of darkness. Is a life of fear and anguish the reward of loyalty and heroism?

It is our honest desire to lessen tension among the nations and to strengthen ties of friendship with Russia. Still on this issue we cannot refrain from uttering our pain. Our conscience is in distress. The liquidation of Russian Jewry is a disaster. Their agony fills us with dismay. How can we remain silent?

The consistent policy of discrimination against the Jews is hard to fathom. The attitude that certain Soviet officials display toward the Jews is more appropriate to Tsarist Russia than it is to a Socialist society. We are at a loss to understand why the Soviet power is bent on destroying Jewish culture. In what way are Jews different from everyone else in Russia? Why can every other minority group enjoy the right to maintain its identity—but not the Jews? Why are Jewish values singled out for derision and contempt? Why foster hatred for a people which only recently suffered untold disaster and has not recovered from the Nazi nightmare? We are gripped with horror. Is this the Utopian plan of Russian policy: for Russia to be a graveyard for our people? Is this the will, the vision, and the design of the Russian government, to complete the work started by the Nazis: the spiritual liquidation as an epilogue to physical extermination? Do houses of worship or courses for the study of Hebrew and Yiddish represent a menace to the security of that mighty land? Is the misery and resentment of three million citizens an asset to her power? If cultural and religious oppression are not wrong, nothing is wrong. I do not see how cultural oppression and scientific progress can long be together.

A soul divided against itself cannot stand. No person can endure permanently half-slave and half-free. Where spiritual slavery is, there intellectual creativity cannot be. For a person is effective when he is allowed to be what he wants to be. Inner turbulence and bitterness in the hearts of so many human beings, though not capable of being reported in surveys and statistics, are a malignant disease in the body politic. What would Russia gain if that senseless oppression were to be victorious and the Jewish minority were to lose its identity and eventually perish?

Or is there perhaps no such deliberate plan? It is a moot question whether the central government of the Soviet Union has no more important problem to worry about than whether or not Jews are to be permitted to eat a piece of matzah on Passover; or whether they might be permitted to receive a couple of prayer books from abroad; or whether or not to allow the reprinting of the Bible, or the publication of a book presenting a true picture of Jewish history. Perhaps the present oppressions are merely the actions of petty-minded bureaucrats. A fool can be worse than a scoundrel, and fools are always around in abundance.

The oppressions may turn out to be the chicanery of petty tyrants, the type of functionary who:

> Drest in a little brief authority,
> Most ignorant of what he's most assur'd,
> His glassy essence like an angry ape,
> Plays such fantastic tricks before high heaven . . .
> As make the angels weep.[1]

But do the actions of petty bureaucrats represent the carefully worked out and deliberate policy of the upper echelons?

The problems of state faced by any government in the age of intercontinental missiles, of constantly changing international constellations and technological revolutions, are so complex and vast that we can hardly expect the members of the Supreme Soviet to debate the issue of whether to prevent a synagogue from being closed down in Charkhow or Lvov, how many students should be permitted to study at the Moscow Yeshivah, or whether a bakery is to be permitted to produce matzoth for Passover. Common sense tells us that the leaders of Russia are unfamiliar with the spiritual significance of Jewish existence. Their approach to the Jewish problem is influenced by informers, mercenary souls, former members of Yevsekecya, individuals who are notorious for their pathological self-hatred and who evoke nothing but revulsion among the Jewish masses in Russia.

Jews are here to stay. We have outlived the persecutions of the

Crusaders, the brutal dreadfulness of the Spanish Inquisition, even the holocaust of Hitler, and we will outlive the sadism of Stalin's disciples. To be sure, some Jews may succumb in spiritual suffocation and surrender their integrity. Yet while suffering passes, *having suffered* never passes. The acid memories of contempt and discrimination will live on in the souls for generations to come as incessant gall, corroding every thought, blasting inner peace, a thorn in the flesh of humanity.

Three million souls will not be blackmailed into spiritual suicide. They may pretend to be silent, but they will not betray their dignity. Communist Russia would then repeat the example of Spain: a land full of crypto-Jews, marranos, living in fear in the shadow of the Inquisition. At a time of world-shaking events and stunning anticipations of things to come—astronauts within the orbit of the moon, the production of nuclear bombs within the power of more and more nations, Telstar and supersonic planes—one is inclined to utter surprise at the fact that so many men of wisdom and sensitivity all over the world have joined in protest against the persecution of Russian Jews.

The issue of human rights, the issue of human dignity, seems to be trivial and light in terms of megatons and space rockets, yet it is the heart of all national and international problems. If the elementary rights and the dignity of so many human beings can be consistently trampled upon in the open view of all humanity, then such cruelty and such indifference to cruelty indicate a sickness that may forecast doom and disaster for all of us.

An old proverb says: If you wish to imagine or to attain a conception of *infinitude,* think of human *stupidity.* The stupidity of the persecution of the Jewish minority which stands in such loathsome contrast to the generosity and grandeur of the Russian soul remains an excruciating puzzle to all sensitive citizens living in Russia and a source of weary bewilderment to decent people all over the world.

Often one is not sure whether these acts of liquidating Jewish culture are burlesque or macabre, a travesty of what Russia represents or a sign of spiritual decay, a joke which a great civilization is perpetrating on itself or simple ruthlessness proceeding from vile minds or cowardly hearts.

It is not our prudence or power that will help them; it is the heart and conscience of men all over the world, the sense of outrage, of moral indignation, that will pierce that armor of callousness and reach the heart and conscience of the people who rule the Soviet land.

What is it that we plead for? *Equality.* The right to teach, to hear, to read the songs and the words of our literature; the right to meet, to communicate with those who have a spiritual and cultural heritage in common. Why are books on Jewish history, why are the books of the prophets put on the index? I ask again: Would the teaching of Hebrew or Yiddish, the printing of the Bible or the publication of a daily newspaper represent a danger to the mighty Soviet Union? The demands we make are so modest that one cannot but regard the present policy as odd.

A sense of humor could be of supreme utility. A meeting of a few fresh minds, immune to delusion and exaggeration, might be of help in alleviating the present agony. Some evils are ephemeral, other evils have a dreadful permanence and the tendency to increase, particularly when they are senseless, devoid of social meaning, evil for the sake of evil. The present policy of the Soviet government, forcing millions of human beings to keep their spiritual character and identity an unpleasant *secret,* to force them to forget what they cherish, to cast their inwardness into oblivion, is a kind of sadism which goes back to Stalin and is in effect the survival of Stalinism, the great curse, the enormous and innermost perversion, the blind hatred for which no means are too venomous, too underhanded, too underground and too petty.

We abhor any form of cold war, any act of aggression, any utterance of hatred. We do not attack, we only plead, addressing ourselves to the conscience of the Russian people. I speak as one who ardently desires friendship between our two countries. Yet how can we cultivate friendship for Russia, knowing that our fellow Jews are being kept in agony, jailed for teaching the language of the prophets or for preparing matzoth? To express what we Jews of America feel about our being disjoined from the Jews of Russia, I may use an ancient saying: it is so hard for us to be apart and separated from you. There is no greater agony for those in love than parting without hope of meeting. What an act of cruelty to impose separation upon those who belong together! One cannot rejoice and be alone. A Jew must never be alone. It is with all Jews that he stands before God. Our prayers are uttered in the first person plural. For us, Jews of America, to be able to recite our prayers and to know that the Jews in other lands are denied their right to celebrate and to worship is a joy mixed with sorrow, is worship alloyed with anguish. This is our situation today. We have all the privileges and liberties in this great land of America, but at the same time there are millions of Jews who live in anguish and are denied the right to be what they are; deprived of the right to teach their children their heritage.

"Ye are My witnesses, saith the Lord, and I am God" (Isaiah 43:12). A rabbi of the second century took the statement to mean, if you are my witnesses, I am God; if you cease to be my witnesses, I am not God. This is one of the boldest utterances in Jewish literature and is full of meaning. If there are no witnesses, there is no God to be met. There is a mystery, an enigma, a darkness past finding out. For God to be present we have to be witnesses. Without the people, Israel, the Bible is mere literature. Through Israel, the Bible is a voice, a demand, a challenge.

The same applies to the individual and the people Israel. If we individual Jews are witnesses to the people, then there will be a people Israel. If we individual Jews fail to be witnesses, there will be no people. To be a witness means to be involved, to accept responsibility. Upon the involvement in the responsibility of the individual Jews the very existence of the people depends. To witness man's cruelty to man and to remain indifferent is an act of betrayal of the legacy of Judaism; it would be a grave sin for the Jews of our day to go on enjoying the prosperity and comforts of this age and to remain deaf to the sufferings of our brethren, not to care when they are oppressed, not to feel hurt when they are molested. There is a voice that calls: "It is so hard for me to part from you."

We feel hurt because they are hurt. We are with them in their agony. The vast majority of American Jewry are descendants of that great community. Virtues that distinguish the best of the Jews of America we owe to that great community: generosity, noble pride in being a Jew, readiness for sacrifice, appreciation of learning, magnanimity of heart are qualities inherited from that great old community.

The records left by historians tell us of Jewish settlements appearing in the Caucasus and in Transcaucasia soon after the destruction of Jerusalem in 586 B.C.E., and they record that by the end of the fourth century B.C.E. cities in Armenia had large Jewish populations. From the ruins of tombstones, synagogue inscriptions, and Greek sources, we learn that in the Crimea more than two thousand years ago there were well-organized Jewish communities whose origin undoubtedly dates back many centuries. Thus, outside Israel, Russian Jewry is the oldest major Jewish settlement in existence today, with local traditions, memories, and customs, with roots in Russian soil and Russian history.

If compassion and cruelty are taken as standards by which to judge the light and the darkness of a period in history, then the twentieth century, specifically 1914–1945, must be regarded, as the darkest age in the annals of history, particularly in the history of the Jewish people. The Jewish world as it existed in 1914, with its thousand-year-old communities, tradition, and institutions, is now a vast cemetery. Every one of us who survived the holocaust of 1939–1945 is a "brand plucked out of the fire."

Compassion is power. In the presence of increasing agony, of violation of justice, it becomes an incurable condition and may overcome sober thought. We do not wish to see it exploited by demagogues or to see it descending to the level of suspicion and vulgar manifestations. Yet under no circumstances will our conscience permit us to suppress our concern, or even to conceal our compassion.

Out of this assembly goes a call to every Jew in the United States: Thou shalt not forget thy brother's agony! And out of our hearts goes a call to our brethren, the Jews of Soviet Russia: You are not alone! In your affliction we are afflicted. We are involved in your plight and we know that to ignore your suffering is to betray our dignity, to taint our integrity.

The Russian Jews are in distress and are even deprived of the right to speak of their being in distress. So here is another meaning for this gathering here tonight. We must speak, because the Jews of Russia have no voice. We must cry in public because they can only cry in secrecy.

We plead, we implore the leaders of Russia: Let our people live in dignity or let our people go! *Let them live or let them leave!*

The Jews of Russia are deprived of the right to express themselves, so we American Jews must utter their cry, must serve as their voice. We shall not be quiet. We shall not keep our peace until we pierce the crust of the world's conscience and the Russian Jews are granted their rights.

The time to act is now. A few years hence and there may be no Jews left in Russia to be saved. We must be prepared for a long and bitter battle that will require all our heart and all our strength. Our spiritual integrity is at stake. To fight for human rights is to save our own souls.

I do not want future generations to spit on our graves, saying: "Here lies a community which living in comfort and prosperity, kept silent while millions of their brothers were exposed to spiritual extermination."

America is committed to the proposition that the world cannot endure permanently half-slave and half-free. Discrimination against the religious and cultural rights of the Jews in the Soviet Union is a

disease that sooner or later will affect the human situation everywhere.

NOTE

1. Shakespeare, *Measure for Measure*, Act 2, Section 2, line 117.

20 / The Last Days of Maimonides

The life of Maimonides seems to be more plausible as a legend than as a fact of history. The achievements that came out of the years 1135–1204 seem so incredible that one is almost inclined to believe that Maimonides is the name of a whole academy of scholars rather than the name of an individual.

The most distinguished physician of his time, the most creative rabbinic scholar of the millennium, an epoch-making philosopher, a notable mathematician, a natural scientist and jurist, an authority and pioneer in the field of comparative religion, a supreme master and perhaps the finest stylist in Hebrew since the days of the Bible, an adviser to his own community as well as to communities in many distant lands; he also had the patience to respond to numerous scholarly inquiries that came to him from distinguished rectors and obscure judges. His unparalleled achievements in Jewish learning evoked astonishment in the eyes of experts in a variety of fields far beyond the borders of Egypt where he lived, and remain incomparable and unsurpassed to this day.

The substance of his work is like granite; its form is solemn. As a result, students have always seen in him the model of serenity, an unmoved mover, a person who had reached intellectual positions early in life and once and for all. The truth, however, is that behind the façade was a life full of drama.

An architect of intellectual systems, an example of a well-planned life, a master of scholarly organization as well as a person involved in social action, his inner existence was full of searching, seeking, striving, self-questing. It is such inner wrestling that must have preceded the dramatic change in his way of living in the last ten years or so of his life.

His life had been rich in achievements; yet many goals, important projects conceived and worked on for many years, were still to be attained. A commentary on all the homilies of the Talmud and other sources, the translation into Hebrew of the works he had written in Arabic, the completion of the commentaries on the Babylonian Talmud already begun as well as his work on the Jerusalem Talmud[1]—all these plans were abandoned for the sake of another goal. The ardent and passionate dedication to study and scholarship which had dominated him since the days of his youth and which had resulted in immortal works now gave way to another exclusive dedication: *the healing of the sick,* the momentary relief from suffering of mortal men. He continued to respond to inquiries and to compose some corrections to earlier writings, but found no time to carry out any major design after the last chapters of *The Guide of the Perplexed.* He did, however, compose a considerable number of treatises on medicine. Indeed, he seems to have given more years of his life to the healing of the sick than to his most important work *Mishneh Torah,* the code of law, which took ten years of labor.

Of the two great achievements of his life, the *Mishneh Torah* or the *summa* of Jewish law was written for the entire people, as a textbook for laymen and rabbis alike, while *The Guide of the Perplexed,* a system of the philosophy of Judaism, was written for the few. The *Mishneh Torah* was not only his *magnum opus.* Designed to bring about a revolution in Jewish studies, a major reformation in Judaism,[2] its acceptance was to change in a radical way the intellectual and spiritual way of the Jewish people; it was to transform Jewish history.

Would this book—the result of his greatest effort, the embodiment of his central dedication—be accepted by the people? This question must have deeply agitated the author. Yet the answer was soon forthcoming. Within a short time after publication this extraordinary opus became the object of lavish praise, but also the target for sharp criticisms. These attacks threatened to disqualify the work as a reliable and authoritative code of Jewish law.

Especially sharp was the blame heaped upon Maimonides for having neglected to cite his sources in his vast code. In the words of his illustrious opponent, Rabbi Abraham Ben David of Posquières, this omission made it difficult, if not impossible, to verify his statements and compelled them to accept his decisions on authority.

> He intended to improve but did not improve, for he forsook the way of all authors who preceded him. They always adduced proof for their statements and cited the proper authority for each statement; this was very useful, for sometimes the judge would be inclined to forbid or permit something and his proof was based on some other authority. Had he known that there was a greater authority who interpreted the law differently, he might have retracted. Now, therefore, I do not know why I should reverse my tradition or my corroborative views because of the compendium of this author. If the one who differs with me is greater than I—fine; and, if I am greater than he, why should I annul my opinion in deference to his? Moreover, there are matters concerning which the Geonim disagree and this author has selected the opinion of one and incorporated it in his compendium. Why should I rely upon his choice when it is not acceptable to me and I do not know whether the contending authority is competent to differ or not. It can only be that an overbearing spirit is in him.[3]

While unimpressed by other criticisms, Maimonides conceded that his omission of sources, though motivated entirely by a desire for brevity, was a serious mistake. He expressed the hope that he might some day write a supplementary work, citing authorities for decisions wherever the sources were not evident from the context.[4] So why did he fail to write the footnotes or the source-book on which the fate of his life work hinged?

In a letter to Joseph Ibn Gabir in Bagdad, Maimonides remarked: "Of the man who discontinues his studies or has never studied, it is said in the Torah: 'he has despised the word of the Lord' (Numbers 15:31); this applies also to a man who fails to continue his studies even if he has become a great scholar, for study of Torah is the highest commandment."[5] And yet while continuously stressing the fundamental importance of study and the advancement of learning, Maimonides himself changed his own mode of living in a way not compatible with his earlier commitment to the supremacy of intellectual pursuits. This important change, which may explain his failure to write the footnotes to his great code, is alluded to in the concluding chapter of *The Guide of the Perplexed.*

In a letter of September, 1199, Maimonides describes how his time was occupied during the last years of his life. The Provençal scholar, Samuel Ibn Tibbon, who was engaged in preparing a Hebrew translation of *The Guide of the Perplexed,* sent a letter to the author consulting him on some difficulties and also expressing a desire to visit him. This is Maimonides' reply:

> With respect to your wish to come here to me, I cannot but say how greatly your visit would delight me, for I truly long to commune with you, and would anticipate our meeting with even greater joy than you. Yet I must advise you not to expose yourself to the perils of the voyage, for, beyond seeing me, and my doing all I could to honor you, you would not derive any advantage from your visit. Do not expect to be able to confer with me on any scientific subject for even one hour, either by day or by night. For the following is my daily occupation:
>
> I dwell at Mizr [Fostat] and the Sultan resides at Kahira [Cairo]; these two places are two Sabbath days' journey distant from each other. My duties to the Sultan are very heavy. I am obliged to visit him every day, early in the morning; and when he or any of his children, or any of the inmates of

his harem, are indisposed, I dare not quit Kahira, but must stay during the greater part of the day in the palace. It also frequently happens that one or two royal officers fall sick, and I must attend to their healing. Hence, as a rule, I repair to Kahira very early in the day, and even if nothing unusual happens, I do not return to Mizr until the afternoon. Then I am almost dying with hunger. . . . I find the antechambers filled with people, both Jews and Gentiles, nobles and common people, judges and bailiffs, friends and foes—a mixed multitude who await the time of my return.

I dismount from my animal, wash my hands, go forth to my patients, and entreat them to bear with me while I partake of some slight refreshment, the only meal I take in the twenty-four hours. Then I go forth to attend to my patients, and write prescriptions and directions for their various ailments. Patients go in and out until nightfall, and sometimes even, I solemnly assure you, until two hours or more in the night. I converse with and prescribe for them while lying down from sheer fatigue; and when night falls, I am so exhausted that I can scarcely speak.

In consequence of this, no Israelite can have any private interview with me, except on the Sabbath. On that day the whole congregation, or at least the majority of the members, come to me after the morning service, when I instruct them as to their proceedings during the whole week; we study together a little until noon, when they depart. Some of them return, and read with me after the afternoon service until evening prayers. In this manner I spend that day. I have here related to you only a part of what you would see if you were to visit me.

Now, when you have completed for our brethren the translation you have commenced, I beg that you will come to me, but not with the hope of deriving any advantage from your visit as regards your studies; for my time is, as I have shown you, excessively occupied.[6]

This is Maimonides' last metamorphosis: From metaphysics to medicine, from contemplation to practice, from speculation to the imitation of God. God is not only the object of knowledge; He is the example one is to follow. Human beings whom He seeks to guide in this providence take the place of abstract concepts which constitute the means of the intellectual perception of God. Preoccupation with the concrete man and the effort to aid him in his suffering is now the form of religious devotion.

The tendency of neo-Platonism toward gnosis, stressing the total absorption in the contemplation of God as man's chief and, indeed, only goal—and which often leads to the disparagement of life and flight from the world—had in earlier days created in Maimonides a tension with the biblical and rabbinic emphasis on ethos, on the primacy of the sacred deed. This has now been resolved. The meaning of his last years is found in overcoming the tension of these tendencies. Contemplation of God and service to man are combined and become one.

His life-long search for personal perfection seems to have found fulfillment in the imitation of God. Personal achievement is abandoned for the sake of enhancing God's presence in human deeds, "to be like God in his actions."[7]

He had insisted that since "total devotion to Him and the employment of intellectual thought in constantly loving Him" is the aim of man, and this is generally achieved by "solitude and isolation," one should "associate with other people only in case of necessity."[8] Now, however, he renounced the postulate of seclusion and was all the time occupied with people. He may perhaps have aspired or come close to the state in which one talks with other people and at the same time thinks constantly of God, being in the presence of God constantly in the heart even though in the body among men—in the way described by the parable: "I sleep, but my heart is awake" (Song of Songs 5:2).[9] It took a life-long dedication to intellectual pursuits to be able to attain simultaneity of involvement with people and being absorbed in the contemplation of God.

In *The Guide of the Perplexed,* Maimonides, following Aristotle, proposes two ideals or perfections which man must strive to achieve. The first ideal is physical, economic, and moral advancement which will offer the serenity of mind to attain the second and ultimate ideal, namely intellectual perfection. Man's ultimate perfection "consists in his knowing about things all that a person perfectly developed is capable of knowing. It is clear that this *ultimate perfection does not include either actions or moral qualities* and that *it consists only of knowledge* arrived at by speculation or established by research . . . and is alone the source of eternal life. Thus the purpose of the Torah is to enable us to attain both perfections. It aims first at the establishment of good mutual relations among men by removing injustice, and through the acquisition of a noble and excellent character. Secondly, it seeks to impart in us correct and true views through which ultimate perfection is achieved."[10]

In the concluding chapter, however, Maimonides offers again a hierarchy of ideals, in which the highest perfection is defined in a new way. It is no more defined as consisting of "knowing about the things in existence all that a person perfectly developed is capable of knowing." "The true human perfection," he now says, "consists in the acquisition of rational virtues—I refer to the possession of notions, which teach true opinions *concerning divine matters.*" In contrast to his earlier view that man's ultimate perfection is purely intellectual—it does not include either actions or moral qualities, but only knowledge—he now defines man's ultimate end as *the imitation of God's ways* and actions, namely, kindness, justice, righteousness.

This radical change in his philosophy of life is brought to expression in explaining the words of Jeremiah.

Thus says the Lord: Let not the wise man glory in his wisdom, let not the mighty man glory in his might, let not the rich man glory in his riches; but let him who glories glory in this, that he understands and knows me, that I am the Lord who practice kindness, justice and righteousness in the earth; for in these things I delight, says the Lord. Jeremiah 9:23–24.

The prophet does not say that knowledge of God is man's most noble end. For were this his intention, he would have said: *But let him who glories glory in this, that he understands and knows Me,* and have stopped there; or he would have said: *That he understands and knows Me that I am One;* or he would have said: *That I have no figure,* or *That there is none like Me,* or something similar. But he says that one should glory in the apprehension of Myself and in the knowledge of My ways and attributes, by which he means His actions. When Moses prayed: "Let me know Thy ways" (Exodus 33:13), he was told that God's ways or actions that ought to be known and imitated are (in the paraphrase of Jeremiah) kindness, justice, righteousness. Then the prophet says in conclusion: *For in these things I delight, says the Lord.* He means that it is My design that there should come from you kindness, justice, righteousness, that man should imitate them, that they should be his way of life.[11]

Maimonides' life, achievements, drives, and decisions cannot be understood without an appreciation of his central concern, his concern for God, which he describes as love of God, as thirst "for the living God" (Psalm 42:3). What is the way that leads to the love of God? Maimonides maintains that contemplation and knowledge are the cause of love. "When a person contemplates the great and wondrous works He has created and thereby comes to realize His incomparable and infinite wisdom, he will love, praise, and glorify Him and desire most ardently to know Him."[12] "This love is only possible when we comprehend the real nature of things, and understand the divine wisdom displayed therein."[13] "One cannot love God except through the knowledge with which one knows Him, and the love is in proportion with the knowledge; the less of the latter, the less of the former, and the more of the latter, the more of the former."[14]

The climax of Maimonides' efforts in trying to obtain knowledge of God, however, is in the admission that "all we understand, is the fact that He exists, that He is a Being to whom none of His creatures is similar, who has nothing in common with them, who does not include plurality, who is never too feeble to produce other beings, and whose relation to the universe is that of a captain to a ship. Even this is not the true relation and a correct likeness, but serves only to convy to us the idea that God rules the universe; that is, that He gives it duration, and preserves its necessary arrangement."[15]

Positive rational knowledge of the essence of God is beyond the bounds of human intelligence. For He is such that when the minds contemplate His essence, knowledge turns into ignorance; and when the tongues aspire to magnify Him, all eloquence turns into weariness.[16]

The mind is a failure in trying to comprehend *God's essence*, yet it is the most marvelous instrument by which we come upon *God's presence*.

The mystery of thought is the deepest and most immediate experience of God's presence. For thought comes about through the contact of the mind with the Active Intellect, a transcendent immaterial entity placed next to the sphere of the moon and acting as an intermediary between the divine Mind and the human intellect in transmitting the divine emanations to the human soul once it has reached the stage of the acquired intellect.

The universe is the work of God as the efficient cause; it has been created by the divine emanation, and all changes in it emanate from Him.[17] It is divine emanation which enables us to think and through which we attain intellectual cognition. Although the emanation—which reaches all men through the Active Intellect—is invariable, its effect on the mind of an individual varies according to the particular nature or receptivity of the individual. The Active Intellect which emanates from God toward us is the link that joins us to God. We have in our power to strengthen and fortify the link or to make it weaker and weaker until we cut it. It will become strong when we employ it in the love of God; it will become weak when we direct our thoughts to other things.[18]

Thought itself is holy. Thought itself is the presence of God.

Man does not sit, move, and occupy himself when he is alone in his house, as he sits, moves, and occupies himself when he is in the presence of a great king; nor does he speak and rejoice while he is with his family and relatives, as he speaks in the king's council. Therefore he who chooses to achieve human perfection and to be in true reality *a man of God* must give heed and know that the great king who always accompanies him and cleaves to him is greater than any human individual, even if the latter be *David* and *Solomon*. This king who cleaves to him and accompanies him is the intellect that overflows toward us and is the bond between us and Him, may He be exalted. Just as we apprehend Him by means of that light which He caused to overflow toward us —as it says, *In Thy light do we see light* (Psalm 36:10)—so does He by means of this selfsame light examine us; and because of it, He, may He be exalted, is constantly with us, examining from on high: *Can any hide himself in secret places that I shall not see him?* Understand this well. Know that when perfect men understand this, they achieve such humility, such awe and fear of God, such reverence and such shame before Him, may He be exalted—and this in ways that pertain to true reality, not to imagination—that their secret conduct with their wives and in latrines is like their public conduct with other people.[19]

For all his dedication to the healing of the human body and the acknowledgment of the value of physical welfare, Maimonides insists that man's being within a body prevents the mind from grasping what is above nature.

"I say that there is a limit to human reason and as long as the soul resides within the body, it cannot grasp what is above nature, for nothing that is immersed in nature can see above it. Reason is limited to the sphere of nature and it is unable to understand that which is above its limits."[20]

". . . as long as the soul resides within the body, it cannot grasp what is above nature." "Matter is a mighty veil and barrier, preventing the apprehension of that which is separate from matter. This applies to the noblest and purest matter, namely that of the heavenly spheres. All the more is this true for the dark and turbid body of man. Hence, whenever our intellect aspires to apprehend God, we come upon a mighty veil and barrier. This is alluded to in all the books of the prophets, namely, that we are separated by a veil from God and that He is hidden from us by a heavy cloud, or by darkness, or by a mist, or by an enveloping cloud—and similar allusions to our incapacity to apprehend Him because of matter. . . . the obstacle consists in the tenebrous character of our substance."[21] Imperfection, corruption, deficiency are due solely to matter.

Every living being dies and suffers illness solely because of the substance of the body and not because of its form. Man's shortcomings and sins are all due to the substance of the body and not to his form, whereas all his virtues are due to his form. For example, knowledge of God, the formation of ideas, the mastery of desire and passion, the ability to decide what ought to be preferred and what ought to be avoided—all are due to his form. On the other hand, eating, drinking, copulation, excessive lust, passion, all vices—all originate in the substance of the body. Since it is impossible for the body to exist without form, or for the form to exist without matter, it was necessary that man's very noble form, the *image of God and His likeness,* should be bound to earthy, turbid, and dark matter. The Creator, therefore, granted to the human form power, dominion, rule, and control over matter in order that it subjugate matter, quell its impulses, and bring it back to the best and most harmonious state possible.

In this respect human beings differ. There are individuals who aspire always to that which is most noble. Their thoughts are engaged in the formation of ideas, the acquisition of true knowledge about everything, and the *union with the divine intellect,* which flows down upon them and which is the source of man's form. Whenever the impulses of the body impel such an individual toward the dirt and the avowedly disgraceful inherent in matter, he feels pain because of his entanglement, is ashamed and abashed because of what he has gone through, and desires to diminish this disgrace with all his power and to be preserved from it in every way.[22]

Growing old was an experience Maimonides seemed to welcome. "For the thing that is acquired through mere old age is a disposition to achieve moral virtues."[23]

The philosophers have already explained that bodily faculties impede in the days of youth man's attainment of moral virtues and, even more, the attainment of pure thought, leading to the passionate love of God. In the measure in which these faculties are weakened and the fire of desires quenched, the intellect gains in strength and light; knowledge becomes purer and the mind delights in what it apprehends. The result is that when a perfect man is stricken with years and approaches death, his apprehension increases very powerfully; joy over his apprehension and a great love for the object of apprehension become stronger, and the soul is separated from the body in a state of delight. Of Moses, Aaron, and Miriam the rabbis said that they died of a kiss, they died "in the delight of this apprehension due to the intensity of passionate love. . . ." The intellect remains forever in the same state, since the screen and the obstacle have been removed, and the person endures permanently in that state of intense delight.[24]

In the light of such meditation the thought of death is a thought of anticipation. For death thus conceived ushers in a new and higher kind of being which is acquired through the actualization of man's intellectual faculty. For it is knowledge and the love of God that endow man with eternal life. The immortality of the soul is the immortality of the acquired spirit. Thus the soul that remains after the death of man is not the soul that comes into being at the time a man is born; the latter is a mere faculty, while that which has a separate existence after death is a reality.[25]

During the night of the twentieth of Tebet, 4965 (the 13th of December, 1204), "a magnificent pillar of cloud ascended to heaven: Moses ben Maimon, the servant of God in Fostat," we read in a medieval chronicle. Jews and Arabs mourned him for three days. There was great sorrow when the news reached Alexandria; a fast was ordered, and the cantor read from Leviticus 26:2 to the end of the threats of punishment, and the last one called up to the Torah read from the first book of Samuel, chapter 4, up to the words: *For the ark of God is taken.*

According to legend, years later, when Maimonides' body was brought to Palestine, robbers attacked the cortege. They wanted to throw the coffin into the sea, but they could not lift it, although there were more than thirty of them. After beholding this they said: That was a godly man. They sent after the Jews they had dispersed by their attack and then acted as escort themselves.

According to his own wish, it is claimed, Maimonides was buried in Tiberias at the place where Rabbi Yehuda Hanassi had so often sojourned. Someone unknown to us placed the following inscription on his tombstone:

Here lies a man, and yet not a man;
Wert thou a man, then heavenly beings produced thee.

Later this inscription was erased and in its place appeared:

Here lies Maimuni, the banished heretic.

The people set up a monument to their teacher with the words:

From Moses to Moses there has been no one like Moses.

Samuel Ibn Tibbon completed his translation of *The Guide of the Perplexed* on the thirtieth of November, 1204, two weeks before Maimonides' death. He boarded a ship immediately and journeyed to Fostat to meet the master. It was too late.

NOTES

1. Rabbi Moses ben Maimon, *Responsa*, ed. J. Blau, p. 725, No. 447; *Kovets*, ed. Lichtenberg, Leipzig, 1859, part II, p. 15c; see part II, p. 44a (hereafter referred to as *Kovets*).

2. See A. Heschel, *Maimonides*, Berlin 1935, pp. 92-110.

3. Rabad, last objection (*hassagah*) on the introduction, in the translation by Isadore Twersky, *Rabad of Posquières*, Cambridge, 1962, p. 131.

4. *Kovets,* part I, p. 26a.

5. *Kovets,* part II, p. 15c.

6. *Kovets,* part II, pp. 6c; see A. Marx, *Jewish Quarterly Review,* vol. XXV (NS), 1935, p. 375 ff. I used in part the translation found in *A Treasury of Jewish Letters,* edited by Franz Kobler, Philadelphia, 1953, vol. I, pp. 211–212.

7. *The Guide of the Perplexed,* part II, ch. 54 (hereafter referred to as *The Guide*). I used the translation of both Sh. Pines and M. Friedlaender.

8. *Ibid.,* part III, ch. 51.

9. *Ibid.,* part III, ch. 51.

10. *Ibid.,* part III, ch. 27.

11. *Ibid.,* part III, ch. 54.

12. *Mishneh Torah, Yesode ha-Torah,* II, 2.

13. *The Guide,* part III, ch. 28.

14. *Mishneh Torah, Teshubah,* X, 6.

15. *The Guide,* part I, ch. 58.

16. *Ibid.,* part II, ch. 58.

17. *Ibid.,* part II, ch. 12.

18. *Ibid.,* part II, ch. 37.

19. *Ibid.,* part III, ch. 52.

20. *Kovets,* part II, p. 23c.

21. *The Guide,* part III, ch. 9.

22. *Ibid.,* part III, ch. 8.

23. *Ibid.,* part I, ch. 54; see also *Kovets,* part II, p. 30c.

24. *The Guide,* part I, ch. 51.

25. *Ibid.,* part I, ch. 70; part III, ch. 27.

SUBJECT INDEX

INDEX OF BIBLICAL PASSAGES